THE CELEBRATIONS LIBRARY

Volume 1

Halloween Program Sourcebook

The Story of Halloween, Including Excerpts of Stories and Legends, Strange Happenings, Poems, Plays, Activities, and Recipes Focusing on Halloween from the Eighteenth Century to the Present, Supplemented with a Bibliography and Indexes

Sue Ellen Thompson, *Editor*

Illustrated by Mary Ann Stavros-Lanning

Omnigraphics, Inc.

Penobscot Building • Detroit, MI 48226

Sue Ellen Thompson, *Editor*

Omnigraphics, Inc.

* * *

Peter E. Ruffner, *Senior Vice President*
Matt Barbour, *Vice President, Operations*
Laurie Lanzen Harris, *Vice President, Editorial*
Thomas J. Murphy, *Vice President, Finance*
Jane Steele, *Marketing Coordinator*

* * *

Frederick G. Ruffner, Jr., Publisher

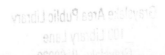

Contents

Contents (*Continued*)

Contents *(Continued)*

Section 5: Plays

Section 6: Activities

Contents (Continued)

Section 7: Recipes

Section 8: Indexes

Preface

The celebration of Halloween — from the ancient Celtic observance of Samhain in Great Britain, from which the holiday derives, to the modern-day trick-or-treating ritual in the United States — has generated a wealth of stories, legends, poetry, and traditions. These legends and lore offer insights into the historical eras and customs from which they come, as well as the significance and traditions of the present.

Halloween Program Sourcebook presents a selection of Halloween-related material to be read, spoken, or performed, as well as activities and recipes to enhance its celebration. *Halloween Program Sourcebook* is the first volume of *The Celebrations Library*, a collection of anthologies on major holidays, ethnic and religious celebrations, and other recurring events celebrated in the United States. Inspired by Robert Haven Schauffler's series of holiday anthologies published early in the twentieth century, *The Celebrations Library* adds new material that reflects each holiday's history, observance, spirit, and significance.

The Plan of the Work

Halloween Program Sourcebook opens with a comprehensive introduction to the origins, evolution, and significance of the holiday, including a perspective on the historical Halloween celebrations in the United States and around the world. The material included is grouped into the following sections: Stories and Legends, Strange Happenings, Poems, Plays, Activities, and Recipes. These selections represent both traditional and contemporary expressions of the mood of the season. Though not all the stories and accounts refer explicitly to Halloween, all contain themes symbolic of the holiday, such as witches, black cats, and ghostly phenomena.

The book ends with an Author and Title Index, listing the titles and authors of the selections appearing within the volume.

Audience

Halloween Program Sourcebook is intended for upper elementary and middle school readers, teachers, librarians, and the general public seeking information and program materials about Halloween.

Acknowledgments

The articles appearing in the *Halloween Program Book* were reprinted from the following sources. We would like to thank the permissions coordinators at the publishing houses contacted for their help in obtaining reprint rights. Every effort has been made to trace copyright. However, if any omissions have been made, contact Omnigraphics so that corrections can be made to future editions of this book.

Text and Illustrations © Susan Gold Purdy, from *Halloween Cookbook*, Franklin Watts 1977. Used with permission of the author/ illustrator.

Behn, Harry, "Hallowe'en" from *The Little Hill*. Copyright 1949 Harry Behn. © Renewed 1977 by Alice L. Behn. Used by permission of Marian Reiner.

Behn, Harry, "Ghosts" from *The Golden Hive*. Copyright © 1957, 1962, 1966 by Harry Behn. Renewed by Pamela Behn Adam, Prescott Behn and Peter Behn. Used by permission of Marian Reiner.

Brokaw, Meredith and Annie Gilbar. From *The Pennywhistle Halloween Book*. Simon & Schuster, 1989. Copyright © 1989 by Meredith Brokaw and Annie Gilbar. Reprinted with permission of Simon & Schuster, Inc.

Cohen, Daniel. *America's Very Own Ghosts*. Dodd, Mead & Co., 1985. Copyright © 1985 by Daniel Cohen. Used by permission of Putnam Berkley, a division of Penguin Putnam Inc.

Crume, Vic, "The Haunted House." From *Haunted House and Other Spooky Poems and Tales*, edited by Gladys Schwartz and Vic Crume. Copyright © 1970 by Scholastic Magazines, Inc. Reprinted by permission of Scholastic Inc.

Di Pasquale, Emanuel, "All Hallow's Eve." From *Halloween Poems*, by Myra Cohn Livingston. Holiday House, 1989. Copyright © 1989 Emanuel di Pasquale. Reprinted by permission of Marian Reiner for the author. All rights reserved.

Harper, Wilhemina. *Ghosts and Goblins*. Dutton, 1965.

Hathaway, Nancy. From *Halloween Crafts and Cookbook*. Harvey House, 1979.

Hunt, Roderick. From *Ghosts, Witches, and Things Like That*. Copyright © Oxford University Press, 1984. Oxford University Press, 1984. Reprinted by permission of Roderick Hunt.

Kennedy, X. J., "Wicked Witch's Kitchen." From *Halloween Poems* by Myra Cohn Livingston, Atheneum, 1975. Copyright © 1975 by X. J. Kennedy. Reprinted by permission of Curtis Brown, Ltd.

Linton, Ralph and Adelin Linton. From *Halloween through Twenty Centuries*. Henry Schuman, 1950.

Livingston, Myra Cohn, "Wailed a Ghost in a Graveyard at Kew." From *A LollyGag of Limericks*. Copyright © 1978 Myra Cohn Livingston. (A Margaret K. McElderry Book). Used with permission of Marian Reiner.

Maguire, Jack. From *The Halloween Book*. Copyright © Philip Lief Group, Inc., 1992. Philip Lief Group, Inc., 1992. Reprinted by permission of the publisher.

Schauffler, Robert H. *Halloween: Its Origin, Spirit, Celebration, and Significance as Related in Prose, Verse, Together with Halloween Stories, Plays, Pantomimes, and Suggestions for Games, Stunts, Parties, Feasts, and Decorations*. Dodd, Mead & Co., 1958.

Walker, Mark. *The Great Halloween Book*. Liberty Publishing, 1983.

Worth, Valerie, "Pumpkin." From *More Small Poems*. Copyright ©
1976 by Valerie Worth. Reprinted by permission of Farrar,
Straus & Giroux, Inc.

The illustrations appearing in the *Halloween Program Sourcebook*
were created using images from the following sources: Corel Draw,
Image Club Graphics' Hypnoclips, Eyewire's Art Parts Holidays
and Holiday's Revisited, and Dynamic Graphics' Artworks Series.

Our Advisors

This publication was reviewed by an Advisory Board comprised
of librarians to assist us in assessing its usefulness and accessibility.
They evaluated the title as it developed, and their suggestions
have proved invaluable. Any errors, however, are ours alone. We'd
like to list the Advisory Board members and thank them for their
efforts.

Gail Beaver
Ann Arbor Huron High School Library and the University of
Michigan School of Information and Library Studies
Ann Arbor, Michigan

Linda Carpino
Detroit Public Library
Detroit, Michigan

Helen Gregory
Grosse Pointe Public Library
Grosse Pointe, Michigan

Rosemary Orlando
St. Clair Shores Public Library
St. Clair Shores, Michigan

Introduction

The Story of Halloween

o understand where our modern celebration of Halloween originated, it is necessary to go back in time to the Celts. These were the people who lived in the British Isles, France, and other parts of northern and western Europe three thousand years ago. They worshipped the sun, the moon, and other forces of nature. Their white-robed priests were called Druids.

November 1 was the first day of the Celtic new year, and it was considered an auspicious day on which to begin a journey or fight a battle. From sundown on October 31 through sunset on November 2, the Celts observed a festival named after Samhain (pronounced SAH-wen), the Lord of the Dead. Of the four major festivals of the Celtic year—which included Imbolc (February 1), Beltane (May 1), and Lughnasa (August 1)—Samhain was the most important. It was during this time of year that the Lord of the Dead opened up the gates of the underworld, and the spirits of the dead were free to roam the earth and visit their former homes and families. It was also on Samhain that the souls of those who had died during the year just ending would assemble and travel together to the land of the dead.

The Celts had mixed feelings about the spirits of the dead who wandered the earth at Samhain. On the one hand, they wanted to keep them happy; so they built bonfires to light their way and prepared special foods as offerings. But they were also terrified of them, so they disguised themselves as whatever they thought these wandering spirits might look like, in the hope that they might blend in with the ghostly crowd. Some scholars say that the Samhain bonfires were designed to scare off any evil spirits that might have escaped from the underworld when the gates were opened.

In addition to being a time when the barriers between this world and the next were dissolved, Samhain also served an important seasonal purpose. November 1 was the day by which all the crops had to be harvested and the best of the farm animals brought into their winter shelters. The others were slaughtered for meat, and there was usually a great feast dedicated to the Lord of the Dead. Winter came early to most of northern Europe, and it was important to get the crops stored and the livestock into the barn or shed where it could be hand-fed during the cold, snowy months ahead.

Celtic householders extinguished their hearth-fires on the night of October 31 and then gathered in a circle while the Druid priests solemnly quenched the sacred altar fire and lit a new one by rubbing two pieces of oak together. The head of each family took some of the live embers from this fire home and used them to kindle a new fire on the hearth, which had to be kept burning until the next year's festival. Fire that had been blessed in this way was considered protection against evil spirits and danger throughout the year. Sparks from the altar fire were also used to light the huge bonfires that had been built especially for this festival in the surrounding hilltops.

It isn't difficult to see how the modern celebration of Halloween emerged from some of these ancient Celtic rites. But the Romans who lived in Great Britain during the first century A.D. observed their own autumn festival, dedicated to the harvest goddess Pomona, at this same time of year. When the Romans conquered Great Britain in the first century A.D., they brought many of their harvest festival customs with them. The most popular involved nuts and apples, which were sacred to Pomona. It is believed that many of our modern-day Halloween games, including bobbing for apples, can be traced back to Pomona's festival.

Although ancient Celtic and Roman customs merged to a large degree, there was one pagan practice that the Romans wouldn't tolerate: the sacrifice of human victims to the Lord of the Dead. Usually these victims were criminals, confined in cages made out of wicker and thatch to resemble giants or huge animals. The cages were then set on fire by the Druid priests, and the victims were roasted alive. The Romans outlawed such sacrifices, although the practice re-appeared in medieval times, when black cats were put into wicker cages and burned alive on Halloween.

The Christianization of Halloween

Christianity arrived in the British Isles during the third and fourth centuries. The Catholic church knew better than to try to stamp out native customs and beliefs, so it encouraged its missionaries to try to put a Christian "spin" on established pagan festivals. This involved persuading the Celts that the supernatural presences they encountered on the night of October 31 were actually hallucinations sent by the Christian devil. The Druids were declared to be devil-worshippers, and the Celtic underworld ruled by Samhain became associated with the Christian Hell.

To further discourage the celebration of Samhain, the Christian church replaced it with the Feast of All Saints, also known as All Saints' Day, All Hallows' Day (*hallow* is an Old English word meaning "holy"), or Hallowmas. This was a catch-all festival designed to honor all the Christian saints, particularly those who had no special feast days of their own. Originally observed in the spring but then moved to November 1, it became a churchwide holiday in 837 A.D. The evening before All Hallows' Day became All Hallows' Even or Eve—eventually shortened to "Halloween"— and it was observed in many western European countries with extra masses and prayers at the graves of deceased friends and relatives.

In the tenth century St. Odilo, the abbot of Cluny in France, proposed that the day after All Saints' Day be set aside in honor of the faithful departed, particularly those whose souls were still in purgatory. November 2 became known as All Souls' Day. People went to church, where the altar was draped in black, and visited their family graves to honor their ancestors. On the evening of November 1, or All Souls' Eve, it was customary to decorate the graveyards and light candles in memory of the dead. In many ways, All Souls' Day was much closer in spirit to the old Celtic Samhain than All Saints' Day was.

The process of incorporating October 31 into the Christian calendar as All Hallows' Eve took several centuries and was never entirely successful. In the British Isles particularly, October 31 continued to flourish as a more or less pagan celebration. Well into the 18th and, in some areas, even the 19th century, people living in rural areas lit bonfires on Halloween to scare off the spirits who were out destroying the crops and harming the cattle. They also set pitchforks braided with straw on fire to singe the brooms of any witches who might happen to be flying by.

Halloween and Guy Fawkes Day

While Halloween remained popular in Ireland, Scotland, and Wales, in England it gradually gave way to the celebration of Guy Fawkes Day on November 5. This holiday commemorates the 1605 event known as the "Gunpowder Plot," in which a group of pro-Catholic conspirators tried to blow up the Houses of Parliament in London to get even with King James I and his government for their laws against Roman Catholics. The plot was discovered and eight of the conspirators — Guy Fawkes among them — were beheaded. Perhaps because All Hallows' Eve was identified with the Roman Catholic church and England wanted to show its independence from the Pope, the celebration of Guy Fawkes Day came to be regarded as the more prominent holiday. The bonfires that once blazed on the night of October 31 were moved up to November 5, and they became a way of remembering the failure of the Gunpowder Plot. To this day, Halloween is not widely celebrated in England.

There are other links between Halloween and Guy Fawkes Day as well. For centuries, English children have built huge bonfires,

Procession of "Guys"

dressed up rag effigies as "Guys," and begged money from strangers to buy fireworks. Some think that the custom of begging "a penny for the Guy" played a part in the increasing popularity of trick-or-treating on Halloween (see below). Others see a parallel between the effigies of Guy Fawkes that are traditionally burned in bonfires on November 5 and the scarecrow-like figures that people make on Halloween by raking up leaves and stuffing them into an old pair of jeans and a checkered flannel shirt. There is no real name for these pumpkin-headed harvest figures, although they are sometimes called Jack-o'-Lanterns.

Guy Fawkes Day was celebrated in the American colonies up until the time of the American Revolution, when such distinctly British commemorations fell out of favor.

Divining the Future

Another custom characteristic of Halloween in the British Isles is the games that are played with nuts and apples, which are used to make predictions about affairs of the heart. In Ireland, for example, it is traditional for a young woman who wants to know if the men she loves are faithful to put three nuts on the fire, naming one for herself and the other two for her admirers. If one of the nuts burns quietly next to hers, it means that the man is true to her and that they will be married within the year; if one cracks or jumps away, it means that he is unfaithful. If all three nuts are separated, she will find no lasting happiness with either of her lovers. Divination games involving nuts were so popular at one time in the north of England that Halloween was known as "Nutcrack Night." A vivid description of the Halloween game involving nuts can be found in Robert Burns's well-known poem, "Hallowe'en" (see page 137).

Robert Burns

Burns's poem also refers to young people who "pou their stocks" (pull their stalks) on Halloween—a reference to another popular divination game played in the Scottish highlands. Boys and girls go out hand-in-hand in the dark to a kale or cabbage patch, where they shut their eyes and at random grab for a stalk and pull. Then they examine the stalk they've chosen for hints about their future spouses. If the stalk is tall and straight, their future mate will be strong and well-built. If it is shriveled or crooked, it means they will marry a hunchback or a sickly person. If a lot of earth clings to the roots, the marriage will be a prosperous one; if the roots are bare and clean, the future mate will not have any money. Sometimes the stalk itself is cut open so that pith inside can be tasted. If it is sweet and tender, the mate will be gentle and kind; if it is sour or bitter, the mate will be difficult to live with.

Burns also describes the custom of having an unmarried girl go off on her own to a "kiln" (barn), taking with her a "clue" or ball of yarn. She throws the yarn over a rafter or crossbeam, holding on to one end. She begins to rewind it, and when the yarn catches or jerks, the young woman asks, "Who is down there at the end of my rope?" According to Scottish folklore, her future husband will respond with his name. Of course, a young man didn't have to be very clever to follow his girlfriend down to the barn and be ready to catch the ball of yarn when it came flying over the rafters. A similar game, played by either men or women, involves arranging three "luggies" (wooden dishes with handles) on the hearth: one with clean water, one with dirty water, and one empty. After being blindfolded, the person gropes for the dishes. If he or she dips into the clean water, he/she will marry a virgin; if into the dirty water, a widow or widower. The person who dips into the empty dish will not marry at all.

Apples

Apples have been a part of Halloween celebrations in the British Isles for centuries. It was believed that if a girl went into her room at midnight on October 31, sat down in front of her mirror, cut an apple into nine slices and held each slice on the point of her knife before eating it, she could look in the mirror and see the face of her future husband peering over her shoulder. Another method was to place apple seeds on her eyelids and name them after her two lovers. The one that dropped from her eye first would not be faithful — although a carefully timed wink might easily affect the outcome.

Bobbing for apples is still a favorite Halloween pastime, particularly at Halloween parties in the United States. Apples are set afloat in a tub of cold water and must be caught with the teeth and not with the hands. Several people bob for apples simultaneously, and the first to snag an apple is believed to be the one who will marry soonest. Sometimes the apple that is caught is then peeled in one continuous piece. The apple peel is thrown over the head, and the guests take turns interpreting the shape that the peel makes on the floor. If it resembles a letter of the alphabet, it is supposed to indicate the name of the person's future mate. Both dunking for apples and using the parings to foretell the future appear to be largely American customs. The English "snap" for apples by placing an apple and a lit candle at opposite ends of a pole suspended from the ceiling. As the pole spins, the player has to brave the flame and bite the apple to win. It is for this reason that Halloween is often referred to as "Snap-Apple Night" in parts of England and as "Apple and Candle Night" in Wales.

Divining the future on Halloween began as a Celtic practice, with the Druid priests looking for indications of what the future might hold in the entrails of the animals sacrificed in the Samhain fires. But the use of nuts and apples to make such predictions may well be a survival of the Romans' festival in honor of the harvest goddess Pomona.

The Irish in the United States

The observance of Halloween came relatively late to the United States. Most of the early settlers, the majority of whom were Protestant, did not observe either Halloween or All Saints' Day. But between 1825 and 1845, more than 700,000 Irish Catholics emigrated to North America — many of them driven from their homeland by famine. The Irish not only celebrated the Catholic All Saints' and All Souls' Days but also preserved elements of the pagan Samhain in their 19th century Halloween rituals. These new Irish settlers brought with them their divination games involving nuts, apples, mirrors, and yarn. They also introduced the jack o' lantern, which was originally a carved-out turnip with a candle inside (see below). When they saw the round, orange pumpkins that grew in America, the Irish knew they had found the ideal vegetable for carving.

Trick or Treat?

The Irish are also given at least partial credit for the practice of trick-or-treating on Halloween. Some scholars say that trick-or-treating originated in the English celebration of All Souls' Day, when children went around asking for "soul cakes" as payment for the prayers they promised to say for the souls of the dead, or in the

Guy Fawkes Day custom of begging "a penny for the Guy." But others say that it can be traced back to an ancient Irish practice where groups of peasants went from house to house on the eve of Samhain soliciting contributions in the name of Muck Olla, a shadowy figure of possibly Druid origins who would take vengeance on those who failed to make a generous enough contribution. Over the centuries, Muck Olla's vengeful behavior was gradually transferred to fairies and goblins, and ultimately into the "tricks" that young people played on their friends and neighbors. (See below for more information on trick-or-treating.)

Halloween in the United States

Although the earliest Halloween celebrations in the American colonies were scattered at best, and usually reflected the ethnic and regional heritage of a particular group of settlers, by the turn of the century Halloween had become a full-fledged American holiday. Although at first it was celebrated primarily by children, adults eventually got caught up in Halloween as well. Today, even grown-up Americans enjoy carving pumpkins, giving masquerade parties, decorating their houses and yards, and participating in parades and street celebrations.

Trick or Treat?

Trick-or-treating was actually one of the last customs to emerge in the American celebration of Halloween. It became popular between 1920 and 1950, starting in the wealthier areas of the East and spreading slowly to more remote areas of the West and South. By the 1950s, however, every child in America was familiar with the custom.

Before trick-or-treating became well established, children in homemade costumes carrying jack o'lanterns would ring doorbells and hold the pumpkin up to the door in an attempt to scare the resident. Since Halloween is a night on which the regular rules of society are suspended and roles are often reversed, adults began thinking of ways to frighten the children that came to their doors. They would dress up as witches, hide in the bushes and make ghostly noises, or drape their doorways in thread to resemble spider webs.

Halloween trick-or-treating is actually a form of "mumming," an ancient custom that involves giving a performance in return for a reward, usually food and drink. What makes Halloween mummers stand out, of course, is the costumes they wear. These can be traced back to the Celtic celebration of Samhain, in which masked and costumed villagers representing the souls of the dead were led to the outskirts of town — a symbolic way of getting rid of ghosts and keeping evil spirits at bay. The Christian celebration of All Hallows' Eve maintained the custom but attempted to put a more religious spin on it, with worshippers parading around the church dressed as angels, patron saints, and occasionally devils. In America, Halloween costumes came back into style in the late Victorian era, when people started wearing them to the Halloween parties that were so popular in the early 1900s. Although Halloween costumes have changed over the years, the classic costumes imitating the spirits of the dead — ghosts and skeletons—have never gone out of style.

For the first several years of their lives, children usually go out trick-or-treating with their parents. Then, as they become pre-adolescents and teenagers, they go out with their friends. College students and young adults usually prefer masquerade parties. Then they become parents, and the entire cycle begins all over again. In this way, trick-or-treating has become an informal rite of passage for American children everywhere, a yardstick by which they measure their maturity

Pranking

The phrase "trick or treat" means "Give me a treat or I'll play a trick on you." In rural areas of the British Isles, roaming groups of young people often dressed up in masks and clothing of the opposite sex and then played tricks on their neighbors. Most Halloween pranks were attacks on domestic order, designed to cause inconvenience rather than destruction. Many were "threshold tricks," which included removing gates and fences, soaping or rattling windows, tying doors shut, blocking chimneys with turf, and jamming doorbells so they wouldn't stop ringing. In America, such mayhem was tolerated throughout the 19th century by adults, many of whom were Irish and Scottish immigrants, who had played the same kind of pranks themselves when they were young. The idea that Halloween is a time of year when what is vulnerable must be protected goes all the way back to Samhain, when the mischief that was done on Halloween was ascribed to wandering spirits from the underworld. Some of these tricks — thumping a farmer's door with a head of cabbage, for example — served as a reminder that the harvest should be in by this time of year.

Traditional Halloween pranks in the United States usually fell into one of three categories: (1) moving a large piece of equipment to an unlikely place (e.g., taking apart a car or piece of farm equipment and reassembling it on top of a barn); (2) moving outhouses or tipping them over, often trapping someone inside; (and 3) making a loud or unstoppable noise (typically by vibrating a notched spool on a window or pelting it with corn kernels). In the 1940s, 50s, and 60s, painted tin Halloween noise-makers were a popular way to irritate people who answered a Halloween knock on the door.

Over a period of time, the "trick" part of the Halloween equation gradually moved up a night, to October 30, while the "treats" were reserved for Halloween proper. Mischief Night in England, which was the night before Guy Fawkes Day, was very similar to the Mischief Night that evolved in the U.S. It was a night when young people ran about the neighborhood soaping windows, pelting cars and houses with raw eggs, and lacing the trees and shrubbery with toilet paper. In the city of Detroit, Michigan, Mischief Night became known as Devil's Night, when fires were lit throughout the city during the 1970s-80s, recalling the fires of hell.

The increase in the urban population in America meant that there were more opportunities for anonymous pranks, many of which resulted in vandalism. By the 1920s, Halloween mischief had gotten out of hand, and adults started looking for ways to discourage it. Handing out candy was one solution, because getting something they wanted became an incentive for young people not to go out and soap windows or ring doorbells. Community Halloween celebrations have also helped to curtail unnecessary mischief. When the residents of Anoka, Minnesota, organized the first city-wide Halloween party in the early 1920s, it was largely an attempt to draw attention away from the mischief-making aspects of the holiday. Today, such community celebrations often include costume parades with prizes, dramatic skits, carnival booth, refreshments (candied apples, popcorn, candy corn, and peanuts), and traditional games such as bobbing for apples.

The Legend of Jack-o'-Lantern

In England and Ireland, people often saw a pale, eerie light moving over the bogs and marshes that resembled a lantern held in someone's hand. They referred to the phenomenon as "Lantern Men," "Hob-o'-Lantern," "Jack-o'-Lantern," or "Will-o'-the-Wisp." Similarly, the ghostly lights that seemed to hover over graves dug in marshy places were called "Corpse Candles." It is likely that these strange lights were the result of the spontaneous combustion of methane or marsh gas given off by rotting plant and animal life. But some people thought that Jack-o'-Lanterns were the souls of sinners condemned to walk the earth, or the souls of men who had been lost at sea.

In Great Britain, Jack-o'-Lantern became a legendary folk figure, the spirit of a blacksmith named Jack. Jack ran into the Devil in a pub on Halloween night, and the Devil was about to claim his doomed soul when Jack convinced him that he should be allowed one last drink. Since Jack had no money, he asked the Devil to transform himself into a sixpence. The Devil, who couldn't resist showing off how skillful he was at shape-shifting, complied. Jack

promptly put the sixpence in his purse, which had a clasp in the shape of a cross, so the Devil couldn't escape. He wouldn't let the Devil out until he promised not to claim Jack's soul for another 10 years.

Ten years later, Jack was walking near an orchard when the Devil came to collect. This time, Jack asked him to please fetch him an apple first. The Devil was climbing up on Jack's shoulders to reach a branch on the apple tree when Jack suddenly whipped out his penknife and carved a cross on the tree trunk. This left the Devil stranded in the air; and as a condition of getting him down, Jack made him promise never to ask for his soul again.

When Jack finally died, he was turned away from Heaven for his sins. When he tried to get into Hell, the Devil said, "I cannot break my word" (since he'd promised never to ask for Jack's soul again). Doomed to wander the earth forever, Jack scooped up a glowing ember from the fires of hell and placed it in the turnip he had been eating so he could see where he was going. This, according to the legend, was the first Jack-o'-Lantern.

Jack-o'-Lanterns were originally made from turnips in Scotland, potatoes in Ireland, and large beets known as mangel-wurzels in England. The ancient celebration of Samhain may also have included the carving of special lanterns to symbolize the life-giving energy of the sun and to encourage it to return at the end of winter. Folklorists have remarked on the resemblance between the typical Jack-o'-Lantern and the human head or skull. Although nowadays the skull is regarded as a frightening symbol of death, the ancient Celts saw it as a lucky charm that could protect people against evil spirits or the power of witches.

Jack-o'-Lanterns are often placed on top of the stuffed harvest dummies that can be seen sitting outside houses or on porches during Halloween. Although the harvest figure itself is a symbol of autumn, carving the head into a frightening face serves as a reminder of the wandering souls who roam the earth on October 31. Unfortunately, few Jack-o'-Lanterns or harvest dummies survive the Halloween season. The tradition of smashing pumpkins on Halloween night is a strong one in the United States, and the larger and more elaborately carved it is, the more tempting a target it makes.

In the English village of Hinton St. George, it is traditional for both children and adults to walk through town on Halloween night carrying "punkies" or lanterns made from carved-out mangel-wurzels with candles in them. The word "punky" may have come from the Scottish term "spunkie," which was another name for Will-o'-the-Wisp. Although this custom is observed in other English towns, the celebration at Hinton St. George is by far the most famous one. Children carrying punkies form a procession through the streets, begging for money and singing the "punky song." A prize is awarded for the best carving job.

Witches and Their Familiars

The word "witch" comes from the Saxon word *wica*, meaning "wise one." Witches were at one time respected women who healed the sick with herbs and who had special knowledge about the moon and stars. It wasn't until the Middle Ages, when Europe was in the midst of a huge struggle between Christianity and paganism, that witches emerged as a force of evil. Those who still clung to their pagan beliefs developed the cult of witchcraft. The most important of the witches' Sabbaths — as the periodic gatherings of witches were called — was on October 31, perhaps to mock the feast of All Saints. The witches who flew through the sky on their broomsticks this night were believed to be on the lookout for souls to steal.

The early Americans' belief in witchcraft came from the European continent, particularly from Scottish and Irish immigrants. Farmers in the Pennsylvania Dutch country painted hex signs on their barns to scare off witches. Iron and salt — two things that witches wouldn't touch — were often placed by the beds of newborn babies to protect them. Elsewhere, people hung other protec-

tive charms — an iron horseshoe, a string of garlic bulbs, or crossed branches of juniper and ash, for example — outside their houses and barns.

Between 1450 and 1750, women who were suspected of being witches were arrested and put on trial all over Europe and even in the United States. In some countries, the suspects were tortured before their trials to the point where they would confess to almost anything. If no confession were obtained, the suspected witch would be examined for a "Devil's mark," which could be any small wart or blemish on her body. When such marks were found, they were pricked with a special pin. If no pain was felt or if the wound did not bleed, this was taken as evidence that the person was a witch. Despite the hysteria that surrounded the famous Salem witchcraft trials in New England, relatively few people were put to death in the United States for being suspected of witchcraft when compared to the estimated hundreds of thousands who died in Europe.

All witches were thought to have "familiars" or pet animals who did their bidding and helped them work their mischief. The black cat, the dog, the sow, and the goat were widely regarded as witches' familiars because they were seen as unusually fertile — and everyone knew that the Devil encouraged witches to have as many offspring as possible so they would eventually outnumber the Christians. Cats were particularly suspect because it was widely believed that witches and devils could transform themselves into cats at will. People were especially wary of cats at Halloween, when witches were known to be out riding their broomsticks. Since most cats looked black at night, the witch's cat was always thought of as being black. The fact that cats could see in the dark and move without making any noise added to their reputation as animals that couldn't be trusted. In Ireland, black cats were thrown into the Samhain bonfires. Elsewhere in Europe, they were burned on the eve of May Day.

Bats were also associated with witches, perhaps because they flew around only at night and draped their wings around their bodies like witches' cloaks when they slept. Early pictures of witches show them worshipping a horned figure with the wings of a bat—mostly likely the Devil. Before attending a Sabbath, witches would rub a special ointment containing bats' blood into their bodies. The wings and entrails of bats were also an important ingredient in their stews.

Halloween Today

Halloween has always been associated with basic human fears: of darkness, death, and supernatural beings. But in recent years, those fears have focused on threats much closer to home. The first stories about booby-trapped goodies—mostly razor blades concealed in apples—appeared in the media in the 1960s. In nearly all of these cases, the razor blade was discovered before anyone was injured, and follow-up investigations concluded that most of the reports were hoaxes. Nevertheless, the news stories changed the course of future Halloween celebrations in this country. By 1970, reports of pins and razor blades hidden in Halloween treats had become so common that children were warned not to eat any of their candy until it had been carefully examined by an adult. Local hospitals even offered to x-ray candy before it was taken home to eat—a practice that has since fallen out of favor.

New fears about the safety of young trick-or-treaters prompted many communities to publish lists of "Halloween Do's and Don'ts," which included wearing only flameproof costumes, using make-up instead of masks (which can make it hard to see cars and other hazards), carrying a flashlight, wearing reflective tape, traveling in groups, and avoiding the homes of strangers. Parents were advised to cut up any fruit that their children brought home and to throw away unwrapped or loosely wrapped treats in case they had been tampered with.

In the wake of the razor blade panic, there were a number of rumors in the 1980s about satanic cults trying to abduct blond-haired, blue-eyed children on Halloween. Several communities in Florida, Texas, and Maryland banned Halloween celebrations altogether in 1989, replacing them with "harvest festivals" or "pumpkin days" that downplayed traditional occult symbols like witches and black cats. Although this hysteria, too, has passed, there is no denying that American parents today are far more cautious about letting their children go out trick-or-treating. Local Halloween parades and parties in schools and community centers have cut down on the amount of time left for trick-or-treating, and in some cases, have replaced door-to-door visits altogether. This is particularly true in urban areas, where people live in large apartment buildings and where they don't always know their neighbors well enough to trust them.

Halloween costumes have changed over the years as well. While traditional costumes representing the symbols of death (skeletons, ghosts) and evil (witches, devils) remain popular, there are also costumes that reflect more contemporary fears. Children and adults have dressed up as Tylenol capsules (after the poisoning scares in 1982 and 1986), as nuclear waste, and as other harbingers of death and destruction. While fads in costumes come and go, most reflect the fear of the unknown and uncontrollable which has always been the essence of Halloween observances.

Halloween Bibliography

Bannatyne, Leslie Pratt. *Halloween: An American Holiday, An American History*. Facts on File, 1990.

Barth, Edna. *Witches, Pumpkins, and Grinning Ghosts: The Story of the Halloween Symbols*. Clarion Books, 1972.

Bauer, Caroline Feller. *Halloween Stories and Poems*. Lippincott, 1989.

Big Book of Halloween Entertainments: A Collection of Original Plays, Poems, and Novelties Written Especially for This Book. Beckley-Cardy Company, 1944.

Brokaw, Meredith, and Annie Gilbar. *The Pennywhistle Halloween Book*. Simon & Schuster, 1989.

Casey, Beatrice Marie. *Good Things for Halloween: Recitations, Monologues, Dialogues, Plays, Exercises, and Drills for All Ages*. T. S. Denison & Company, 1929.

Cohen, Daniel. *America's Very Own Ghosts*. Dodd, Mead & Company, 1985.

Corwin, Judith Hoffman. *Halloween Fun*. Julian Messner, 1984.

Harper, Wilhemina. *Ghosts and Goblins*. Dutton, 1965.

Hatch, Jane M. *The American Book of Days*. H.W. Wilson, 1978.

Hathaway, Nancy. *Halloween Crafts and Cookbook*. Harvey House, 1979.

Herda, D. J. *Halloween*. Franklin Watts, 1983.

Hintz, Martin, and Kate Hintz. *Halloween: Why We Celebrate It the Way We Do*. Capstone Press, 1996.

Hoffman, Phyllis. *Happy Halloween*. Charles Scribner's Sons, 1982.

Hole, Christina. *English Custom and Usage*. Omnigraphics, 1990.

Hunt, Roderick. *Ghosts, Witches, and Things Like That*. Oxford University Press, 1984.

King, John. *The Celtic Druids' Year: Seasonal Cycles of the Ancient Celts*. Blandford, 1994.

Linton, Ralph, and Adelin Linton. *Halloween through Twenty Centuries*. Henry Schuman, 1950.

Livingston, Myra Cohn. *Halloween Poems*. Holiday House, 1939.

Long, George. *The Folklore Calendar*. Omnigraphics, 1990.

Maguire, Jack. *The Halloween Book*. Philip Lief Group, Inc., 1992.

Purdy, Susan. *Halloween Cookbook*. Franklin Watts, 1977.

Sandak, Cass R. *Halloween*. Crestwood House/Macmillan, 1990.

Santino, Jack. *All Around the Year: Holidays & Celebrations in American Life*. University of Illinois Press, 1994.

———. *Halloween and Other Festivals of Death and Life*. University of Tennessee Press, 1994.

Schauffler, Robert H. *Halloween: Its Origin, Spirit, Celebration, and Significance as Related in Prose and Verse, Together with Halloween Stories, Plays, Pantomimes; and Suggestions for Games, Stunts, Parties, Feasts and Decorations*. Dodd, Mead & Company, 1958.

Tuleja, Tad. *Curious Customs: The Stories Behind 296 Popular American Rituals*. Stonesong Press, 1987.

Walker, Mark. *The Great Halloween Book*. Liberty Publishing Company, 1983.

ꙮ

Halloween Web Sites

Booville, a Halloween City . . . . http://www.usacitylink.com/boo/

Halloween . . . . http://holidays.net/halloween/index.htm

Stories and Legends

The Black Cat

By Edgar Allan Poe

☞☜

or the most wild, yet most homely narrative which I am about to pen, I neither expect nor solicit belief. Mad indeed would I be to expect it in a case where my very senses reject their own evidence. Yet, mad am I not—and very surely do I not dream. But to-morrow I die, and to-day I would unburthen my soul. My immediate purpose is to place before the world plainly, succinctly, and without comment, a series of mere household events. In their consequences these events have terrified—have tortured—have destroyed me. Yet I will not attempt to expound them. To me they have presented little but Horror—to many they will seem less terrible than *baroques*. Hereafter, perhaps, some intellect may be found which will reduce my phantasm to the commonplace—some intellect more calm, more logical, and far less excitable than my own, which will perceive, in the circumstances I detail with awe, nothing more than an ordinary succession of very natural causes and effects.

From my infancy I was noted for the docility and humanity of my disposition. My tenderness of heart was even so conspicuous as to make me the jest of my companions. I was especially fond of animals, and was indulged by my parents with a great variety of pets. With these I spent most of my time, and never was so happy as when feeding and caressing them. This peculiarity of character grew with my growth, and in my manhood I derived from it one of my principal sources of pleasure. To those who have cherished an affection for a faithful and sagacious dog, I need hardly be at the trouble of explaining the nature or the intensity of the gratification thus derivable. There is something in the unselfish and self-sacrificing love of a brute which goes directly to the heart of him who has had frequent occasion to test the paltry friendship and gossamer fidelity of mere *Man*.

I married early, and was happy to find in my wife a disposition not uncongenial with my own. Observing my partiality for domestic pets, she lost no opportunity of procuring those of the most agreeable kind. We had birds, gold-fish, a fine dog, rabbits, a small monkey, and *a cat*.

This latter was a remarkably large and beautiful animal, entirely black, and sagacious to an astonishing degree. In speaking of his intelligence, my wife, who at heart was not a little tinctured with superstition, made frequent allusion to the ancient popular notion which regarded all black cats as witches in disguise. Not that she was ever *serious* upon this point, and I mention the matter at all for no better reason than that it happens just now to be remembered.

Pluto—this was the cat's name—was my favorite pet and playmate; I alone fed him, and he attended me whereever I went about the house. It was even with difficulty that I could prevent him from following me through the streets.

Our friendship lasted in this manner for several years, during which my general temperament and character—through the instrumentality of the Fiend Intemperance—had (I blush to confess it) experienced a radical alteration for the worse. I grew, day by day, more moody, more irritable, more regardless of the feelings of others. I suffered myself to use intemperate language to my wife. At length, I even offered her personal violence. My pets of course were made to feel the change in my disposition. I not only neglected, but ill-used them. For Pluto, however, I still retained sufficient regard to restrain me from maltreating him, as I made no scruple of maltreating the rabbits, the monkey, or even the dog, when by accident, or through affection, they came in my way. But my disease grew upon me — for what disease is like Alcohol! — and at length even Pluto, who was now becoming old, and consequently somewhat peevish — even Pluto began to experience the effects of my ill-temper.

One night returning home much intoxicated from one of my haunts about town, I fancied that the cat avoided my presence. I seized him, when, in his fright at my violence, he inflicted a slight wound upon my hand with his teeth. The fury of a demon instantly possessed me. I knew myself no longer. My original soul seemed at once to take its flight from my body, and a more than fiendish malevolence, gin-nurtured, thrilled every fiber of my frame. I took from my waistcoast pocket a penkife, opened it, grasped the poor beast by the throat, and deliberately cut one of its eyes from the socket! I blush, I burn, I shudder, while I pen the damnable atrocity.

When reason returned with the morning — when I had slept off the fumes of the night's debauch — I experienced a sentiment half of horror, half of remorse, for the crime of which I had been guilty, but it was at best a feeble and equivocal feeling, and the soul remained untouched. I again plunged into excess, and soon drowned in wine all memory of the deed.

In the meantime the cat slowly recovered. The socket of the lost eye presented, it is true, a frightful appearance, but he no longer appeared to suffer any pain. He went about the house as usual, but, as might be expected, fled in extreme terror at my approach. I had so much of my old heart left as to be at first grieved by this evident dislike on the part of the creature which had once so loved me. But this feeling soon gave place to irritation. And then came, as if to my final and irrevocable overthrow, the spirit of PERVERSENESS. Of this spirit philosophy takes no account. Yet I am not more sure that my soul lives that I am that perverseness is one of the primitive impulses of the human heart — one of the indivisible primary faculties or sentiments which give direction to the character of Man. Who has not, a hundred times,

found himself committing a vile or a silly action for no other reason than because he knows he should *not?* Have we not a perpetu-
al inclination, in the teeth of our best judgment to violate that
which is *Law,* merely because we understand it to be such? This
spirit of perverseness, I say, came to my final overthrow. It was this
unfathomable longing of the soul to *vex* itself — to offer violence
to its own nature — to do wrong for the wrong's sake only — that
urged me to continue and finally to consummate the injury I had
inflicted upon the unoffending brute. One morning, in cool blood,
I slipped a noose about its neck and hung it to the limb of a
tree; — hung it with tears streaming from my eyes, and with the
bitterest remorse at my heart; hung it *because* I knew that it had
loved me, and *because* I felt it had given me no reason for offence;
hung it *because* I knew that in so doing I was committing a sin — a
deadly sin that would so jeopardize my immortal soul as to place it,
if such a thing were possible, even beyond the reach of the infinite
mercy of the Most Merciful and Most Terrible God.

On the night of the day on which this cruel deed was done, I
was aroused from sleep by the cry of fire. The curtains of my bed
were in flames. The whole house was blazing. It was with great difficulty that my wife, a servant, and myself, made our escape from
the conflagration. The destruction was complete. My entire worldly wealth was swallowed up, and I resigned myself thence-forward
to despair.

I am above the weakness of seeking to establish a sequence of
cause and effect between the disaster and the atrocity. But I am
detailing a chain of facts, and wish not to leave even a possible
link imperfect. On the day succeeding the fire, I visited the ruins.
The walls with one exception had fallen in. This exception was
found in a compartment wall, not very thick, which stood about
the middle of the house, and against which had rested the head of
my bed. The plastering had here in great measure resisted the
action of the fire, a fact which I attributed to its having been
recently spread. About this wall a dense crowd were collected, and
many persons seemed to be examining a particular portion of it

with very minute and eager attention. The words "strange!" "singular!" and other similar expressions, excited my curiosity. I approached and saw, as if graven in *bas relief* upon the white surface, the figure of a gigantic *cat*. The impression was given with an accuracy truly marvellous. There was a rope about the animal's neck.

When I first beheld this apparition — for I could scarcely regard it as less — my wonder and my terror were extreme. But at length reflection came to my aid. The cat, I remembered, had been hung in a garden adjacent to the house. Upon the alarm of fire this garden had been immediately filled by the crowd, by some one of whom the animal must have been cut from the tree and thrown through an open window into my chamber. This had probably been done with the view of arousing me from sleep. The falling of other walls had compressed the victim of my cruelty into the substance of the freshly-spread plaster; the lime of which, with the flames and the *ammonia* from the carcase, had then accomplished the portraiture as I saw it.

Although I thus readily accounted to my reason, if not altogether to my conscience, for the startling fact just detailed, it did not the less fail to make a deep impression upon my fancy. For months I could not rid myself of the phantasm of the cat, and during this period there came back into my spirit a half-sentiment that seemed, but was not, remorse. I went so far as to regret the loss of the animal, and to look about me among the vile haunts which I now habitually frequented for another pet of the same species, and of somewhat similar appearance, with which to supply its place.

One night as I sat half-stupefied in a den of more than infamy, my attention was suddenly drawn to some black object, reposing upon the head of one of the immense hogsheads of gin or of rum, which constituted the chief furniture of the apartment. I had been looking steadily at the top of this hogshead for some minutes, and what now caused me surprise was the fact that I had not sooner perceived the object thereupon. I approached it, and touched it with my hand. It was a black cat — a very large one — fully as large as Pluto, and closely resembling him in every respect but one. Pluto had not a white hair upon any portion of his body; but this cat had a large although indefinite splotch of white covering nearly the whole region of the breast.

Upon my touching him he immediately arose, purred loudly, rubbed against my hand, and appeared delighted with my notice. This, then, was the very creature of which I was in search. I at once offered to purchase it of the landlord; but this person made no claim to it — knew nothing of it — had never seen it before.

I continued my caresses, and when I prepared to go home the animal evinced a disposition to accompany me. I permitted it to do so, occasionally stooping and patting it as I proceeded. When it reached the house it domesticated itself at once, and became immediately a great favorite with my wife.

For my own part, I soon found a dislike to it arising within me. This was just the reverse of what I had anticipated, but — I know not how or why it was — its evident fondness for myself rather disgusted and annoyed. By slow degrees these feelings of disgust and annoyance rose into the bitterness of hatred. I avoided the creature; a certain sense of shame, and the remembrance of my former deed of cruelty, preventing me from physically abusing it. I did not, for some weeks, strike or otherwise violently ill-use it, but gradually — very gradually — I came to look upon it with unutterable loathing, and to flee silently from its odious presence as from the breath of a pestilence.

What added, no doubt, to my hatred of the beast was the discovery, on the morning after I brought it home, that, like Pluto, it also had been deprived of one of its eyes. This circumstance, however, only endeared it to my wife, who, as I have already said, possessed in a high degree that humanity of feeling which had once been my distinguishing trait, and the source of many of my simplest and purest pleasures.

With my aversion to this cat, however, its partiality for myself seemed to increase. It followed my footsteps with a pertinacity which it would be difficult to make the reader comprehend. Whenever I sat, it would crouch beneath my chair or spring upon my knees, covering me with its loathsome caresses. If I arose to walk it would get between my feet and thus nearly throw me down, or fastening its long and sharp claws in my dress, clamber in this manner to my breast. At such times, although I longed to destroy it with a blow, I was yet withheld from so doing, partly by a memory of my former crime, but chiefly — let me confess it at once — by absolute *dread* of the beast.

This dread was not exactly a dread of physical evil — and yet I should be at a loss how otherwise to define it. I am almost ashamed to own — yes, even in this felon's cell, I am almost ashamed to own — that the error and horror with which the animal inspired me, had been heightened by one of the merest chimeras it would be possible to conceive. My wife had called my attention more than once to the character of the mark of white hair, of which I have spoken, and which constituted the sole visible difference between the strange beast and the one I had destroyed. The reader will remember that this mark, although large, had been originally very indefinite, but by slow degrees — degrees nearly imperceptible, and which for a long time my reason struggled to reject as fanciful — it had at length assumed a rigorous distinctness of outline. It was now the representation of an object that I shudder to name — and for this above all I loathed and dreaded, and would have rid myself of the monster *had I dared* — it was now, I say, the image of a hideous — of a ghastly thing — of the GALLOWS! — oh, mournful and terrible engine of Horror and of Crime — of Agony and Death!

And now was I indeed wretched beyond the wretchedness of mere Humanity. And a *brute beast* — whose fellow I had contemptuously destroyed — a *brute beast* to work out for *me* — for me, a man, fashioned in the image of the High God — so much of insufferable woe! Alas! neither by day nor by night knew I the blessing of rest any more! During the former the creature left me no moment alone; and in the latter I started hourly from dreams of unutterable fear, to find the hot breath of *the thing* upon my face, and its vast weight — an incarnate night-mare that I had no power to shake off — incumbent eternally upon my *heart!*

Beneath the pressure of torments such as these, the feeble remnant of the good within me succumbed. Evil thoughts became my sole intimates — the darkest and most evil of thoughts. The moodiness of my usual temper increased to hatred of all things and of all mankind; while from the sudden frequent and ungovernable outbursts of a fury to which I now blindly abandoned myself, my uncomplaining wife, alas! was the most usual and the most patient of sufferers.

One day she accompanied me upon some household errand into the cellar of the old building which our poverty compelled us to inhabit. The cat followed me down the steep stairs, and nearly throwing me headlong, exasperated me to madness. Uplifting an axe, and forgetting in my wrath the childish dread which had hitherto stayed my hand, I aimed a blow at the animal, which of course would have proved instantly fatal had it descended as I wished. But this blow was arrested by the hand of my wife. Goaded by the interference into a rage more than demoniacal, I withdrew my arm from her grasp and buried the axe in her brain. She fell dead upon the spot without a groan.

This hideous murder accomplished, I set myself forthwith and with entire deliberation to the task of concealing the body. I knew that I could not remove it from the house, either by day or by night, without the risk of being observed by the neighbors. Many projects entered my mind. At one period I thought of cutting the corpse into minute fragments and destroying them by fire. At another I resolved to dig a grave for it in the floor of the cellar. Again, I deliberated about casing it in the well in the yard — about packing it in a box, as if merchandise, with the usual arrangements, and so getting a porter to take it from the house. Finally I hit upon what I considered a far better expedient than either of these. I determined to wall it up in the cellar — as the monks of the middle ages are recorded to have walled up their victims.

For a purpose such as this the cellar was well adapted. Its walls were loosely constructed and had lately been plastered throughout with a rough plaster, which the dampness of the atmosphere had prevented from hardening. Moreover, in one of the walls was a projection caused by a false chimney or fireplace, that had been filled up and made to resemble the rest of the cellar. I made no doubt that I could readily displace the bricks at this point, insert the corpse, and wall the whole up as before, so that no eye could detect anything suspicious.

And in this calculation I was not deceived. By means of a crow-bar I easily dislodged the bricks, and having carefully deposited the body against the inner wall, I propped it in that position, while with little trouble I relaid the whole structure as it originally stood. Having procured mortar, sand, and hair, with every possible precaution, I prepared a plaster which could not be distinguished from the old, and with this I very carefully went over the new brick-work. When I had finished I felt satisfied that all was right. The wall did not present the slightest appearance of having been disturbed. The rubbish on the floor was picked up with the minutest care. I looked around triumphantly, and said to myself—"Here at last, then, my labor has not been in vain."

My next step was to look for the beast which had been the cause of so much wretchedness; for I had at length firmly resolved to put it to death. Had I been able to meet with it at the moment there could have been no doubt of its fate, but it appeared that the crafty animal had been alarmed at the violence of my previous anger, and forbore to present itself in my present mood. It is impossible to describe or to imagine the deep, the blissful sense of relief which the absence of the detested creature occasioned in my bosom. It did not make its appearance during the night—and thus for one night at least, since its introduction into the house, I soundly and tranquilly slept; ay, *slept* even with the burden of mur-der upon my soul!

The second and the third day passed, and still my tormentor came not. Once again I breathed as a freeman. The monster, in terror, had fled the premises for ever! I should behold it no more! My happiness was supreme! The guilt of my dark deed disturbed me but little. Some few inquiries had been made, but these had been readily answered. Even a search had been instituted — but of course nothing was to be discovered. I looked upon my future felicity as secured.

Upon the fourth day of the assassination, a party of police came very unexpectedly into the house, and proceeded again to make rigorous investigation of the premises. Secure, however, in the inscrutability of my place of concealment, I felt no embarrassment whatever. The officers bade me accompany them in their search. They left no nook or corner unexplored. At length, for the third or fourth time, they descended into the cellar. I quivered not in a muscle. My heart beat calmly as that of one who slumbers in innocence. I walked the cellar from end to end. I folded my arms upon my bosom, and roamed easily to and fro. The police were thoroughly satisfied, and prepared to depart. The glee of my heart was too strong to be restrained. I burned to say if but one word by way of triumph, and to render doubly sure their assurance of my guiltlessness.

"Gentlemen," I said at last, as the party ascended the steps, "I delight to have allayed your suspicions. I wish you all health, and a little more courtesy. By-the-by, gentlemen, this — this is a very well constructed house." [In the rabid desire to say something easily, I scarcely knew what I uttered at all.] — "I may say an *excellently* well-constructed house. These walls — are you going, gentlemen? — these walls are solidly put together"; and here, through the mere frenzy of bravado, I rapped heavily with a cane which I held in my hand upon that very portion of the brick-work behind which stood the corpse of the wife of my bosom.

But may God shield and deliver me from the fangs of the Arch-Fiend! No sooner had the reverberation of my blows sunk into silence than I was answered by a voice from within the tomb! — by a cry, at first muffled and broken, like the sobbing of a child, and then quickly swelling into one long, loud, and continuous scream, utterly anomalous and inhuman—a howl—a wailing shriek, half of horror and half of triumph, such as might have arisen only out of hell, conjointly from the throats of the damned in their agony and of the demons that exult in the damnation.

Of my own thoughts it is folly to speak. Swooning, I staggered to the opposite wall. For one instant the party upon the stairs remained motionless, through extremity of terror and of awe. In the next a dozen stout arms were toiling at the wall, It fell bodily. The corpse, already greatly decayed and clotted with gore, stood erect before the eyes of the spectators. Upon its head, with red extended mouth and solitary eye of fire, sat the hideous beast whose craft had seduced me into murder, and whose informing voice had consigned me to the hangman. I had walled the monster up with the tomb!

The Legend of Sleepy Hollow

(Found among the Papers of the Late Diedrich Knickerbocker)

By Washington Irving

ઉ૭

A pleasing land of drowsy-head it was,
Of dreams that wave before the half-shut eye,
And of gay castles in the clouds that pass,
For ever flushing round a summer sky.

— CASTLE OF INDOLENCE

In the bosom of one of those spacious coves which indent the eastern shore of the Hudson, at that broad expansion of the river denominated by the ancient Dutch navigators the Tappan Zee, and where they always prudently shortened sail and implored the protection of St. Nicholas when they crossed, there lies a small market-town or rural port which by some is called Greensburg, but which is more generally and properly known by the name of Tarry Town. This name was given, we are told, in former days by the good housewives of the adjacent country from the inveterate propensity of their husbands to linger about the village tavern on marketdays. Be that as it may, I do not vouch for the fact, but merely advert to it for the sake of being precise and authentic. Not far from this village, perhaps about two miles, there is a little valley, or rather lap of land, among high hills, which is one of the quietest places in the whole world. A small brook glides through it, with just murmur enough to lull one to repose, and the occasional whistle of a quail or tapping of a woodpecker is almost the only sound that ever breaks in upon the uniform tranquillity.

I recollect that when a stripling my first exploit in squirrel-shooting was in a grove of tall walnut trees that shades one side of the valley. I had wandered into it at noontime, when all Nature is peculiarly quiet, and was startled by the roar of my own gun as it broke the Sabbath stillness around and was prolonged and reverberated by the angry echoes. If ever I should wish for a retreat whither I might steal from the world and its distractions and dream quietly away the remnant of a troubled life, I know of none more promising than this little valley.

From the listless repose of the place and the peculiar character of its inhabitants, who are descendants from the original Dutch settlers, this sequestered glen has long been known by the name of SLEEPY HOLLOW, and its rustic lads are called the Sleepy Hollow Boys throughout all the neighboring country. A drowsy, dreamy influence seems to hang over the land and to pervade the very atmosphere. Some say that the place was bewitched by a High German doctor during the early days of the settlement; others, that an old Indian chief, the prophet or wizard of his tribe, held his powwows there before the country was discovered by Master Hendrick Hudson. Certain it is, the place still continues under the sway of some witching power that holds a spell over the minds of the good people, causing them to walk in a continual reverie. They are given to all kinds of marvellous beliefs, are subject to trances and visions, and frequently see strange sights and hear music and voices in the air. The whole neighborhood abounds with local tales, haunted spots, and twilight superstitions; stars shoot and meteors glare oftener across the valley than in any other part of the country, and the nightmare, with her whole ninefold, seems to make it the favorite scene of her gambols.

The dominant spirit, however, that haunts this enchanted region, and seems to be commander-in-chief of all the powers of the air, is the apparition of a figure on horseback without a head. It is said by some to be the ghost of a Hessian trooper whose head had been carried away by a cannon-ball in some nameless battle during the Revolutionary War, and who is ever and anon seen by the countryfolk hurrying along in the gloom of night as if on the wings of the wind. His haunts are not confined to the valley, but extend at times to the adjacent roads, and especially to the vicinity of a church at no great distance. Indeed, certain of the most authentic historians of those parts, who have been careful in collecting and collating the floating facts concerning this spectre, allege that the body of the trooper, having been buried in the churchyard, the ghost rides forth to the scene of battle in nightly quest of his head, and that the rushing speed with which he sometimes passes along the Hollow, like a midnight blast, is owing to his being belated and in a hurry to get back to the churchyard before daybreak.

Such is the general purport of this legendary superstition, which has furnished materials for many a wild story in that region of shadows; and the spectre is known at all the country firesides by the name of the Headless Horseman of Sleepy Hollow.

It is remarkable that the visionary propensity I have mentioned is not confined to native inhabitants of the valley, but is unconsciously imbibed by every one who resides there for a time. However wide awake they may have been before they entered that sleepy region, they are sure in a little time to inhale the witching influence of the air and begin to grow imaginative — to dream dreams and see apparitions.

I mention this peaceful spot with all possible laud, for it is in such little retired Dutch valleys, found here and there embosomed in the great State of New York, that population, manners, and customs remain fixed, while the great torrent of migration and improvement, which is making such incessant changes in other parts of this restless country, sweeps by them unobserved. They are like those little nooks of still water which border a rapid stream where we may see the straw and bubble riding quietly at anchor or slowly revolving in their mimic harbor, undisturbed by the rush of the passing current. Though many years have elapsed since I trod the drowsy shades of Sleepy Hollow, yet I question whether I should not still find the same trees and the same families vegetating in its sheltered bosom.

In this by-place of Nature there abode, in a remote period of American history — that is to say, some thirty years since — a worthy wight of the name of Ichabod Crane, who sojourned, or, as he expressed it, "tarried," in Sleepy Hollow for the purpose of instructing the children of the vicinity. He was a native of Connecticut, a State which supplies the Union with pioneers for the mind as well as for the forest, and sends forth yearly its legions of frontier woodmen and country schoolmasters. The cognomen of Crane was not inapplicable to his person. He was tall, but exceedingly lank, with narrow shoulders, long arms and legs, hands that dangled a mile out of his sleeves, feet that might have served for shovels, and his whole frame most loosely hung together. His head was small, and flat at top, with huge ears, large green glassy eyes, and a long snipe nose, so that it looked like a weather-cock perched upon his spindle neck to tell which way the wind blew. To see him striding along the profile of a hill on a windy day, with his clothes bagging and fluttering about him, one might have mistaken him for the genius of Famine descending upon the earth or some scarecrow eloped from a cornfield.

His school-house was a low building of one large room, rudely constructed of logs, the windows partly glazed and partly patched with leaves of old copy-books. It was most ingeniously secured at vacant hours by a withe twisted in the handle of the door and stakes set against the window-shutters, so that, though a thief might get in with perfect ease, he would find some embarrassment in getting out — an idea most probably borrowed by the architect, Yost Van Houten, from the mystery of an eel-pot. The school-house stood in a rather lonely but pleasant situation, just at the foot of a woody hill, with a brook running close by and a formidable birch tree growing at one end of it. From hence the low murmur of his pupils' voices, conning over their lessons, might be heard in a drowsy summer's day like the hum of a bee-hive, interrupted now and then by the authoritative voice of the master in the tone of menace or command, or, peradventure, by the appalling sound of the birch as he urged some tardy loiterer along the flowery path of knowledge. Truth to say, he was a conscientious man, and ever bore in mind the golden maxim, "Spare the rod and spoil the child." Ichabod Crane's scholars certainly were not spoiled.

I would not have it imagined, however, that he was one of those cruel potentates of the school who joy in the smart of their subjects; on the contrary, he administered justice with discrimination rather than severity, taking the burden off the backs of the weak and laying it on those of the strong. Your mere puny stripling, that winced at the least flourish of the rod, was passed by with indulgence; but the claims of justice were satisfied by inflicting a double portion on some little tough, wrong-headed broad-skirted Dutch urchin, who sulked and swelled and grew dogged and sullen beneath the birch. All this he called "doing his duty by their parents"; and he never inflicted a chastisement without following it by the assurance, so consolatory to the smarting urchin, that "he would remember it and thank him for it the longest day he had to live."

When school-hours were over he was even the companion and playmate of the larger boys, and on holiday afternoons would convoy some of the smaller ones home who happened to have pretty sisters or good housewives for mothers noted for the comforts of the cupboard. Indeed it behooved him to keep on good terms with his pupils. The revenue arising from his school was small, and would have been scarcely sufficient to furnish him with daily bread, for he was a huge feeder, and, though lank, had the dilating powers of an anaconda; but to help out his maintenance he was, according to country custom in those parts, boarded and lodged at the houses of the farmers whose children he instructed. With these he lived successively a week at a time, thus going the rounds of the neighborhood with all his worldly effects tied up in a cotton handkerchief.

That all this might not be too onerous on the purses of his rustic patrons, who are apt to consider the costs of schooling a grievous burden and schoolmasters as mere drones, he had various ways of rendering himself both useful and agreeable. He assisted the farmers occasionally in the lighter labors of their farms, helped to make hay, mended the fences, took the horses to water, drove the cows from pasture, and cut wood for the winter fire. He laid aside, too, all the dominant dignity and absolute sway with which he lorded it in his little empire, the school, and became wonderfully gentle and ingratiating. He found favor in the eyes of the mothers by petting the children, particularly the youngest; and like the lion bold, which whilom so magnanimously the lamb did hold, he would sit with a child on one knee and rock a cradle with his foot for whole hours together.

In addition to his other vocations, he was the singing-master of the neighborhood and picked up many bright shillings by instructing the young folks in psalmody. It was a matter of no little vanity to him on Sundays to take his station in front of the churchgallery with a band of chosen singers, where, in his own mind, he completely carried away the palm from the parson. Certain it is, his voice resounded far above all the rest of the congregation, and there are peculiar quavers still to be heard in that church, and which may even be heard half a mile off, quite to the opposite side of the mill-pond on a still Sunday morning, which are said to be legitimately descended from the nose of Ichabod Crane. Thus, by divers little makeshifts in that ingenious way which is commonly denominated "by hook and by crook," the worthy pedagogue got on tolerably enough, and was thought, by all who understood nothing of the labor of headwork, to have a wonderfully easy life of it.

The schoolmaster is generally a man of some importance in the female circle of a rural neighborhood, being considered a kind of idle, gentleman-like personage of vastly superior taste and accomplishments to the rough country swains, and, indeed, inferior in learning only to the parson. His appearance, therefore, is apt to occasion some little stir at the tea-table of a farm-house and the addition of a supernumerary dish of cakes or sweetmeats, or, peradventure, the parade of a silver tea-pot. Our man of letters, therefore, was peculiarly happy in the smiles of all the country damsels. How he would figure among them in the churchyard between services on Sundays, gathering grapes for them from the wild vines that overrun the surrounding trees; reciting for their amusement all the epitaphs on the tombstones; or sauntering, with a whole bevy of them, along the banks of the adjacent mill-pond, while the more bashful country bumpkins hung sheepishly back, envying his superior elegance and address.

From his half-itinerant life, also, he was a kind of travelling gazette, carrying the whole budget of local gossip from house to house, so that his appearance was always greeted with satisfaction. He was, moreover, esteemed by the women as a man of great erudition, for he had read several books quite through, and was a perfect master of Cotton Mather's *History of New England Witchcraft*, in which, by the way, he most firmly and potently believed.

He was, in fact, an odd mixture of small shrewdness and simple credulity. His appetite for the marvellous and his powers of digesting it were equally extraordinary, and both had been increased by his residence in this spellbound region. No tale was too gross or monstrous for his capacious swallow. It was often his delight, after his school was dismissed in the afternoon, to stretch himself on the rich bed of clover bordering the little brook that whimpered by his schoolhouse, and there con over old Mather's direful tales until the gathering dusk of the evening made the printed page a mere mist before his eyes. Then, as he wended his way by swamp and stream and awful woodland to the farm-house where he happened to be quartered, every sound of Nature at that witching hour fluttered his excited imagination—the moan of the whippoor-will from the hillside; the boding cry of the tree-toad, that harbinger of storm; the dreary hooting of the screech-owl, or the sudden, rustling in the thicket of birds frightened from their roost.

The fire-flies, too, which sparkled most vividly in the darkest places, now and then startled him as one of uncommon brightness would stream across his path; and if, by chance, a huge blockhead of a beetle came winging his blundering flight against him, the poor varlet was ready to give up the ghost, with the idea that he was struck with a witch's token. His only resource on such occasions, either to drown thought or drive away evil spirits, was to sing psalm tunes; and the good people of Sleepy Hollow, as they sat by their doors of an evening, were often filled with awe at hearing his nasal melody, "in linked sweetness long drawn out," floating from the distant hill or along the dusky road.

Another of his sources of fearful pleasure was to pass long winter evenings with the old Dutch wives as they sat spinning by the fire, with a row of apples roasting and spluttering along the hearth, and listen to their marvellous tales of ghosts and goblins, and haunted fields, and haunted brooks, and haunted bridges, and haunted houses, and particularly of the headless horseman, or Galloping Hessian of the Hollow, as they sometimes called him. He would delight them equally by his anecdotes of witchcraft and of the direful omens and portentous sights and sounds in the air which prevailed in the earlier times of Connecticut, and would frighten them woefully with speculations upon comets and shooting stars, and with the alarming fact that the world did absolutely turn round and that they were half the time topsy-turvy.

But if there was a pleasure in all this while snugly cuddling in the chimney-corner of a chamber that was all of a ruddy glow from the crackling wood-fire, and where, of course, no spectre dared to show its face, it was dearly purchased by the terrors of his subsequent walk homewards. What fearful shapes and shadows beset his path amidst the dim and ghastly glare of a snowy night! With what wistful look did he eye every trembling ray of light streaming across the waste fields from some distant window! How often was he appalled by some shrub covered with snow, which, like a sheeted spectre, beset his very path! How often did he shrink with curdling awe at the sound of his own steps on the frosty crust beneath his feet, and dread to look over his shoulder, lest he should behold some uncouth being tramping close behind him! And how often was he thrown into complete dismay by some rushing blast howling among the trees, in the idea that it was the Galloping Hessian on one of his nightly scourings!

All these, however, were mere terrors of the night, phantoms of the mind that walk in darkness; and though he had seen many spectres in his time, and been more than once beset by Satan in divers shapes in his lonely perambulations, yet daylight put an end to all these evils; and he would have passed a pleasant life of it, in despite of the devil and all his works, if his path had not been crossed by a being that causes more perplexity to mortal man than ghosts, goblins, and the whole race of witches put together, and that was — a woman.

Among the musical disciples who assembled one evening in each week to receive his instructions in psalmody was Katrina Van Tassel, the daughter and only child of a substantial Dutch farmer. She was a blooming lass of fresh eighteen, plump as a partridge, ripe and melting and rosy-cheeked as one of her father's peaches, and universally famed, not merely for her beauty, but her vast expectations. She was withal a little of a coquette, as might be perceived even in her dress, which was a mixture of ancient and modern fashions, as most suited to set off her charms. She wore the ornaments of pure yellow gold which her great-great-grand-mother had brought over from Saardam, the tempting stomacher of the olden time, and withal a provokingly short petticoat to display the prettiest foot and ankle in the country round.

Ichabod Crane had a soft and foolish heart towards the sex, and it is not to be wondered at that so tempting a morsel soon found favor in his eyes, more especially after he had visited her in her paternal mansion. Old Baltus Van Tassel was a perfect picture of a thriving, contented, liberal-hearted farmer. He seldom, it is true, sent either his eyes or his thoughts beyond the boundaries of his own farm, but within those everything was snug, happy, and well-conditioned. He was satisfied with his wealth, but not proud of it, and piqued himself upon the hearty abundance, rather than the style in which he lived. His stronghold was situated on the banks of the Hudson, in one of those green, sheltered, fertile nooks in which the Dutch farmers are so fond of nestling. A great elm tree spread its broad branches over it, at the foot of which bubbled up a spring of the softest and sweetest water in a little well formed of a barrel, and then stole sparkling away through the grass to a neighboring brook that bubbled along among alders and dwarfwillow. Hard by the farm-house was a vast barn, that might have served for a church, every window and crevice of which seemed bursting forth with the treasures of the farm; the flail was busily resounding within it from morning to night; swallows and martins skimmed twittering about the eaves; and rows of pigeons, some with one eye turned up, as if watching the weather, some with their heads under their wings or buried in their bosoms, and others, swelling, and cooing, and bowing about their dames, were enjoying the sunshine on the roof. Sleek, unwieldy porkers were grunting in the repose and abundance of their pens, whence sallied forth, now and then, troops of sucking pigs as if to snuff the air. A stately squadron of snowy geese were riding in an adjoining pond, conveying whole fleets of ducks; regiments of turkeys were gobbling through the farm-yard, and guinea-fowls fretting about it, like ill-tempered housewives, with their peevish, discontented cry. Before the barn-door strutted the gallant cock, that pattern of a husband, a warrior, and a fine gentleman, clapping his burnished wings and crowing in the pride and gladness of his heart — sometimes tearing up the earth with his feet, and then generously calling his ever-hungry family of wives and children to enjoy the rich morsel which he had discovered.

The pedagogue's mouth watered as he looked upon his sumptuous promise of luxurious winter fare. In his devouring mind's eye he pictured to himself every roasting-pig running about with a pudding in his belly and an apple in his mouth; the pigeons were snugly put to bed in a comfortable pie and tucked in with a coverlet of crust; the geese were swimming in their own gravy; and the ducks pairing cosily in dishes, like snug married couples, with a decent competency of onion sauce. In the porkers he saw carved out the future sleek side of bacon and juicy relishing ham; not a turkey but he beheld daintily trussed up, with its gizzard under its wing, and, peradventure, a necklace of savory sausages; and even bright Chanticleer himself lay sprawling on his back in a side-dish, with uplifted claws, as if craving that quarter which his chivalrous spirit disdained to ask while living.

As the enraptured Ichabod fancied all this, and as he rolled his great green eyes over the fat meadow-lands, the rich fields of wheat, of rye, of buckwheat, and Indian corn, and the orchards burdened with ruddy fruit, which surrounded the warm tenement of Van Tassel, his heart yearned after the damsel who was to inherit these domains, and his imagination expanded with the idea how they might be readily turned into cash and the money invested in immense tracts of wild land and shingle palaces in the wilderness. Nay, his busy fancy already realized his hopes, and presented to him the blooming Katrina, with a whole family of children, mounted on the top of a wagon loaded with household trumpery, with pots and kettles dangling beneath, and he beheld himself bestriding a pacing mare, with a colt at her heels, setting out for Kentucky, Tennessee, or the Lord knows where.

When he entered the house the conquest of his heart was complete. It was one of those spacious farm-houses with high-ridged but lowly-sloping roofs, built in the style handed down from the first Dutch settlers, the low projecting eaves forming a piazza along the front, capable of being closed up in bad weather. Under this were hung flails, harness, various utensils of husbandry, and nets for fishing in the neighboring river. Benches were built along the sides for summer use, and a great spinning-wheel at one end and a churn at the other showed the various uses to which this important porch might be devoted. From this piazza the wondering Ichabod entered the hall, which formed the centre of the mansion and the place of usual residence. Here rows of resplendent pewter, ranged on a long dresser, dazzled his eyes. In one corner stood a huge bag of wool ready to be spun; in another a quantity of linsey-woolsey just from the loom; ears of Indian corn and strings of dried apples and peaches hung in gay festoons along the walls, mingled with the gaud of red peppers; and a door left ajar gave him a peep into the best parlor, where the clawfooted chairs and dark mahogany tables shone like mirrors; andirons, with their accompanying shovel and tongs, glistened from their covert of asparagus tops; mock-oranges and conch-shells decorated the mantelpiece; strings of various-colored birds' eggs were suspended above it; a great ostrich egg was hung from the centre of the room, and a corner cupboard, knowingly left open, displayed immense treasures of old silver and well-mended china.

From the moment Ichabod laid his eyes upon these regions of delight the peace of his mind was at an end, and his only study was how to gain the affections of the peerless daughter of Van Tassel. In this enterprise, however, he had more real difficulties than generally fell to the lot of a knight-errant of yore, who seldom had anything but giants, enchanters, fiery dragons, and suchlike easily-conquered adversaries to contend with, and had to make his way merely through gates of iron and brass and walls of adamant to the castle keep, where the lady of his heart was confined; all which he achieved as easily as a man would carve his way to the centre of a Christmas pie, and then the lady gave him her hand as a matter of course. Ichabod, on the contrary, had to win his way to the heart of a country coquette beset with a labyrinth of whims and caprices, which were for ever presenting new difficulties and impediments; and he had to encounter a host of fearful adversaries of real flesh and blood, the numerous rustic admirers who beset every portal to her heart, keeping a watchful and angry eye upon each other, but ready to fly out in the common cause against any new competitor.

Among these the most formidable was a burly, roaring, roystering blade of the name of Abraham — or, according to the Dutch abbreviation, Brom — Van Brunt, the hero of the country round, which rang with his feats of strength and hardihood. He was broad-shouldered and double-jointed, with short curly black hair and a bluff but not unpleasant countenance, having a mingled air of fun and arrogance. From his Herculean frame and great powers of limb, he had received the nickname of BROM BONES, by which he was universally known. He was famed for great knowledge and skill in horsemanship, being as dextrous on horseback as a Tartar. He was foremost at all races and cock-fights, and, with the ascendancy which bodily strength acquires in rustic life, was the umpire in all disputes, setting his hat on one side and giving his decisions with an air and tone admitting of no gainsay or appeal. He was always ready for either a fight or a frolic, but had more mischief than ill-will in his composition; and with all his overbearing roughness there was a strong dash of waggish good-humor at bottom. He had three or four boon companions who regarded him as their model, and at the head of whom he scoured the country, attending every scene of feud or merriment for miles around. In cold weather he was distinguished by a fur cap surmounted with a flaunting fox's tail; and when the folks at a country gathering descried this well-known crest at a distance, whisking about among a squad of hard riders, they always stood by for a squall. Sometimes his crew would be heard dashing along past the farmhouses at midnight with hoop and halloo, like a troop of Don Cossacks, and the old dames, startled out of their sleep, would listen for a moment till the hurryscurry had clattered by, and then exclaim, "Ay, there goes Brom Bones and his gang!" The neighbors looked upon him with a mixture of awe, admiration, and good-will, and when any madcap prank or rustic brawl occurred in the vicinity always shook their heads and warranted Brom Bones was at the bottom of it.

This rantipole hero had for some time singled out the blooming Katrina for the object of his uncouth gallantries, and, though his amorous toyings were something like the gentle caresses and endearments of a bear, yet it was whispered that she did not altogether discourage his hopes. Certain it is, his advances were signals for rival candidates to retire who felt no inclination to cross a lion in his amours; insomuch, that when his horse was seen tied to Van Tassel's paling on a Sunday night, a sure sign that his master was courting — or, as it is termed, "sparking" — within, all other suitors passed by in despair and carried the war into other quarters.

Such was the formidable rival with whom Ichabod Crane had to contend, and, considering all things, a stouter man than he would have shrunk from the competition and a wiser man would have despaired. He had, however, a happy mixture of pliability and per-severance in his nature; he was in form and spirit like a supple jack — yielding, but tough; though he bent, he never broke; and though he bowed beneath the slightest pressure, yet the moment it was away, jerk! he was as erect and carried his head as high as ever.

To have taken the field openly against his rival would have been madness; for he was not a man to be thwarted in his amours, any more than that stormy lover, Achilles. Ichabod, therefore, made his advances in a quiet and gently insinuating manner. Undercover of his character of singing-master he made frequent visits at the farm-house; not that he had anything to apprehend from the meddlesome interference of parents, which is so often a stumbling-block in the path of lovers. Balt Van Tassel was an easy, indulgent soul; he loved his daughter better even than his pipe, and, like a reasonable man and an excellent father, let her have her way in everything. His notable little wife, too, had enough to do to attend to her housekeeping and manage her poultry; for, as she sagely observed, ducks and geese are foolish things and must be looked after, but girls can take care of themselves. Thus while the busy dame bustled about the house or plied her spinning-wheel at one end of the piazza, honest Balt would sit smoking his evening pipe at the other, watching the achievements of a little wooden warrior who, armed with a sword in each hand, was most valiantly fighting the wind on the pinnacle of the barn. In the mean time, Ichabod would carry on his suit with the daughter by the side of the spring under the great elm or sauntering along in the twilight, that hour so favorable to the lover's eloquence.

I profess not to know how women's hearts are wooed and won. To me they have always been matters of riddle and admiration. Some seem to have but one vulnerable point or door of access, while others have a thousand avenues and may be captured in a thousand different ways. It is a great triumph of skill to gain the former, but a still greater proof of generalship to maintain possession of the latter, for a man must battle for his fortress at every door and window. He who wins a thousand common hearts is therefore entitled to some renown, but he who keeps undisputed sway over the heart of a coquette is indeed a hero. Certain it is, this was not the case with the redoubtable Brom Bones; and from the moment Ichabod Crane made his advances the interests of the former evidently declined; his horse was no longer seen tied at the palings on Sunday nights, and a deadly feud gradually arose between him and the preceptor of Sleepy Hollow.

Brom, who had a degree of rough chivalry in his nature, would fain have carried matters to open warfare, and have settled their pretensions to the lady according to the mode of those most concise and simple reasoners, the knights-errant of yore — by single combat; but Ichabod was too conscious of the superior might of his adversary to enter the lists against him: he had overheard a boast of Bones, that he would "double the schoolmaster up and lay him on a shelf of his own school-house"; and he was too wary to give him an opportunity. There was something extremely provoking in this obstinately pacific system; it left Brom no alternative but to draw upon the funds of rustic waggery in his disposition and to play off boorish practical jokes upon his rival. Ichabod became the object of whimsical persecution to Bones and his gang of rough riders. They harried his hitherto peaceful domains; smoked out his singing school by stopping up the chimney; broke into the school-house at night, in spite of its formidable fastenings of withe and window stakes, and turned everything topsy-turvy; so that the poor schoolmaster began to think all the witches in the country held their meetings there. But, what was still more annoying, Brom took all opportunities of turning him into ridicule in presence of his mistress, and had a scoundrel dog whom he taught to whine in the most ludicrous manner, and introduced as a rival of Ichabod's to instruct her in psalmody.

In this way matters went on for some time without producing any material effect on the relative situation of the contending powers. On a fine autumnal afternoon Ichabod, in pensive mood, sat enthroned on the lofty stool whence he usually watched all the concerns of his little literary realm. In his hand he swayed a ferrule, that sceptre of despotic power; the birch of justice reposed on three nails behind the throne, a constant terror to evil-doers; while on the desk before him might be seen sundry contraband articles and prohibited weapons detected upon the persons of idle urchins, such as half-munched apples, pop-guns, whirligigs, fly-cages, and whole legions of rampant little paper game-cocks. Apparently there had been some appalling act of justice recently inflicted, for his scholars were all busily intent upon their books or slyly whispering behind them with one eye kept upon the master, and a kind of buzzing stillness reigned throughout the schoolroom. It was suddenly interrupted by the appearance of a negro in tow-cloth jacket and trowsers, a round-crowned fragment of a hat like the cap of Mercury, and mounted on the back of a ragged, wild, half-broken colt, which he managed with a rope by way of halter. He came clattering up to the school door with an invitation to Ichabod to attend a merry-making or "quilting frolic" to be held that evening at Mynheer Van Tassel's; and, having delivered his message with that air of importance and effort at fine language which a negro is apt to display on petty embassies of the kind, he dashed over the brook, and was seen scampering away up the hollow, full of importance and hurry of his mission.

All was now bustle and hubbub in the late quiet school-room. The scholars were hurried through their lessons without stopping at trifles; those who were nimble skipped over half with impunity, and those who were tardy had a smart application now and then in the rear to quicken their speed or help them over a tall word. Books were flung aside without being put away on the shelves, inkstands were overturned, benches thrown down, and the whole school was turned loose an hour before the usual time, bursting forth like a legion of young imps, yelping and racketing about the green in joy at their early emancipation.

The gallant Ichabod now spent at least an extra half-hour at his toilet, brushing and furbushing up his best, and indeed only, suit of rusty black, and arranging his looks by a bit of broken looking-glass that hung up in the school-house. That he might make his appearance before his mistress in the true style of a cavalier, he borrowed a horse from the farmer with whom he domiciliated, a choleric old Dutchman of the name of Hans Van Ripper, and, thus gallantly mounted, issued forth like a knight-errant in quest of adventures. But it is meet I should, in the true spirit of romantic story, give some account of the looks and equipments of my hero and his steed. The animal he bestrode was a broken-down plough-horse that had outlived almost everything but his viciousness. He was gaunt and shagged, with a ewe neck and a head like a hammer; his rusty mane and tail were tangled and knotted with burrs; one eye had lost its pupil and was glaring and spectral, but the other had the gleam of a genuine devil in it. Still, he must have had fire and mettle in his day, if we may judge from the name he bore of Gunpowder. He had, in fact, been a favorite steed of his master's, the choleric Van Ripper, who was a furious rider, and had infused, very probably, some of his own spirit into the animal; for, old and broken down as he looked, there was more of the lurking devil in him than in any young filly in the country.

Ichabod was a suitable figure for such a steed. He rode with short stirrups, which brought his knees nearly up to the pommel of the saddle; his sharp elbows stuck out like grasshoppers'; he carried his whip perpendicularly in his hand like a sceptre; and as his horse jogged on the motion of his arms was not unlike the flapping of a pair of wings. A small wool hat rested on the top of his nose, for so his scanty strip of forehead might be called, and the skirts of his black coat fluttered out almost to his horse's tail. Such was the appearance of Ichabod and his steed as they shambled out of the gate of Hans Van Ripper, and it was altogether such an apparition as is seldom to be met with in broad daylight.

It was, as I have said, a fine autumnal day, the sky was clear and serene, and Nature wore that rich and golden livery which we always associate with the idea of abundance. The forests had put on their sober brown and yellow, while some trees of the tenderer kind had been nipped by the frosts into brilliant dyes of orange, purple, and scarlet. Streaming files of wild-ducks began to make their appearance high in the air; the bark of the squirrel might be heard from the groves of beech and hickory nuts, and the pensive whistle of the quail at intervals from the neighboring stubble-field.

The small birds were taking their farewell banquets. In the fulness of their revelry they fluttered, chirping and frolicking, from bush to bush and tree to tree, capricious from the very profusion and variety around them. There was the honest cock-robin, the favorite game of stripling sportsmen, with its loud querulous note; and the twittering blackbirds, flying in sable clouds; and the golden-winged woodpecker, with his crimson crest, his broad black gorget, and splendid plumage; and the cedar-bird, with its red-tipt wings and yellow-tipt tail and its little monteiro cap of feathers; and the blue jay, that noisy coxcomb, in his gay light-blue coat and white underclothes, screaming and chattering, nodding and bobbing and bowing, and pretending to be on good terms with every songster of the grove.

As Ichabod jogged slowly on his way his eye, ever open to every symptom of culinary abundance, ranged with delight over the treasures of jolly Autumn. On all sides he beheld vast store of apples — some hanging in oppressive opulence on the trees, some gathered into baskets and barrels for the market, others heaped up in rich piles for the ciderpress. Farther on he beheld great fields of Indian corn, with its golden ears peeping from their leafy coverts and holding out the promise of cakes and hasty pudding; and the yellow pumpkins lying beneath them, turning up their fair round bellies to the sun, and giving ample prospects of the most luxurious of pies; and anon he passed the fragrant buckwheat-fields, breathing the odor of the bee-hive, and as he beheld them soft anticipations stole over his mind of dainty slapjacks, well buttered and garnished with honey or treacle by the delicate little dimpled hand of Katrina Van Tassel.

Thus feeding his mind with many sweet thoughts and "sugared suppositions," he journeyed along the sides of a range of hills which look out upon some of the goodliest scenes of the mighty Hudson. The sun gradually wheeled his broad disk down into the west. The wide bosom of the Tappan Zee lay motionless and glassy, excepting that here and there a gentle undulation waved and prolonged the blue shadow of the distant mountain. A few amber clouds floated in the sky, without a breath of air to move them. The horizon was of a fine golden tint, changing gradually into a pure apple green, and from that into the deep blue of the mid-heaven. A slanting ray lingered on the woody crests of the precipices that overhung some parts of the river, giving greater depth to the dark gray and purple of their rocky sides. A sloop was loitering in the distance, dropping slowly down with the tide, her sail hanging uselessly against the mast, and as the reflection of the sky gleamed along the still water it seemed as if the vessel was suspended in the air.

It was toward evening that Ichabod arrived at the castle of the Heer Van Tassel, which he found thronged with the pride and flower of the adjacent country — old farmers, a spare leathern-faced race, in homespun coats and breeches, blue stockings, huge shoes, and magnificent pewter buckles; their brisk withered little dames, in close crimped caps, longwaisted shortgowns, homespun petticoats, with scissors and pincushions and gay calico pockets hanging on the outside; buxom lasses, almost as antiquated as their mothers, excepting where a straw hat, a fine ribbon, or perhaps a white frock, gave symptoms of city innovation; the sons, in short squareskirted coats with rows of stupendous brass buttons, and their hair generally queued in the fashion of the times, especially if they could procure an eel-skin for the purpose, it being esteemed throughout the country as a potent nourisher and strengthener of the hair.

Brom Bones, however, was the hero of the scene, having come to the gathering on his favorite steed Daredevil — a creature, like himself, full of metal and mischief, and which no one but himself could manage. He was, in fact, noted for preferring vicious animals, given to all kinds of tricks, which kept the rider in constant risk of his neck, for he held a tractable, well-broken horse as unworthy of a lad of spirit.

Fain would I pause to dwell upon the world of charms that burst upon the enraptured gaze of my hero as he entered the state parlor of Van Tassel's mansion. Not those of the bevy of buxom lasses with their luxurious display of red and white, but the ample charms of a genuine Dutch country tea-table in the sumptuous time of autumn. Such heaped-up platters of cakes of various and almost indescribable kinds, known only to experienced Dutch housewives! There was the doughty doughnut, the tenderer oly koek, and the crisp and crumbling cruller; sweet cakes and short cakes, ginger cakes and honey cakes, and the whole family of cakes. And then there were apple pies and peach pies and pumpkin pies, besides slices of ham and smoked beef; and moreover delectable dishes of preserved plums and peaches and pears and quinces, not to mension broiled shad and roasted chickens, together with bowls of milk and cream — all mingled higgledy-piggledy, pretty much as I have enumerated them, with the motherly tea-pot sending up its clouds of vapor from the midst. Heaven bless the mark! I want breath and time to discuss this banquet as it deserves, and am too eager to get on with my story. Happily, Ichabod Crane was not in so great a hurry as his historian, but did ample justice to every dainty.

He was a kind and thankful creature, whose heart dilated in proportion as his skin was filled with good cheer, and whose spirits rose with eating as some men's do with drink. He could not help, too, rolling his large eyes round him as he ate, and chuckling with the possibility that he might one day be lord of all this scene of almost unimaginable luxury and splendor. Then, he thought, how soon he'd turn his back upon the old school-house, snap his fingers in the face of Hans Van Ripper and every other niggardly patron, and kick any itinerant pedagogue out of doors that should dare to call him comrade!

Old Baltus Van Tassel moved about among his guests with a face dilated with content and good humor, round and jolly as the harvest moon. His hospitable attentions were brief, but expressive, being confined to a shake of the hand, a slap on the shoulder, a loud laugh, and a pressing invitation to. "fall to and help themselves."

And now the sound of music from the common room, or hall, summoned to the dance. The musician was an old grayheaded negro who had been the itinerant orchestra of the neighborhood for more than half a century. His instrument was as old and battered as himself. The greater part of the time he scraped on two or three strings, accompanying every movement of the bow with a motion of the head, bowing almost to the ground and stamping with his foot whenever a fresh couple were to start.

Ichabod prided himself upon his dancing as much as upon his vocal powers. Not a limb, not a fibre about him was idle; and to have seen his loosely hung frame in full motion and clattering about the room you would have thought Saint Vitus himself, that blessed patron of the dance, was figuring before you in person. He was the admiration of all the negroes, who, having gathered, of all ages and sizes, from the farm and the neighborhood, stood forming a pyramid of shining black faces at every door and window, gazing with delight at the scene, rolling their white eyeballs, and showing grinning rows of ivory from ear to ear. How could the flogger of urchins be otherwise than animated and joyous! The lady of his heart was his partner in the dance, and smiling graciously in reply to all his amorous oglings, while Brom Bones, sorely smitten with love and jealousy, sat brooding by himself in one corner.

When the dance was at an end Ichabod was attracted to a knot of the sager folks, who, with old Van Tassel, sat smoking at one end of the piazza gossiping over former times and drawing out long stories about the war.

This neighborhood, at the time of which I am speaking, was one of those highly favored places which abound with chronicle and great men. The British and American line had run near it during the war; it had therefore been the scene of marauding, and infested with refugees, cow-boys, and all kinds of border chivalry. Just sufficient time had elapsed to enable each story-teller to dress up his tale with a little becoming fiction, and in the indistinctness of his recollection to make himself the hero of every exploit.

There was the story of Doffue Martling, a large blue-bearded Dutchman, who had nearly taken a British frigate with an old iron nine-pounder from a mud breastwork, only that his gun burst at the sixth discharge. And there was an old gentleman who shall be nameless, being too rich a mynheer to be lightly mentioned, who, in the battle of Whiteplains, being an excellent master of defence, parried a musket-ball with a small sword, insomuch that he absolutely felt it whiz round the blade and glance off at the hilt: in proof of which he was ready at any time to show the sword, with the hilt a little bent. There were several more that had been equally great in the field, not one of whom but was persuaded that he had a considerable hand in bringing the war to a happy termination.

But all these were nothing to the tales of ghosts and apparitions that succeeded. The neighborhood is rich in legendary treasures of the kind. Local tales and superstitions thrive best in these sheltered, long-settled retreats, but are trampled under foot by the shifting throng that forms the population of most of our country places. Besides, there is no encouragement for ghosts in most of our villages, for they have scarcely had time to finish their first nap and turn themselves in their graves before their surviving friends have travelled away from the neighborhood; so that when they turn out at night to walk their rounds they have no acquaintance left to call upon. This is perhaps the reason why we so seldom hear of ghosts except in our long-established Dutch communities.

The immediate cause, however, of the prevalence of supernatural stories in these parts was doubtless owing to the vicinity of Sleepy Hollow. There was a contagion in the very air that blew from that haunted region; it breathed forth an atmosphere of dreams and fancies infecting all the land. Several of the Sleepy Hollow people were present at Van Tassel's, and, as usual, were doling out their wild and wonderful legends. Many dismal tales were told about funeral trains, and mourning cries and wailings heard and seen about the great tree where the unfortunate Major André was taken, and which stood in the neighborhood. Some mention was made also of the woman in white that haunted the dark glen at Raven Rock, and was often heard to shriek on winter nights before a storm, having perished there in the snow. The chief part of the stories, however, turned upon the favorite spectre of Sleepy Hollow, the headless horseman, who had been heard several times of late patrolling the country, and, it was said, tethered his horse nightly among the graves in the churchyard.

The sequestered situation of this church seems always to have made it a favorite haunt of troubled spirits. It stands on a knoll surrounded by locust trees and lofty elms, from among which its decent whitewashed walls shine modestly forth, like Christian purity beaming through the shades of retirement. A gentle slope descends from it to a silver sheet of water bordered by high trees, between which peeps may be caught at the blue hills of the Hudson. To look upon its grass-grown yard, where the sunbeams seem to sleep so quietly, one would think that there at least the dead might rest in peace. On one side of the church extends a wide woody dell, along which raves a large brook among broken rocks and trunks of fallen trees. Over a deep black part of the stream, not far from the church, was formerly thrown a wooden bridge; the road that led to it and the bridge itself were thickly shaded by overhanging trees, which cast a gloom about it even in the daytime, but occasioned a fearful darkness at night. Such was one of the favorite haunts of the headless horseman, and the place where he was most frequently encountered. The tale was told of old Brouwer, a most heretical disbeliever in ghosts, how he met the horseman returning from his foray into Sleepy Hollow, and was obliged to get up behind him; how they galloped over bush and brake, over hill and swamp, until they reached the bridge, when the horseman suddenly turned into a skeleton, threw old Brouwer into the brook, and sprang away over the tree-tops with a clap of thunder.

This story was immediately matched by a thrice-marvellous adventure of Brom Bones, who made light of the galloping Hessian as an arrant jockey. He affirmed that on returning one night from the neighboring village of Sing-Sing he had been overtaken by this midnight trooper; that he had offered to race with him for a bowl of punch, and should have won it too, for Daredevil beat the goblin horse all hollow, but just as they came to the church bridge the Hessian bolted and vanished in a flash of fire.

All these tales, told in that drowsy undertone with which men talk in the dark, the countenances of the listeners only now and then receiving a casual gleam from the glare of a pipe, sank deep in the mind of Ichabod. He repaid them in kind with large extracts from his invaluable author, Cotton Mather, and added many marvellous events that had taken place in his native state of Connecticut, and fearful sights which he had seen in his nightly walks about Sleepy Hollow.

The revel now gradually broke up. The old farmers gathered together their families in their wagons, and were heard for some time rattling along the hollow roads and over the distant hills. Some of the damsels mounted on pillions behind their favorite swains, and their light-hearted laughter, mingling with the clatter of hoofs, echoed along the silent woodlands, sounding fainter and fainter until they gradually died away, and the late scene of noise and frolic was all silent and deserted. Ichabod only lingered behind, according to the custom of country lovers, to have a tête-à-tête with the heiress, fully convinced that he was now on the high road to success. What passed at this interview I will not pretend to say, for in fact I do not know. Something, however, I fear me, must have gone wrong, for he certainly sallied forth, after no very great interval, with an air quite desolate and chop-fallen. Oh these women! these women! Could that girl have been playing off any of her coquettish tricks? Was her encouragement of the poor pedagogue all a mere sham to secure her conquest of his rival? Heaven only knows, not I! Let it suffice to say, Ichabod stole forth with the air of one who had been sacking a hen-roost rather than a fair lady's heart. Without looking to the right or left to notice the scene of rural wealth on which he had so often gloated, he went straight to the stable, and with several hearty cuffs and kicks roused his steed most uncourteously from the comfortable quarters in which he was soundly sleeping, dreaming of mountains of corn and oats and whole valleys of timothy and clover.

It was the very witching time of night that Ichabod, heavy-hearted and crest-fallen, pursued his travel homeward along the sides of the lofty hills which rise above Tarry Town, and which he had traversed so cheerily in the afternoon. The hour was as dismal as himself. Far below him the Tappan Zee spread its dusky and indistinct waste of waters, with here and there the tall mast of a sloop riding quietly at anchor under the land. In the dead hush of midnight he could even hear the barking of the watchdog from the opposite shore of the Hudson; but it was so vague and faint as only to give an idea of his distance from this faithful companion of man. Now and then, too, the long-drawn crowing of a cock, accidentally awakened, would sound far, far off, from some farm-house away among the hills; but it was like a dreaming sound in his ear. No signs of life occurred near him, but occasionally the melancholy chirp of a cricket, or perhaps the guttural twang of a bull-frog from a neighboring marsh, as if sleeping uncomfortably and turning suddenly in his bed.

All the stories of ghosts and goblins that he had heard in the afternoon now came crowding upon his recollection. The night grew darker and darker; the stars seemed to sink deeper in the sky, and driving clouds occasionally hid them from his sight. He had never felt so lonely and dismal. He was, moreover, approaching the very place where many of the scenes of the ghost-stories had been laid. In the centre of the road stood an enormous tulip tree which towered like a giant above all the other trees of the neighborhood and formed a kind of landmark. Its limbs were gnarled and fantastic, large enough to form trunks for ordinary trees, twisting down almost to the earth and rising again into the air. It was connected with the tragical story of the unfortunate André, who had been taken prisoner hard by, and was universally known by the name of Major André's tree. The common people regarded it with a mixture of respect and superstition, partly out of sympathy for the fate of its ill-starred namesake, and partly from the tales of strange sights and doleful lamentations told concerning it.

As Ichabod approached this fearful tree he began to whistle: he thought his whistle was answered; it was but a blast sweeping sharply through the dry branches. As he approached a little nearer he thought he saw something white hanging in the midst of the tree: he paused and ceased whistling, but on looking more narrowly perceived that it was a place where the tree had been scathed by lightning and the white wood laid bare. Suddenly he heard a groan; his teeth chattered and his knees smote against the saddle; it was but the rubbing of one huge bough upon another as they were swayed about by the breeze. He passed the tree in safety, but new perils lay before him.

About two hundred yards from the tree a small brook crossed the road and ran into a marshy and thickly wooded glen known by the name of Wiley's Swamp. A few rough logs, laid side by side, served for a bridge over this stream. On that side of the road where the brook entered the wood a group of oaks and chestnuts, matted thick with wild grape-vines, threw a cavernous gloom over it. To pass this bridge was the severest trial. It was at this identical spot that the unfortunate André was captured, and under the covert of those chestnuts and vines were the sturdy yeomen concealed who surprised him. This has ever since been considered a haunted stream, and fearful are the feelings of a schoolboy who has to pass it alone after dark.

As he approached the stream his heart began to thump; he summoned up, however, all his resolution, gave his horse half a score of kicks in the ribs, and attempted to dash briskly across the bridge; but instead of starting forward, the perverse old animal made a lateral movement and ran broadside against the fence. Ichabod, whose fears increased with the delay, jerked the reins on the other side and kicked lustily with the contrary foot: it was all in vain; his steed started, it is true, but it was only to plunge to the opposite side of the road into a thicket of brambles and alderbushes. The schoolmaster now bestowed both whip and heel upon the starveling ribs of old Gunpowder, who dashed forward, snuffing and snorting, but came to a stand just by the bridge with a suddenness that had nearly sent his rider sprawling over his head. Just at this moment a plashy tramp by the side of the bridge caught the sensitive ear of Ichabod. In the dark shadow of the grove on the margin of the brook he beheld something huge, misshapen, black, and towering. It stirred not, but seemed gathered up in the gloom, like some gigantic monster ready to spring upon the traveller.

The hair of the affrighted pedagogue rose upon his head with terror. What was to be done? To turn and fly was now too late; and besides, what chance was there of escaping the ghost or goblin, if such it was, which could ride upon the wings of the wind? Summoning up, therefore, a show of courage, he demanded in stammering accents, "Who are you?" He received no reply. He repeated his demand in a still more agitated voice. Still there was no answer. Once more he cudgelled the sides of the inflexible Gunpowder, and, shutting his eyes, broke forth with involuntary fervor into a psalm tune. Just then the shadowy object of alarm put itself in motion, and with a scramble and a bound stood at once in the middle of the road. Though the night was dark and dismal, yet the form of the unknown might now in some degree be ascertained. He appeared to be a horseman of large dimensions and mounted on a black horse of powerful frame. He made no offer of molestation or sociability, but kept aloof on one side of the road, jogging along on the blind side of old Gunpowder, who had now got over his fright and waywardness.

Ichabod, who had no relish for this strange midnight companion, and bethought himself of the adventure of Brom Bones with the Galloping Hessian, now quickened his steed in hopes of leaving him behind. The stranger, however, quickened his horse to an equal pace. Ichabod pulled up, and fell into a walk, thinking to lag behind; the other did the same. His heart began to sink within him; he endeavored to resume his psalm tune, but his parched tongue clove to the roof of his mouth and he could not utter a stave. There was something in the moody and dogged silence of this pertinacious companion that was mysterious and appalling. It was soon fearfully accounted for. On mounting a rising ground, which brought the figure of his fellow-traveller in relief against the sky, gigantic in height and muffled in a cloak, Ichabod was horrorstruck on perceiving that he was headless! but his horror was still more increased on observing that the head, which should have rested on his shoulders, was carried before him on the pommel of the saddle. His terror rose to desperation; he rained a shower of kicks and blows upon Gunpowder, hoping by a sudden movement to give his companion the slip; but the spectre started full jump with him. Away, then, they dashed through thick and thin, stones flying and sparks flashing at every bound. Ichabod's flimsy garments fluttered in the air as he stretched his long, lank body away over his horse's head in the eagerness of his flight.

They had now reached the road which turns off to Sleepy Hollow; but Gunpowder, who seemed possessed with a demon, instead of keeping up it, made an opposite turn and plunged headlong down hill to the left. This road leads through a sandy hollow shaded by trees for about a quarter of a mile, where it crosses the bridge famous in goblin story, and just beyond swells the green knoll on which stands the whitewashed church.

As yet the panic of the steed had given his unskilful rider an apparent advantage in the chase; but just as he had got halfway through the hollow the girths of the saddle gave way and he felt it slipping from under him. He seized it by the pommel and endeavored to hold it firm, but in vain, and had just time to save himself by clasping old Gunpowder round the neck, when the saddle fell to the earth, and he heard it trampled under foot by his pursuer. For a moment the terror of Hans Van Ripper's wrath passed across his mind, for it was his Sunday saddle; but this was no time for petty fears; the goblin was hard on his haunches, and (unskilled rider that he was) he had much ado to maintain his seat, sometimes slipping on one side, sometimes on another, and sometimes jolted on the high ridge of his horse's back-bone with a violence that he verily feared would cleave him asunder.

An opening in the trees now cheered him with the hopes that the church bridge was at hand. The wavering reflection of a silver star in the bosom of the brook told him that he was not mistaken. He saw the walls of the church dimly glaring under the trees beyond. He recollected the place where Brom Bones' ghostly competitor had disappeared. "If I can but reach that bridge," thought Ichabod, "I am safe." Just then he heard the black steed panting and blowing close behind him; he even fancied that he felt his hot breath. Another convulsive kick in the ribs, and old Gunpowder sprang upon the bridge; he thundered over the resounding planks; he gained the opposite side; and now Ichabod cast a look behind to see if his pursuer should vanish, according to rule, in a flash of fire and brimstone. Just then he saw the goblin rising in his stirrups and in the very act of hurling his head at him. Ichabod endeavored to dodge the horrible missile, but too late. It encountered his cranium with a tremendous crash; he was tumbled headlong into the dust, and Gunpowder, the black steed, and the goblin rider passed by like a whirlwind.

The next morning the old horse was found, without his saddle and with the bridle under his feet, soberly cropping the grass at his master's gate. Ichabod did not make his appearance at breakfast;

dinner-hour came, but no Ichabod. The boys assembled at the school-house and strolled idly about the banks of the brook, but no schoolmaster. Hans Van Ripper now began to feel some uneasiness about the fate of poor Ichabod and his saddle. An inquiry was set on foot, and after diligent investigation they came upon his traces. In one part of the road leading to the church was found the saddle trampled in the dirt; the tracks of horses' hoofs, deeply dented in the road and evidently at furious speed, were traced to the bridge, beyond which, on the bank of a broad part of the brook, where the water ran deep and black, was found the hat of the unfortunate Ichabod, and close beside it a shattered pumpkin.

The brook was searched, but the body of the schoolmaster was not to be discovered. Hans Van Ripper, as executor of his estate, examined the bundle which contained all his worldly effects. They consisted of two shirts and a half, two stocks for the neck, a pair or two of worsted stockings, an old pair of corduroy small-clothes, a rusty razor, a book of psalm tunes full of dog's ears, and a broken pitch-pipe. As to the books and furniture of the school-house, they belonged to the community, excepting Cotton Mather's *History of Witchcraft*, a *New England Almanac*, and a book of dreams and fortune-telling, in which last was a sheet of foolscap much scribbled and blotted in several fruitless attempts to make a copy of verses in honor of the heiress of Van Tassel. These magic books and the poetic scrawl were forthwith consigned to the flames by Hans Van Ripper, who from that time forward determined to send his children no more to school, observing that he never knew any good come of this same reading and writing. Whatever money the schoolmaster possessed — and he had received his quarter's pay but a day or two before — he must have had about his person at the time of his disappearance.

The mysterious event caused much speculation at the church on the following Sunday. Knots of gazers and gossips were collected in the churchyard, at the bridge, and at the spot where the hat and pumpkin had been found. The stories of Brouwer, of Bones, and a whole budget of others were called to mind, and when they had diligently considered them all, and compared them with the symptoms of the present case, they shook their heads and came to the conclusion that Ichabod had been carried off by the galloping Hessian. As he was a bachelor and in nobody's debt, nobody troubled his head any more about him, the school was removed to a different quarter of the hollow and another pedagogue reigned in his stead.

It is true an old farmer, who had been down to New York on a visit several years after, and from whom this account of the ghostly adventure was received, brought home the intelligence that Ichabod Crane was still alive; that he had left the neighborhood, partly through fear of the goblin and Hans Van Ripper, and partly in mortification at having been suddenly dismissed by the heiress; that he had changed his quarters to a distant part of the country; had kept school and studied law at the same time, had been admitted to the bar, turned politician, electioneered, written for the newspapers, and finally had been made a justice of the Ten Pound Court. Brom Bones, too, who shortly after his rival's disappearance conducted the blooming Katrina in triumph to the altar, was observed to look exceedingly knowing whenever the story of Ichabod was related, and always burst into a hearty laugh at the mention of the pumpkin, which led some to suspect that he knew more about the matter than he chose to tell.

The old country wives, however, who are the best judges of these matters, maintain to this day that Ichabod was spirited away by supernatural means; and it is a favorite story often told about the neighborhood round the winter evening fire. The bridge became more than ever an object of superstitious awe, and that may be the reason why the road has been altered of late years so as to approach the church by the border of the millpond. The school-house, being deserted, soon fell to decay, and was reported to be haunted by the ghost of the unfortunate pedagogue; and the ploughboy, loitering homeward of a still summer evening, has often fancied his voice at a distance chanting a melancholy psalm tune among the tranquil solitudes of Sleepy Hollow.

POSTSCRIPT

*Found in the Handwriting
of Mr. Knickerbocker*

The preceding tale is given almost in the precise words in which I heard it related at a Corporation meeting of the ancient city of Manhattoes, at which were present many of its sagest and most illustrious burghers. The narrator was a pleasant, shabby, gentlemanly old fellow in pepper-and-salt clothes, with a sadly humorous face, and one whom I strongly suspected of being poor, he made such efforts to be entertaining. When his story was concluded there was much laughter and approbation, particularly from two or three deputy aldermen who had been asleep the greater part of the time. There was, however, one tall, dry-looking old gentleman, with beetling eyebrows, who maintained a grave and rather severe face throughout, now and then folding his arms, inclining his head, and looking down upon the floor, as if turning a doubt over in his mind. He was one of your wary men, who never laugh but upon good grounds — when they have reason and the law on their side. When the mirth of the rest of the company had subsided and silence was restored, he leaned one arm on the elbow of his chair, and, sticking the other akimbo, demanded, with a slight but exceedingly sage motion of the head and contraction of the brow, what was the moral of the story and what it went to prove.

The story-teller, who was just putting a glass of wine to his lips as a refreshment after his toils, paused for a moment, looked at his inquirer with an air of infinite deference, and, lowering the glass slowly to the table, observed that the story was intended most logically to prove —

"That there is no situation in life but has its advantages and pleasures — provided we will but take a joke as we find it;

"That, therefore, he that runs races with goblin troopers is likely to have rough riding of it.

"Ergo, for a country schoolmaster to be refused the hand of a Dutch heiress is a certain step to high preferment in the state."

The cautious old gentleman knit his brows tenfold closer after this explanation, being sorely puzzled by the ratiocination of the syllogism, while methought the one in pepper-and-salt eyed him with something of a triumphant leer. At length he observed that all this was very well, but still he thought the story a little on the extravagant — there were one or two points on which he had his doubts.

"Faith, sir," replied the story-teller, "as to that matter, I don't believe one-half of it myself."

—D. K.

The Woodman and the Goblins

By J.B. Esenwein and Marietta Stockard

&

nce on a time a Woodman lived in the heart of a thick wood. He lived all by himself; he did not have any wife to look after him, or any children to look after. But he was a clever old fellow, and managed things somehow. He built his own house, did his own cooking, and mended his own clothes.

He did all the washing he thought necessary, which was not a great deal, so his house was not very clean and tidy, for he thought the best place for things was where they could be picked up easily; and when anything got lost he had no one to blame but himself.

One afternoon he suddenly remembered that he had to go to the village, which was miles and miles away, to get a new ax. His old one was of no use, for he had sharpened it so many times that there was very little left of it. He had some work to do the next day, so a new ax he must have, and he hurried to get ready.

He washed his brown face, combed his gray hair, stuck a skewer through his leather clothes where some buttons were off, and set out for the village.

When the people saw his fat, stumpy little figure coming down the street, they came out to talk to him, for he was a kind old fellow and they all liked him. He was glad to have someone to talk with besides himself, so he stayed quite late in the village. The sun was going down before he put his new ax across his shoulder and started for home.

"Be careful as you go through the woods tonight," his friends called after him, "you know it is Halloween; the witches and goblins will be out."

"I've never seen one of them yet," said the old Woodman, "but I'll try to get home before midnight, so I'll be safe," and he hurried along through the woods.

He would have told you that he could find his way home with his eyes shut, but suddenly, to his great surprise, he saw that the road looked strange and he had not the least idea where he was. As he went forward the woods became thicker and thicker. He could hardly squeeze through the trees, they were so close together. But he walked on, starting at every sound, for it was very dark indeed, and he could not help thinking of all the stories he had ever heard of witches, goblins, and ghosts.

At last he came to a huge beech tree, and as he peered about trying to find a path, he came upon six big eggs. They were in a hollow place between the roots of the tree.

"What thumping big eggs!" he said. "I'll take them home and hatch them out. If I can raise some hens to lay such eggs, I'll not have far to look for breakfast hereafter."

He took up the eggs and carried them carefully, walking very slowly so as not to stumble with his treasures. At last, after some trouble, he found the road and went along home.

When he got into the house he began to look about for some way to hatch the eggs. The cat was soft and warm, but she would never keep still long enough; besides, he dared not trust her. He thought of putting them into bed with himself, but it was out of the question for him to stay in bed three weeks. At last he thought of a piece of red flannel he had bought to make himself some winter shirts. So he cut it up, and wrapped an egg in each piece of it, then set them around the fire.

For three weeks he kept the fire going night and day, and he turned and watched the eggs. It was a tedious job, but of course if one wants something he must work for it, and the Woodman wanted those big hens.

At last the day came when the eggs showed signs of life. They moved a little — just a teeny, tiny bit. He had to look close to be quite sure it was true. One began to chip, then another began to chip. One of the cracks opened, and out came—not a chicken's head as he had expected, but a little squirmy fist, like a baby's hand, only it was a purply black.

Soon there was a crackling and a squealing and a squirming, and out of one egg popped a head, out of another a foot, and soon six little bodies came wriggling out of the six eggs.

The Woodman stood staring at six of the queerest little imps you ever could imagine, sprawling about on the floor. They stretched their necks and tumbled about over one another like young puppies. The poor Woodman did not know what to say or think or do. He stood scratching his head and staring. He had never had a family before, and he did not have any neighbors to come in and give him advice.

He thought the poor things looked cold, for they had hatched out without any clothes on, so he took the pieces of flannel that had been wrapped around the eggs, and snipped a round hole in each piece. Then he slipped the pieces over the little shivering bodies. It was a funny sight, but the Woodman did not laugh. It was a serious matter to get a family like that all at once.

But how was he to feed them? He brought some pans of milk, but they did not know how to drink. At last he thought of a way. He took some of the flannel, dipped it in the milk, and stuck it into their gaping little mouths. After a while he taught them to

drink through a straw. Then they ate and ate and ate. They did not know when to stop.

Of course that made them sick, and there was more trouble for the poor man. He had never been so busy in all his life. Sometimes he was so tired that he thought of running away and leaving them; but he was too kind to do that, for he knew they would freeze and starve if they were left alone.

"Perhaps if I take care of them now, they will help me when they are older," he thought. Then he planned all the ways they could help him, running errands, cooking the food, chopping wood, and going to the spring for the drinking water.

But as they grew older, instead of helping him, they hindered him more and more. They were always playing pranks. They pulled the poor cat's tail, hid the Woodman's glasses — in fact, they were just as bad as bad could be. But bad as they were all day long, when the candles were lit in the evening they all became quiet at once.

No matter what they were doing, the moment they saw the light of the candles, they stopped and gathered around the table. They leaned their elbows on it, propped their chins on their hands, and stared at the candles, each eye like the letter O, with a dot in the middle.

One night when they gathered around the table in this way, an idea came to the Woodman: "I know what I'll do," he thought, "I'll put the candle into this lantern and they will follow it. I will take them to the beech tree where I found the eggs, and I'll leave them there. Some of their own people will be sure to find them."

So he took the candle and put it in the lantern, and all the Goblins — for that is what they were — crowded around to see him do it. They chattered among themselves like bats, never taking their eyes off the light. They did not wink, they did not blink — they just stared and stared at the light until the old

Woodman felt like staring himself. He made for the door and went out into the night.

They all came stumbling after, their eyes glued to the light. Sometimes one stumbled and fell, but he got up again and went bumping on as before. On they went through the dark woods. Shadows danced about their path, twigs crackled under their feet, and now and then there was a dull thud as one stumbled over a root or a stone.

At last the Woodman found the beech tree and hung the lantern on a broken branch, then turned to go home. The little Goblins squatted on the ground in a circle, and sat staring up at the lantern.

But the Woodman turned away and walked into the black night along the tangled path; he stumbled like a blind man. Branches struck him in the face, one hurt his hand as he tried to thrust it aside, and finally he slipped and fell. He tried to crawl forward, but something seized him by the belt. He gave a scream of terror. It was only the limb of a tree, but the poor man was almost frightened out of his wits.

He looked back at the light, and the little Goblins were sitting there still and quiet. When he looked away, the darkness seemed more terrible. He was afraid of every dark shadow.

He looked back at the light again, and it seemed as if he were being drawn back to it and to his Goblin family. The more he looked at their homely little faces, the more he wanted to be there with them, and with the light. So he crawled slowly back toward the circle.

His own eyes began to be glued to the light. They grew big and round, and he stared and stared and stared, unable to turn away from it; the Spell had come upon him, too.

He took his place in the Goblin circle, and if the light still burns, beyond a doubt they are all sitting there still underneath the crooked beech tree.

The King o' the Cats

By Joseph Jacobs

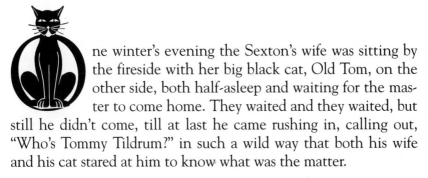

ne winter's evening the Sexton's wife was sitting by the fireside with her big black cat, Old Tom, on the other side, both half-asleep and waiting for the master to come home. They waited and they waited, but still he didn't come, till at last he came rushing in, calling out, "Who's Tommy Tildrum?" in such a wild way that both his wife and his cat stared at him to know what was the matter.

"Why, what's the matter?" said his wife, "and why do you want to know who Tommy Tildrum is?"

"Oh, I've had such an adventure. I was digging away at Old Mr. Fordyce's grave when I suppose I must have fallen asleep, and only woke up by hearing a cat's miaou."

"Miaou!" said Old Tom in answer.

"Yes, just like that! So I looked over the edge of the grave, and what do you think I saw?"

"Now, how can I tell?" said the Sexton's wife.

"Why, nine black cats all like our friend Old Tom here, all with a white spot on their chestesses. And what do you think they were carrying? Why, a small coffin covered with a black velvet pall, and on the pall was a small coronet all of gold, and at every third step they took they cried all together, miaou — !"

"Miaou!" said Old Tom again.

"Yes, just like that!" said the Sexton. "And as they came nearer and nearer to me I could see more distinctly, because their eyes shone out with a sort of green light. Well, they all came toward me, eight of them carrying the coffin, and the biggest cat of all walking in front for all the world like — But look at Old Tom, how he's looking at me. You'd think he knew all I was saying."

"Go on, go on," said his wife, "never mind Old Tom."

"Well, as I was a-saying, they came toward me slowly and solemnly, and at every third step crying all together, miaou — "

"Miaou!" said Old Tom again.

"Yes, just like that, till they came and stood right opposite Mr. Fordyce's grave, where I was, when they all stood still and looked straight at me. I did feel queer, that I did! But look at Old Tom; he's looking at me just like they did."

"Go on, go on," said his wife, "never mind Old Tom."

"Where was I? Oh, they all stood still looking at me, when the one that wasn't carrying the coffin came forward and, staring straight at me, said to me — yes, I tell 'ee, *said* to me, with a squeaky voice, 'Tell Tom Tildrum that Tim Toldrum's dead,' and that's why I asked you if you knew who Tom Tildrum was, for how can I tell Tom Tildrum Tim Toldrum's dead if I don't know who Tom Tildrum is?"

"Look at Old Tom, look at Old Tom!" screamed his wife.

And well he might look, for Old Tom was swelling and Old Tom was staring, and at last Old Tom shrieked out, "What — Old Tim dead! Then I'm the King o' the Cats!" and rushed up the chimney and was never more seen.

The Witchstone of Scrapfaggot Green

By Peter Haining

ଈଔ

The county of Essex, on the outskirts of London, is known in history as "The Witch County." The reason for this is that from the middle of the sixteenth century to the end of the seventeenth, there were more "witches" tried, tortured, and put to death in the area than anywhere else in the British Isles.

We know that many of these poor people were not witches at all, but harmless old men or women who had somehow upset their neighbours and thus been accused of being in league with the Devil. Some of them probably knew all about country cures and used their potions to help relieve minor illnesses at a time when there were no local doctors. But unfortunately when these cures worked, superstitious neighbours thought it was sure proof that they were aided by Satan himself. Anyone who was suspected of being a witch was for most of the time treated with awe and avoided at all costs. But when the authorities began to root out all those who were said to be enemies of the Church, accusing fingers would be raised. And it is a measure of the fear that people had of witches — whether they were real or not — that this fear often continued after the witch was dead.

Just off the A12 road between the towns of Chelmsford and Braintree lies the charming little village of Great Leighs. The village has an impressive Norman church, two fine pubs, and a few shops. It also has a little area of common around a crossroads with the extraordinary name of Scrapfaggot Green. It is here that the story begins back in the year 1944 at the end of the Second World War.

The Americans had joined Britain, and all over England convoys of troops and weapons began to move up and down the roads, and even in the narrow lanes of Essex.

In the first week of June, a particularly large convoy of American tank-carriers passed through the village of Great Leighs. They were east-bound towards the coast from their depot and had already been on the road for almost two days. The weather was hot and close, and the drivers had lost patience with the crawling speed which was the best they could make along the narrow Essex lanes. Just as the leading driver was about to make a turn at the crossroads known as Scrapfaggot Green, he muttered a curse and slammed on his brakes. There was a large stone standing by the roadside, and he knew his load was too wide to get by it.

The American dropped from the cab of his truck and walked forward towards the stone, scratching his head. It was a huge, weathered piece of rock, standing all of eight feet high, and set firmly in the earth. On the top, it had a strange hole. Even at a quick estimate he reckoned it must weigh all of two tons. The man looked around. Even by pulling over to the far side of the road, he could not hope to squeeze by. It looked as if the convoy would have to turn round and find another route. But that would ruin their schedule. As the man stood thinking, a couple of other drivers from vehicles that had pulled up behind came to join him.

"Darned rock," the first American muttered. "We'll never clear it with these wide loads."

One of the other drivers went over to the rock and slapped its smooth grey surface. "Reckon we could shift it to one side? Don't seem to be doing too much here."

The three Americans looked at each other for a moment. It would certainly save them going back—and surely the folk here wouldn't mind them moving the stone? Besides, there didn't seem to be anyone about.

"Right. Let's shift it," the first driver said, making up his mind. He moved quickly back to his cab. From inside he pulled out a steel hawser, and with the help of his two companions this was linked around the stone and joined up to the front bumper of the truck. Back in his cab again, the American applied full power to his truck and began easing backwards. The wire grew taut and for a moment the stone held firm. Increasing his acceleration, the driver felt the wheels of his vehicle slip momentarily. Then, gradually, the stone began to lean over from its standing position. The man pressed his foot down harder and the stone eased out from its resting place. He pulled the rock several yards from its former position and then stopped once more. He released the steel hawser from the stone and the vehicle, and five minutes later all the trucks in the convoy successfully navigated the crossroads and disappeared into the distance.

For the best part of quarter of an hour the stone lay on its side in the sunshine until the first person walked by and saw what had happened. He was an old man, and it took him several moments to fully understand why *something* about the common looked different. When he realized what it was, he hurried off back to the village. There he burst into the public bar of the St. Anne's Castle Inn and announced in a voice that was almost shaking, "Someone's moved the Witch's Stone."

The group of old men who sat enjoying their first pints of beer of the day looked up with puzzled expressions.

"Moved it, George?" one of them said. "Don't be daft. Thing's too heavy to move."

"I tell you it's been shifted," the man insisted. "Over on its side, it is. Come and look if you don't believe me."

Within the hour the story was flying around Great Leighs that the Witch's Stone on Scrapfaggot Green had indeed been removed. Probably something to do with the big convoy that had gone through earlier, one of the locals reckoned.

"No good will come of it," an old woman muttered, shaking her head. She, for one, knew the sinister reputation of the stone which had stood at the crossroads for almost three hundred years. For underneath, it was said, was the body of a witch who had worked such evil in her life that the rock had been put over her grave to ensure she did not rise again to terrify the neighborhood. To the younger people of Great Leighs such a story was just superstitious nonsense. For them the stone was something for children to play on, or courting couples to sit beside.

But over the next few days they were to be made to eat their words. Because within hours of the stone being moved, the village was terrorized by a series of events that are quite unique in supernatural lore.

The incidents began the following night. In the early hours of the morning the bell in the church tower began to chime all of its own accord. And then at 2:30 a.m. the clock on the steeple struck midnight, the twelve chimes ringing eerily out across the village, waking several of its inhabitants. For many nights thereafter the clock was to do exactly the same thing.

In Great Leighs next morning, several people were surprised to find that none of their hens had laid any eggs. And a number of others discovered some of their chickens missing. They later recovered these—all drowned in water butts.

Nor did the strange reports end there. Ernest Withen at Chadwicks Farm awoke to find that the stacks he had built only a few days previously were broken down and spread all over his yard. Yet he knew there had been no strong wind during the night. He was even more puzzled by the fact that all his hay wagons had been moved from the places in which he had left them in his sheds. On another farm, the owner also found some of his haystacks pushed over, and a group of stacks moved from one field to another. A shepherd named Alf Quilter, going to tend his flock, found that half were in their pen, and half out of it—although the hurdle was still closed and the surrounding fence was not damaged in any way. In the local builder's yard belonging to Charlie Dickson, piles of heavy scaffolding poles which normally took strong, fit men to shift them were scattered about the ground like so many matchsticks.

By the mid-morning of the day after the moving of the stone, it was clear that almost everyone in the village had some uncanny story to report. But it was only one or two of the very old people who thought it might have anything to do with the stone. The next night brought another fresh crop of mysterious happenings. Arthur Sykes, the landlord of the St. Anne's Castle Inn, found three geese missing without a trace, and admitted uneasily that during the night furniture had been moved about his premises, seemingly by invisible hands. In one of the bedrooms a chest of drawers had been tipped over, a heavy wardrobe moved across the room, and the bedclothes torn from the bed and strewn about the floor. Bill Reynolds, the landlord of the other pub, the Dog and Gun, had been jovially sceptical of all the stories after the first night. People's imagination playing tricks on them, was his verdict. The next morning he woke up to find a heavy stone that he had never seen before blocking his front door.

Within three days, the story reached the newspapers and made front page news across the country. The reporters who descended on Great Leighs found no evidence of a hoax, and no shortage of new outbreaks to report. But now, they seemed to be getting more dangerous.

Thirty sheep and two horses were found dead in a field, and the disturbances in the bedroom at the St. Anne's Castle Inn were repeated again with still more violent upheaval—leaving Arthur Sykes even more bewildered than before. As he told a friend later,

"I just don't understand it. From the way the room was upset I should certainly have heard something going on. I was sleeping in the next bedroom. But I never heard a thing."

Mr. Sykes had an even stranger experience to recount to one of the newspaper reporters. "It happened out in the street — in broad daylight. I saw this cut-throat razor lying on the ground. I went to pick it up — and it jumped clean away from me. I tried the same thing again and once more it jumped away from me. It couldn't have been a joke — someone pulling it with a piece of thread. For you see it kept jumping up and down, each time about a foot into the air. Frankly it frightened me, so I just left it there and went away."

By now the village was also being investigated by a psychic expert who soon confessed himself just as baffled as the locals. He could find no evidence at all that human agency was involved in any of the incidents.

In the public bar of the St. Anne's Castle Inn, the conviction really began to grow that somehow the mysterious events might all be connected with the moving of the stone.

The men in the bar had all heard the whisper going round the village that it was the witch who was responsible. That by removing the stone, her ghost had been set free and was now wreaking her vengeance on the village. At first hearing, such talk sounded as if it had come straight from the superstitious Middle Ages. But when modern science was baffled by such events — and it was — perhaps it would be as well to take a little bit of notice of it.

"I reckon we should put the stone back where it was." The old man who now spoke had been silent for some time as he listened to the arguments going backwards and forwards in the bar. "Would do no harm, would it? And if things still went on happening it might put an end to the stories about the witch."

It was an idea that had occurred to several of the others, but they had been a bit reluctant to suggest it. It seemed somehow to be giving in to superstition. For a short while, the little group talked about it. They knew the stone was heavy, but if one of them got a tractor they could surely drag it back into its old position by the road? Yes, that was what they would do. At the worst it would tidy up the common again, and at best, well . . .

Later that same evening a group of the men drove out to Scrapfaggot Green on a tractor and successfully hauled the stone back into its slot. It went in easily, one of the men remembered, almost smoothly. In the silence and darkness of night they worked, the men could almost swear they heard a rustling in the undergrowth and then a groan as the massive grey rock dropped back into place. But that could have been just the eeriness of the situation.

What is for sure, though, is that Great Leighs has not been disturbed again from that moment, and if it was the ghost of the old witch whom the Americans unknowingly released, then she has lain quietly ever since. But today, you will not find anyone in that pretty little village who will consider for a moment any suggestion that the rock on Scrapfaggot Green should be moved again . . .

And So To Bed

By Roderick Hunt

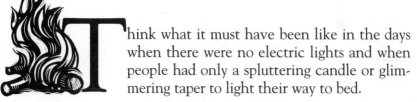

Think what it must have been like in the days when there were no electric lights and when people had only a spluttering candle or glimmering taper to light their way to bed.

Imagine them climbing the dark stairs and seeing only as far ahead as the dim light of the candle would reach. Imagine the wavering shadows as the candle-flame flickered in the draughty bedroom, while outside, in a night as dark as pitch, the wind moaned about the house and sighed through the cracks and crevices in the walls and floors.

People were very careful, especially on All Hallows' Eve, to protect themselves from harmful witches and evil spirits. Doorways would be hung with garlic, laurel or bay leaves, and horseshoes.

Before going to bed the fire was put out to prevent a hobgoblin being attracted inside to warm himself. Fire-irons were placed on the empty grate in the sign of the cross. This was done to keep a witch from entering the house by way of the chimney.

Brooms were carefully put away in cupboards, in case a witch should spirit one out of the house to ride on it and bring bad luck to the household.

Lastly all doors and windows were securely locked and the keys removed. As an added safeguard, the sign of the cross was made over the keyholes to stop some witch or warlock from slipping through them.

Of course there were still dangers, even in sleep. To keep a baby safe from a witch, a knife would be placed at the bottom of the cot. Some parents would slip a piece of bread, blessed by a priest, under a child's pillow. They would say words similar to these as they did so:

> *Bring the holy crust of bread.*
> *Lay it underneath the head.*
> *'Tis a certain charm to keep*
> *Hags away while children sleep.*

Before they went to sleep people would speak the words of a charm. The charm had to be repeated aloud before the eyes closed. This one is said by people, even to this day:

> *Matthew, Mark, Luke and John,*
>   *Bless the bed that I lie on.*
> *If I die before I wake,*
>   *I pray the Lord my soul to take.*
> *Four corners to my bed,*
>   *Four angels round my head,*
> *One to watch and one to pray,*
>   *Two to keep the Devil away.*

The Haunted Waxworks

By Roderick Hunt

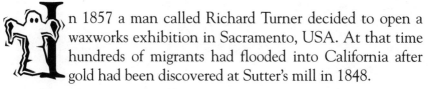

In 1857 a man called Richard Turner decided to open a waxworks exhibition in Sacramento, USA. At that time hundreds of migrants had flooded into California after gold had been discovered at Sutter's mill in 1848.

In those days the famous waxworks of Madame Tussaud in London had been an enormous success and its fame had spread. Waxwork exhibitions had opened in some of the big cities in the USA. Turner was certain that the miners and people of Sacramento would be delighted if such a fashionable and popular form of entertainment could be set up for them to visit.

Accordingly, Turner travelled to London and managed to buy from the Tussaud family a group of waxworks which had not been popular in London. The group was that of six French characters awaiting execution at the guillotine during the French Revolution.

What particularly attracted Turner to these figures was that their faces had been made from moulds pressed from those of the actual victims after death. And the clothes were those taken from the victims' very bodies after the execution.

Turner made these the centrepiece of his exhibition and, just as he hoped, the tough, hard-bitten miners flocked to see it.

About a week after the exhibition opened, however, a strange thing began to happen. Every morning when the doors of the waxworks hall were unlocked, one of the figures from the guillotine group had moved to a new position and its head been removed from its body.

For some weeks, even though the hall was securely locked and a guard patrolled outside, by the next morning, the figure had always moved with the head taken off and placed, undamaged, on the floor.

Turner asked his caretaker to spend the night with him in the hall so that the mystery could be solved. Both men fell asleep and woke up to find that the figure had moved while they slept.

They tried again, and the second time they were more successful. Just before 2:30 in the morning the figure began to move. With mounting horror the men saw first an arm move, then the legs.

After a moment the stiff-looking wax face with its normally staring eyes seemed to come to life. Its features twisted into an angry frown and it said, in French: "Is it not possible to get some peace at night? The people come to see us die. Now they come to see our spirits encased in wax. Come here no more during the hours of darkness or you will regret it."

Turner and the caretaker did not wait in the hall to hear any more angry words from the ghostly figure in wax.

Sometime later, a young reporter from a Sacramento newspaper heard of the strange encounter and asked if he could stay in the hall with the waxworks to see for himself. At first Turner was unwilling, but finally he agreed and the young man was locked in the hall.

At exactly 2:31 the caretaker was aroused by screams and hammerings coming from inside. He quickly unlocked the door and the hysterical figure of the reporter slumped into his arms.

The reporter afterwards told his story.

He was, he said, convinced that the story of the sinister wax figure that came to life was just a tale made up by Richard Turner in the hope that more visitors would be attracted to the waxworks.

He felt sure that he would simply spend an uneventful night among a collection of wax dummies.

Yet as he sat in the eerie hall with its vaulted roof and dim wall lights, he began to grow less sure. The rows of figures were so uncannily like human beings that their complete stillness and the absolute silence made him feel nervous and uneasy.

He looked at the group of executed French men and women. There were five of them in all. They stood on individual stands, each with a neatly printed label at its feet.

There were two aristocrats, a man and a woman in faded silk and lace finery, a priest holding up his Bible, a young lady-in-waiting, and a man in a black suit with a frilled white cravat.

It was the man in the black suit who drew the reporter's attention, for it was about him that all the fuss had been made. It was this rather small figure that had previously come to life in the small hours of the night and from whose waxen face had come the whispered words: "Come here no more during the hours of darkness or you will regret it."

The man's name was Nicodème Léopold-Lépide. He had been a tax collector for a French duke. He had won the hatred of the poor with his greed and dishonesty.

Now, as the reporter stared at the figure, his nervousness increased. There was something about the stiff, waxen face that seemed somehow different to the faces of other effigies.

Was it the shadows, or did the face have an expression of sinister cunning?

The reporter gazed once more round the gloomy hall. Then, he looked again at the man in the black suit. What he saw made him frown. The figure was surely not standing quite like that when he had looked before.

He looked away again. When he looked back, the figure had changed its position once more. The reporter felt a chill creep over him. He stared at the figure and this time he saw it move. Slowly at first, then more quickly until, with a movement of its head, it stared straight at him.

Never had the young man seen a look of such evil and malice. A mist of terror clouded his eyes. And as he looked at the figure its head no longer seemed solid, but appeared ghostly and transparent.

Suddenly the figure stepped down from its stand and moved straight towards him. Backing hastily to the door, the reporter knocked on it urgently in order to call the caretaker.

There was no answer. The caretaker was asleep.

The young man banged harder as the wax figure moved closer. Then he turned and started to hammer with his fists on the door. As the horrid wax hands closed round his neck and the fingers pressed his throat, he screamed.

He remembered no more until he saw the friendly face of the caretaker bending over him anxiously.

As for the figure of M. Léopold-Lépide, it was found the next morning by the door, yet the head was on the floor next to the other figures.

When Richard Turner was replacing the waxwork on its stand he noticed that the fingers were flattened and out-of-shape. Could this have happened when they pressed against the reporter's neck?

In the end the waxwork was melted down and another figure was put in its place. After this there were no more strange movements and Turner's Waxwork Exhibition went on for the next twenty-five years.

The Coach of Death

By Roderick Hunt

ome years ago, a lady called Miss Selwyn, the head-mistress of a girls' school in the south of England, was staying with friends who lived at Belgrade Castle in County Dublin, Southern Ireland.

Like many other buildings of its kind, Belgrade Castle has its share of ghosts, none of which Miss Selwyn knew about at the time of her visit.

It was during the summer, and Miss Selwyn was sleeping in a bedroom on the fourth floor. The room was bright and airy, and it looked out on to a beautiful sunken Italian garden on the southern side of the house. The garden was neatly laid out with paths and formal flowerbeds, and it was surrounded by marble balustrades and stonework.

Just beyond the Italian garden was an avenue of yew trees. Originally this avenue had been part of the main driveway. It led from the road to the south side of the castle and then swept round the corner of the building to the front door.

Later this driveway had been closed, and the nearest trees had been removed to allow the sunken garden to be built. At the far end a ditch with one steep side had been dug to prevent cattle from wandering into the castle grounds. The new drive led directly to the front door across some fields.

One night Miss Selwyn went to bed as usual without any thought of ghosts and quickly went to sleep. Suddenly, in only a few moments it seemed to her, though in fact it was much longer, she woke in a state of great alarm. She did not at first know why. She lay quiet and still in the dark, her hair tingling on her scalp, her feelings on edge, but her mind fully alert and wary, wondering what could have awakened her.

Then suddenly she heard it! A loud and heavy sound of horses hooves clattering along the great Yew Avenue toward the house, accompanied by the constant jingling of harness and the deep rumble of heavy iron-tyred wheels.

A great coach was moving rapidly, the horses almost cantering along the avenue where no coach could possibly go.

Miss Selwyn had awakened in a state of alarm which must have come upon her while she was still asleep. Her alarm increased as she listened to the noise which seemed to rumble through the room, but it was several moments before she fully realized that there was no road outside and consequently nowhere where a heavy carriage and horses — or any kind of vehicle for that mat-ter — could drive.

She suddenly realized that she was faced with some sort of ghostly manifestation. The noises seemed all the more eerie as she called to mind the setting of the old building and exotic garden. At this, she pulled the bedclothes over her head to shut out all sound — and any sight, too, if need be.

After a time, nothing more having happened, Miss Selwyn peeped out of her refuge to find, to her intense relief, that all was now silent and calm. The ghostly coach and four had passed on, leaving everything as quiet and peaceful as if they had never been. Yet Miss Selwyn found it hard to forget those dreadful sounds rum-bling and crashing through the night. She lay still for some time, wondering if they would start again but all continued quiet, and eventually she fell asleep.

As soon as breakfast was over Miss Selwyn tackled her hostess about her terrifying experience during the night. The owner's wife, Mrs. Richards, listened with polite interest but did not show the slightest concern. Then she explained in an almost casual way that the phantom coach was well-known and that every member of the family had heard it so often that they no longer minded it.

She and her husband had just forgotten to warn their guest about it. They told her not to mind it as nothing else ever happened in regard to it. Every now and again at regular intervals it was sure to be heard by someone.

The history of the manifestation as Miss Selwyn was able to piece it together is interesting, though distinctly grim.

It appears that some 150 to 200 years before, the owner of the castle was a judge. At that time the Yew Avenue was still part of the driveway which, running from the lodge gates, went sharply round the house to the front door.

Some disturbances had taken place in the town, and in the course of his duty the judge had tried one of the ringleaders, found him guilty and sentenced him to death. But the rest of the members of his group were still at large and thirsting for revenge.

They did not have to wait long, for shortly after the execution of their leader, they waylaid the judge as he drove late one evening from his club in the town back to his country estate. Men seized the horses and pulled the coachman off his box, while the footman at the rear was wounded by a shot and fell to the ground.

As for the judge, before he could defend himself, fierce bearded faces were thrust through the windows of the coach and he was shot and shot again until his dead body slumped across the seats.

Then the gang made off, and the horses, terrified by the tumult and the firing and with no hand to guide them, set off and galloped along the familiar road home. The lodge gates stood open and the horses continued in their frantic stampede, thundering along the avenue till at last they slowed and came to a stop, sweating and frightened, before the hall door.

The bewildered servants of the house went out to greet their master and saw the great coach standing there with no one in charge. Some ran to the horses' heads and others anxiously looked inside, straining their eyes in the darkness until they made out the blood-stained body of their master, on the seat of his coach, dead. What intense horror and distress must this tragedy have brought to his family and to his household! The old hall and the gardens around it echoed and re-echoed to the cries of his people as they mourned. No wonder then that the terrible event should impregnate the very stones and throughout the centuries re-enact itself, at least in part, for those who are sensitive enough to hear it.

This appears to be a case of a pure echo from the past, the repetition of an incident just as it occurred, without any variation whatsoever. It is strange that it should happen at odd times which are in no way connected with its anniversary, but as far as we logical human beings are concerned, these things are still shrouded in mystery.

Strange
Happenings

The Salem Witch Trials

By Roderick Hunt

ତ୍ତର

 n 1692, the parents of a number of girls at Salem Village in Massachusetts, USA, were alarmed when their daughters began to suffer from the symptoms of a frightening disorder.

The girls would be seized by fits in which their bodies would jerk violently, or be twisted into strange and unnatural shapes. During these fits it took an enormous amount of physical strength from adults to hold the girls still or straighten their rigid bodies and bent limbs.

At other times the girls experienced terrifying hallucinations in which they claimed that they were tormented by weird spectres who pinched and bit them; indeed there were often marks and bruises to be found on the girls' bodies. Such terrors left them temporarily unable to speak, hear, or see.

The girls were suffering from a condition known to doctors today as hysteria. This sometimes happens when a group of people are so badly affected by fear or nervousness that, all at the same time, they feel ill or faint, or suffer from fits. As often happens in cases of group hysteria, the Salem girls were affecting each other. Each time one of them became hysterical she would trigger off the others.

Two of the girls, Elizabeth Parris, aged 9 and Abigail Williams, 11, were the daughter and niece of the Reverend Samuel Parris, a minister at Salem. Extremely worried, Revd. Parris asked the advice of men who had studied medicine, one of whom came to the conclusion that the girls were bewitched. They were, he said, the victims of a spiteful and vicious sort of evil deliberately brought about by someone.

Revd. Parris did not want to think that there were witches in his community. Had the girls somehow disturbed the forces of evil by tampering with the occult? He found out that one of the older girls in the group had tried to tell her own fortune by gazing into the white of an egg placed in a rounded glass. And there she had seen a coffin. This threw her into a state of shock and terror.

It emerged that the girls had been helped in their occult experiments by Parris's own servant, a woman called Tituba. Her lurid stories of ghosts, demons, and the supernatural had overexcited the girls' vivid imaginations and sent them into a turmoil of nervousness.

Nowadays, with our knowledge of medicine and psychology it is hard to imagine why the parents could not put an end to the girls' hysterical behaviour. But it must be remembered that, in those days, people believed very strongly in the power of the supernatural. For over a hundred years people in Europe lived in the fear of witchcraft, and tens of thousands had been hunted down, brought to trial, and executed.

It is hardly surprising, therefore, that the devout, God-fearing Puritans of New England should have shared this dread of witches and have held a deeply rooted belief in the Devil and all his works.

Matters came to a head when one of the girls' aunts baked a witch-cake. This cake, made from barley meal mixed with the girls' urine, was given to a dog in the belief that the evil which possessed the girls would then pass into the dog.

Parris was shocked and angry. He believed in the power of prayer. The witchcake he considered to be a dangerous spell. "The Devil has been raised among us," he announced, ". . . and when he shall be silenced the Lord only knows."

His words started a horrifying chapter in the history of witch-hunts, and the girls became the cause of a tragic drama which was to cost the lives of twenty people. What had begun as a genuine hysteria developed into a frightening sort of game which the girls became unable to control.

The moment that people thought witchcraft was involved, the eyes of the whole community were focused on the girls. They began, secretly, to delight in the sensation they were causing. They started to play up to the adults' fears and to behave in such a way that made sure they were the centre of attention.

As well as Elizabeth Parris and Abigail Williams, there were also Ann Putnam, 12, Mary Walcott, 16, Elizabeth Hubbard, 17, Susan Sheldon and Elizabeth Booth, both 18, Mercy Lewis, 19, and Elizabeth Proctor, 20. As events unfolded, the girls were joined by other impressionable girls, most of them in their late teens.

The question was asked: who had bewitched them? The girls named two simple-minded women, Sarah Osburn and Sarah Good. They also named Tituba.

At the hearing before magistrates, Sarah Good, charged with being a witch, strongly denied that she was in league with the Devil or had done the girls any harm. But the girls, who were at the hearing, took their cue from each other and fell into a fit, claiming that Sarah Good's spirit had left her body and was attacking them by biting and pinching.

Tituba provided the magistrates with an astonishing confession. She had, she said, given herself to the Devil and had signed his book in which were the names of nine other witches.

Her confession was pure fantasy. She alleged that she had ridden on a pole with Sarah Good, Sarah Osburn, and two other witches. They had flown above the rooftops and she had been forced to go with them to torment the girls. Salem was driven into a turmoil of fear and suspicion. People threw sideways glances at each other; Tituba's confession had mentioned nine other witches — who were they?

One of the girls, Ann Putnam, then accused a fourth woman called Martha Corey. Martha was a respectable woman who hotly denied the charges made against her. In her agitated state at the hearing, she wrung her hands and bit her lip. At once several girls complained that they had been bitten and pinched. "Look," they cried. "She is doing it to us now."

All the women, except Tituba, were committed for trial. Amazingly, those who confessed to being witches were not condemned to death, nor indeed sent for trial. It was only those who denied witchcraft and protested their innocence who were tried and executed. Tituba was reprieved, but remained in gaol.

During the months that followed, Salem was gripped by witch-hunt madness. The victims of this madness ranged from the most respected and well-to-do members of the community to the poorest and most humble.

Often, after the girls had named a person, spiteful or wrong-minded people would come forward with lies or ridiculous evidence which in normal times would have been laughed at.

Throughout the trials the magistrates accepted as their main evidence the testimony of the girls, who continued to claim that the spirits of the accused had physically attacked and hurt them.

For example, Elizabeth Proctor made this sworn statement, "That I have been most grievously tormented by my neighbour, John Proctor, or his appearance (spirit). Also I have seen his appearance most grievously torment and afflict Mary Walcott, Mercy Lewis, and Ann Putnam by pinching, twisting, and choking them."

On the basis of this, John Proctor was later convicted of witchcraft and hanged.

The magistrates were even convinced when the girls' fits were brought on by the presence of a complete stranger. They accepted as evidence the "touch test." If the girls in a fit were quietened by a person's touch, that person was sure to be guilty, the evil having been passed back into him.

Over 150 people were arrested during the period of madness at Salem. Of these, thirty-one (six of whom were men) Acre sentenced to death. Nineteen of these unfortunate people were hanged and two died in gaol. One was pressed to death by heavy weights: an ancient form of execution for anyone refusing to plead either guilty or not guilty.

The Salem witch hunt was no more terrible than many of those which took place in Europe between 1450 and 1750, in which 100,000 people were put to death. That people should have been so blinded by fear and superstition, as so many were at Salem in 1692, shows the extraordinary way that people's minds were gripped by a belief in the Devil and the powers of evil.

Nevertheless, the horrors at Salem were recognized by a number of people at the time, many of whom suspected that the girls were only pretending to have fits and were lying about their hallucinations.

In later years, several of those involved in the terrible events made statements saying that they had been wrong in what they said at the trials. In admitting that they had been mistaken, or had given false evidence, they claimed to have acted without fully understanding what they were doing.

This was probably true. Only by looking back at themselves could people fully realize the folly of what had happened and see for themselves that the witch hunts were the result of a delusion.

The Amazing Mr. Home

By Roderick Hunt

୧ଔ

During the second half of the nineteenth century people became fascinated by a phenomenon known as spiritualism. This is the practice of trying to make contact with the dead. Usually this is done through a medium — a person who claims to have special powers which allow the spirits of dead people to talk through him.

It all started with the Fox sisters in Hydesville, New York State, in 1848. Two young girls, Kate and Margarette Fox, caused a sensation by claiming to make contact with the spirit of a man they said had been killed in the house where they were living.

The Fox sisters started a craze which swept through the country and spread to Europe. Soon millions of people were attending meetings called *seances* where they witnessed such things as mysterious rappings on tables, disembodied voices, automatic writing, and luminous apparitions. At some seances heavy objects floated through the air or musical instruments played by themselves.

Unfortunately many mediums were frauds, and people who came to a seance hoping to hear a genuine message from their dead relatives were cheated, often by crude conjuring tricks.

One medium who baffled researchers and scientists was a man called Daniel Dunglas Home (1833-1886). Home was known as a physical *medium*. This is someone who claims that through him the spirit world is able to manipulate things and move objects about.

Home's powers were extraordinary. He was able to make small items vanish and reappear in a different part of the room. He could make objects, some as heavy as a piano, levitate (rise up in the air) all by themselves. In his presence musical instruments would play, as if by invisible hands. Sometimes he himself would levitate, or he would levitate other people.

Throughout his career as a medium Home was never caught in the act of fraud or trickery. He held many seances in bright light and he did not receive payment for them. He was always willing for people to investigate what he did, and he was happy to demonstrate his powers to the most disbelieving of them.

At a seance at the court of Napoleon III in France on 12 January 1863, Home caused a tablecloth to levitate from the table, even though he was some distance away and the room was fully lit. While the table was being examined to see if Home had used trick apparatus, it gave off a series of raps that seemed to come from the wood of the table itself.

One man who investigated Home's amazing ability was a famous scientist called Sir William Crookes (1832-1919). Once Crookes enclosed an accordion in a metal cage so that Home could not reach it. Despite this, during the seance, the accordion rose up in the cage and played a tune.

Another strange phenomenon which Home was able to achieve was that of stretching his body. He would increase his body length by as much as six inches, even though as many as six witnesses were holding on to him.

Home's favourite trick was to levitate himself. It was claimed that people hung on to his legs while he rose up in the air, and Sir William Crookes himself witnessed Home levitate a chair with a woman sitting in it.

Perhaps most amazing of all was Home's apparent ability to handle red-hot coal without burning himself. It seems that he could take a piece of glowing coal from the fire, hold it in both hands, and blow on it until it was almost white hot.

No one has ever been able to explain how Home was able to achieve his astonishing feats. It is unlikely that he used apparatus and he did not have accomplices to help him. Many of his seances were held in other people's homes, so it would have been difficult for him to fake his amazing effects.

How did he do it? The truth is that nobody knows.

The Curse of the Chases

By Roderick Hunt

ରୋ

The entrance slab was slowly drawn back from the tomb, and the men waited, terrified of what they might see. Daylight flooded into the gloomy vault. There was silence for a moment, then gasps of horror broke the stillness. Inside the tomb, there was chaos: the coffins had been hurled about once more. Even the heaviest coffin was upright against the wall. The curse of the Chases had struck again.

The place was Barbados in the West Indies, on a headland above the bay. There was, and still is, a church with a cemetery lying beside it. In the cemetery there is a strongly built stone tomb, the last restingplace of the Chase family.

The tomb is built of large stone blocks which are cemented together. A massive slab of blue marble once acted as a great, unmovable door on top of the entrance. Only when another coffin was ready for the tomb was the door opened by a gang of strong men.

Yet between 1812 and 1820, someone or something opened the tombs. And inside, all the coffins were thrown violently about. Yet the door was untouched.

The vault was built in 1724 for the Hon. John Elliott, but there is no record that he was ever buried there. The first burial took

place on 31 July 1807 when Mrs. Thomasina Goddard was laid to rest. About a year later, the vault passed to new owners, the Chase family.

On 22 February 1808, the tomb was opened, so that the coffin of a small child, Mary Ann Chase, could be lodged there. The only other coffin inside was that of Mrs. Goddard.

In those days mortality was high, especially among very small children. On 6 July, another young Chase was placed in the vault. The inside of the tomb was just as it was before.

But on 9 August 1812 the body of Thomas Chase was carried to the tomb. When the door was opened, the mourners were horrified to find that the coffins of the little Chase girls were both on end and upside down against one of the walls.

The coffins were replaced alongside Mrs. Goddard's, and eight strong men put Thomas Chase's coffin on the floor. It was solid and made of lead. Then the stonemasons scaled up the vault once again.

On 22 September another member of the Chase family was brought to the vault, and the mourners had another shock. All the coffins, including the one made of lead, had been thrown about. On 17 November, exactly the same thing happened again.

By now the whole of Barbados knew the story, and the Chase family were becoming more and more desperate and upset. But no one could offer an explanation.

On 17 July 1819 another member of the family died. The Governor of Barbados, Lord Combermere, attended the funeral. When the vault was opened, he saw for himself that all the coffins, except Mrs. Goddard's, had again been hurled all over the tomb.

The Governor ordered that fine sand should be put down inside the vault to pick up the footsteps of any intruder. Then the tomb was sealed.

On 18 April 1820 the Governor ordered that the Rector should re-open the vault, even though no member of the Chase family had died.

This time the chaos inside was even worse than usual. One of the largest coffins had been flung against the door, which luckily opened outwards. All the sand inside was untouched except where the coffins had been thrown on to it. There were no footprints.

The islanders by this time were becoming more and more alarmed at these strange events. So the Governor decided to re-move all the coffins and bury them in the earth in another corner of the churchyard. And there they remained in peace with no fur-ther trouble.

What possible explanations can be offered? No one believed that anyone had broken into the vault, even if it had been possi-ble to move the heavy stone. It is also hard to imagine who would dare to break in, for superstition was rife on the island.

One writer claimed that Thomas Chase was a hard, cruel man who had many enemies in Barbados. He alleged that Thomas Chase had killed himself and that one of his daughters had starved herself to death. It was claimed that the other corpses had tried to expel her from the vault.

Others said that earthquakes had caused the upheavals. But how can earthquakes be confined to a few square metres of ground?

Another theory was that floods had caused the disturbances. But the tomb was at the very top of a headland. Besides, why were the remains of Mrs. Goddard never disturbed?

The vault still lies in the churchyard in Barbados. But it re-mains empty, and the Chases lie buried peacefully in the earth.

The Stratford Poltergeist

By Roderick Hunt

ଊଡ଼

While the British Isles and Europe are sprinkled with haunted vicarages and rectories, few American churchmen have been harassed by noisy ghosts. But the unseen intruder that invaded the peaceful parsonage of the Reverend Eliakim Phelps in the sleepy town of Stratford, Connecticut, in 1850 ranks second to none as *the* classic American poltergeist.

A respected Presbyterian minister, Dr. Phelps, lived in the parsonage for two years before anything strange started to happen. He had four children, of whom the youngest was a boy of three and the oldest a girl of sixteen. Admittedly, Dr. Phelps was interested in occult matters and sometimes dabbled in amateur mesmerism and hypnosis. But he was in no way eccentric. The spiritualist craze was currently sweeping the country, and no one thought it queer when even a model churchman like Phelps occasionally held home seances and table-rapping experiments to try to contact the dead.

It was on a Sunday, 10 March 1850, that Dr. Phelps's poltergeist troubles began. They would continue for the next eighteen months. That particular morning, Dr. Phelps took his whole family with him to church. Their only servant, an Irish girl, was attending mass in nearby Bridgeport. Since the parsonage would be deserted for a few hours, Phelps locked it securely before leaving.

When he and his family returned, the front door was standing wide open. Dr. Phelps thought this very peculiar, for the servant girl had not yet returned. When they went inside, a strange sight met the family's eyes. Chairs, tables, and other furniture were scattered about in wild disorder. Yet nothing had been stolen. In fact, a solid gold watch was lying exactly where it had been left that morning.

That afternoon, the Phelps family, as was their custom, went to church again. However, Dr. Phelps remained behind, in case their destructive visitor returned. He neither heard nor saw anything out of the ordinary all the time his family was gone. But when they returned and took up their normal activities in various parts of the house, they soon noticed that crockery and other objects were not in their normal places.

Strangest of all was what they found in the master bedroom. A sheet was spread over the bed, outside the counterpane. Underneath it was a nightgown with its arms folded across the breast and stockings placed where the wearer's legs would normally protrude. This crude effigy was laid out in the same fashion as a corpse usually was before it was placed in the coffin.

Next morning, the same sort of pranks continued — with a few new ones added. Furniture and other objects were seen to glide about. Phelps himself saw an umbrella, which was standing in the hall, suddenly rise up and fly across the room for twenty-five feet. A bucket, standing at the top of the parsonage stairs, came crashing down into the room below. Then smaller articles started to sail through the air. Nails, spoons, knives, dishes, forks, keys, bits of iron and tin were thrown about the house in all directions.

Later, the family again found evidence of some strange deathwatch. A piece of black crêpe was discovered twisted about the knocker of the back door. The mirrors in the front rooms were draped with sheets and tablecloths, as was the custom in that part of the country when a dead person lay in a house shrouded for burial.

As these unnerving things continued in his home, Dr. Phelps decided to call in a friend to confirm them. This man, also a clergyman, stayed for three weeks and became convinced that neither the servant girl nor any of the children were in any way responsible for the occurrences. Once, when a large raw potato fell out of nowhere next to Dr. Phelps's plate, the two men experimented with it, dropping it from various heights to find out how high it must have fallen to make such a noise. They concluded that fifteen inches was right. But nobody could possibly have thrown it from that height without being detected.

A few days later, the two ministers saw a large chair rise from the floor and then bang down again. This happened with such violence that members of the family in other parts of the house could hear the whole parsonage shudder. The two dumbfounded clergymen also saw a heavy plated candlestick move from its customary place on the mantelpiece and swoop down onto the floor. There it beat itself continuously against the floor until it was shattered. On that same day, loud pounding noises were heard throughout the house, as if someone were striking the floor with an axe. Several times these sickening thuds were followed by frightful screams.

Day after day, these and other odd happenings plagued the Phelps family. Not surprisingly, word of them spread about the countryside and numbers of people came to see for themselves. Not one of them could account for the weird occurrences by any logical explanation. Yet they all agreed that neither the servant girl nor any of the children could be producing them through trickery or practical jokes. Also, it was becoming more and more apparent that the strange goings-on were centred about two of the Phelps children — twelve-year-old Harry, and sometimes his sister Anna, who was four years older.

Once when Harry was out riding with Dr. Phelps, twenty small stones were hurled at regular intervals into the carriage. Another time, Harry was tied up and suspended bodily in a tree. The boy was also caught up several times from the floor by some mysterious means and transported across the room. Once he was tossed into a cistern of rainwater. On still another occasion, Harry's pants were ripped to ribbons from the cuffs to the knees.

The longer the poltergeist activity went on at the Phelps house, the more destructive were its results. At one period, the poltergeist took to smashing windowpanes—no fewer than seventy-one of them. Dr. Phelps himself witnessed the last one being broken by a flying tumbler that had sailed across the room. Harry was also present but standing a good twenty feet away.

Mysterious messages also began to appear. Often they were insultingly worded and signed with the names of neighbouring clergymen. While writing alone in his study one time, Dr. Phelps paused for a minute and turned his back to the desk. When he resumed writing, he discovered that ten words had been written in large letters on the sheet before him. The message said: "Very nice paper and very nice ink for the Devil." The ink was still wet!

Young Harry continued to be the butt of most of the poltergeist's devilment. In one instance, his bed was set on fire. When eventually he was sent to school in far-off Philadelphia, the poltergeist pursued him even there. His books were ripped, his clothes were torn, and his very presence at the school caused such an uproar that he had to be sent home to Stratford. Strangely, when Harry was absent from the parsonage, comparative peace reigned in the house.

The most bizarre work done by the poltergeist occurred on 16 March, just a few days after its first appearance. Soon after breakfast on that day, Dr. Phelps and some members of his family went into one of the little-used chambers of the parsonage. They were astounded to discover there eleven stuffed effigies—all of quite angelic beauty. All but one were female figures. Most were arranged in attitudes of prayer and devotion. They had been fashioned of clothing found about the house, stuffed to resemble human beings. A woman's dress would be filled with a fur muff, or pillows, or bunches of other dresses; shoes and bonnets were placed in appropriate places to complete the mysterious dummies.

Before many of the figures lay open Bibles; gloves with pointing fingers indicated certain passages of Scripture. Some of the figures knelt by the beds; others bent their "faces" toward the floor in attitudes of deep humility. But all were so arranged that they seemed to be worshipping the central figure of a dwarf, above which hung a flying form, possibly an angel.

One of these fantastic figures was formed from one of Mrs. Phelps's dresses. As Dr. Phelps gazed in awe at this strange sight, his three-year-old son entered the room. Seeing the kneeling figure, whom he assumed to be his mother, he whispered: "Be still, everyone, Ma is saying her prayers."

Many other queer things took place. One evening a "vegetable growth" suddenly appeared on the living room carpet. It spread and seemed to take root; odd symbols appeared on the leaves for several minutes, after which it vanished. Heavy marble-topped tables would rise and crash to the floor. Spoons were bent double and thrown at the family. Turnips fell from the ceiling. The older daughter was frequently pinched. And, while the whole house was watched and doors were kept locked, the invisible sculptor continued creating his tableaux of lifelike effigies.

With the passing of the months, and the frequent absence of Harry and his sister, the "Stratford Poltergeist," as it came to be known, ceased its malicious pranks, and at last the parsonage returned to its peaceful routine.

The intelligent and inquiring Dr. Phelps, who kept many written accounts of the odd happenings, never could find out how they were produced. They were widely written up in the major newspapers and scientific journals of the day, and some of the occurrences were witnessed by news reporters. One of the most colourful figures then investigating psychic phenomena, Andrew Jackson Davis (known as "the Poughkeepsie Seer"), came in person to inspect the Phelps house; he witnessed several occurrences. And Dr. Phelps's own accounts of the disturbances were widely published; their straightforward style strongly indicates that he was perfectly honest in all that he reported. Indeed, Phelps would have had little to gain by falsifying the accounts and stood to forfeit his good reputation had he done so.

In his later years, it was a still-baffled Phelps who wrote: "I witnessed these occurrences hundreds and hundreds of times, and I know that in hundreds of instances they took place when there was no visible power by which the motion could have been produced."

Today the old parsonage, now called the Phelps Mansion, still stands. Boarded up now, it can still be seen not far from the fashionable Shakespeare Theatre, for which the town is famous. As summer visitors watch *Hamlet* or *A Midsummer Night's Dream* in that theatre, few are aware that a stone's throw away there disported a classic American poltergeist whose antics once held the whole countryside in fear and awe.

The Great Houdini

By Daniel Cohen

ᘓᘒ

Harry Houdini was America's greatest magician. Houdini didn't really believe in ghosts. He met a lot of people who said they could talk to ghosts or spirits. Such people are called *mediums*. Houdini thought that most mediums were fakes. He spent a lot of time exposing fake mediums.

Still, Houdini wasn't 100 percent sure that there were no such things as spirits. He really wanted to believe that the living could talk to the dead. He just had no proof that they could.

Harry Houdini died on Halloween in 1926. His death came as a shock. He was not an old man. He had not been sick. And dying on Halloween! It all seemed very strange and mysterious.

Mediums began reporting that they were in touch with Houdini's spirit. Houdini's spirit said that you could talk to the dead. That's what the mediums claimed, anyway. Not many people believed them.

But there was another story. There was a rumor that Houdini had told his wife, Beatrice, he would try to send her a message from beyond the grave if it were possible. He said she would know if the message was a real one because it would be in code. It would be a code that only she and Houdini knew.

A medium named Arthur Ford said he had received Houdini's coded message. Beatrice Houdini seemed to agree.

Then it all became very confusing.

A newspaper reporter said it was all a fake. He said he heard Beatrice Houdini and Ford cooking up the whole story. He said they were trying to make some money from it.

Some of Houdini's magician friends said that the code was not a secret at all. It was a code that a lot of magicians used in their acts. They said there never was a Houdini message.

What did Beatrice Houdini say to all of this? She said she had not plotted with Arthur Ford. But she said there never was a coded message either.

Since her husband's death, Beatrice Houdini had been very ill. She said she had been mixed up and said things she didn't mean.

But for years, Beatrice Houdini would sit alone on Halloween, waiting for a message from her husband. Finally, she gave up.

The idea of Houdini's Halloween message from the dead is still around. Almost every Halloween some medium somewhere says that the ghost of Houdini has spoken to him.

Poems

Hallowe'en [1]

By Robert Burns

With Notes by Robert Chambers

("The following poem will, by many readers, be well enough understood; but for the sake of those who are unacquainted with the manners and traditions of the country where the scene is cast, notes are added, to give some account of the principal charms and spells of that night, so big with prophecy to the peasantry in the west of Scotland. The passion of prying into futurity, makes a striking part of the history of human nature in its rude state, in all ages and nations; and it may be some entertainment to a philosophic mind, if any such should honour the author with a perusal, to see the remains of it among the more unenlightened in our own.") — BURNS.

Upon that night, when fairies light
    On Cassilis Downans'[2] dance,
Or owre the lays, in splendid blaze,   (fields)
    On sprightly courses prance;
Or for Colean the route is ta'en,
    Beneath the moon's pale beams,
There, up the Cove [3] to stray and rove,
    Amang the rocks and streams
        To sport that night,

---

[1] All Hallow Eve, or the eve of All Saints' Day, is thought to be a night when witches, devils, and other mischief-making beings, are all abroad on their baneful midnight errands; particularly those aerial people, the fairies, are said on that night to hold a grand anniversary. — B.

[2] Certain little romantic, rocky, green hills, in the neighborhood of the ancient seat of the Earls of Cassilis. — B.

[3] A noted cavern near Colean House, called the Cove of Colean; which, as well as Cassilis Downans, is famed in country story for being a favorite haunt of fairies. — B.

Amang the bonnie, winding banks,
    Where Doon rins, wimplin', clear,   (wheeling)
Where Bruce [4] ance ruled the martial ranks,
    And shook his Carrick spear,
Some merry, friendly, country-folks
    Together did convene,
To burn their nits, and pou their stocks   (nuts, pull)
    And haud their Hallowe'en
        Fu' blithe that night.

The lasses feat, and cleanly neat,   (trim)
    Mair braw than when they're fine;
Their faces blithe, fu' sweetly kythe,   (show)
    Hearts leal, and warm, and kin':   (true)
The lads sae trig, wi' wooer-babs   (spruce, knots)
    Weel knotted on their garten,   (garter)
Some unco blate, and some wi' gabs   (bashful, talk)
    Gar lasses' hearts gang sartin'
        Whiles fast at night.   (sometimes)

Then, first and foremost, through the kail,   (cabbage)
    Their stocks [5] maun a' be sought ance;
They steek their een, and graip, and wale, (close, grope, choose)

---

   [4] The famous family of that name, the ancestors of Robert, the great deliverer of his country, were Earls of Carrick. —B.

   [5] The first ceremony of Hallowe'en is pulling each a stock, or plant of kail. They must go out, hand in hand, with eyes shut, and pull the first they meet with; its being big or little, straight or crooked, is prophetic of the size and shape of the grand object of all their spells — the husband or wife. If any yird or earth stick to the root, that is tocher or fortune; and the taste of the custoc — that is, the heart of the stem — is indicative of the natural temper and disposition. Lastly, the stems, or, to give them their ordinary appellation, the runts, are placed somewhere above the head of the door, and the Christian names of people whom chance brings into the house are, according to the priority of placing the runts, the names in question. —B.

For muckle anes and straught anes.	(straight)
Poor hav'rel Will fell aft the drift,	(fool)
And wandered through the bow-kail;	(cabbages)
And pou't, for want o' better shift,	
An runt was like a sow-tail,	(stalk)
Sae bow't that night.	(crooked)

Then, straught or crooked, yird or nane,	
They roar and cry a' throu'ther;	(in confusion)
The very wee things, todlin' rin	(tottering)
Wi' stocks out-owre their shouther:	
And gif the custoc's sweet or sour,	
Wi' joctelegs they taste them;	(knives)
Syne cozily aboon the door,	(Then)
Wi' cannie care, they've placed them	(gentle)
To lie that night.	

The lasses staw frae' mang them a'	(stole)
To pou their stalks o' corn;[6]	
But Rab slips out, and jinks about,	(dodges)
Behint the muckle thorn:	
He grippet Nelly hard and fast;	
Loud skirlèd a' the lasses;	(screamed)
But her tap-pickle maist was lost,	
When kuittlin' in the fause-house[7]	(cuddling)
Wi' him that night.	

---

[6] They go [to] the barn-yard, and pull each, at three several times, a stalk of oats. If the third stalk wants the top-pickle — that is, the grain at the top of the stalk — the party in question will not continue spotless until marriage. — B.

[7] When the corn is in a doubtful state, by being too green or wet, the stack-builder, by means of old timber, etc., makes a large apartment in his stack, with an opening in the side which is fairest exposed to the wind: this he calls a fause-house. — B.

The auld guidwife's weel-hoordit nits [8]
  Are round and round divided;
And mony lads' and lasses' fates
  Are there that night decided:
Some kindle couthie, side by side,   (agreeably)
  And burn thegither trimly;
Some start awa' wi' saucy pride,
  And jump out-owre the chimlie
    Fu' high that night.

Jean slips in twa wi' tentie e'e;
  Wha 'twas, she wadna tell;
But this is Jock, and this is me,
  She says in to hersel':
He bleezed owre her, and she owre him,
  As they wad never mair part;
Till, fuff! he started up the lum,   (chimney)
  And Jean had e'en a sair heart
    To see't that night.

Poor Willie, wi' his bow-kail runt,
  Was brunt wi' primsie Mallie;   (demure)
And Mary, nae doubt, took the drunt   (a pet)
  To be compared to Willie.
Mall's nit lap out wi' pridefu' fling,
  And her ain fit it brunt it;   (foot)
While Willie lap, and swore, by jing,
  'Twas just the way he wanted
    To be that night.

[8] Burning the nuts is a famous charm. They name the lad and lass to each particular nut as they lay them in the fire, and accordingly as they burn quietly together, or start from beside one another, the course and issue of the courtship will be. — B.

Nell had the fause-house in her min',
   She pits hersel' and Rob in;
In loving bleeze they sweetly join,
   Till white in ase they're sobbin'.   (ashes)
Nell's heart was dancin' at the view,
   She whispered Rob to leuk for't:
Rob stowlins prie'd her bonny mou'   (stealthily kissed)
   Fu' cozie in the neuk for't,
      Unseen that night.

But Merran sat behint their backs,
   Her thoughts on Andrew Bell;
She lea'es them gashin' at their cracks   (conversing)
   And slips out by hersel':
She through the yard the nearest taks,
   And to the kiln she goes then,
And darklins graipit for the bauks,   (cross-beams)
   And in the blue-clue [9] throws them,
      Right fear't that night.

And aye she win't, and aye she swat,   (winded)
   I wat she made nae jaukin';   (dallying)
Till something held within the pat,
   Guid L——! but she was quakin'!
But whether 'twas the deil himsel',
   Or whether 'twas a bauk-en',   (beam-end)
Or whether it was Andrew Bell,
   She did na wait on talkin'
      To spier that night.   (inquire)

[9] Whoever would with success try this spell, must strictly observe these directions: — Steal out, all alone, to the kiln, and, darkling, throw into the pot a clue of blue yarn; wind it in a clue off the old one, and towards the latter end something will hold the thread; demand "wha hauds?" — that is, Who holds? An answer will be returned from the kiln-pot, by naming the Christian and sur-name of your future spouse. — B.

Wee Jenny to her granny says:
"Will ye go wi' me, granny?
I'll eat the apple [10] at the glass
    I got frae Uncle Johnny:"
She fuff't her pipe wi' sic a lunt,   (smoke)
    In wrath she was sae vap'rin',
She notic't na, an aizle brunt   (cinder)
    Her braw new worset apron
        Out through that night.

"Ye little skelpie-limmer's face! [11]   (young jade)
    I daur you try sic sportin',   (dare)
As seek the foul thief ony place,
    For him to spae your fortune: (tell)
Nae doubt but ye may get a sight!
    Great cause ye hae to fear it;
For mony a ane has gotten a fright,
    And lived and died deleeret   (delirious)
        On sic a night.

"Ae hairst afore the Sherra-moor —   (harvest)
    I mind't as weel's yestreen,
I was a gilpey then, I'm sure   (young girl)
    I was na past fifteen:
The simmer had been cauld and wat,
    And stuff was unco green;
And aye a rantin' kirn we gat,   (noisy harvest-home)
    And just on Hallowe'en
        It fell that night.

[10] Take a candle, and go alone to a looking-glass; eat an apple before it, and some traditions say, you should comb your hair all the time; the face of your conjugal companion to be will be seen in the glass, as if peeping over your shoulder. — B.

[11] "A technical term in female scolding." — B.

"Our stibble-rig [12] was Rab M'Graen,
    A clever sturdy fallow:
His sin gat Eppie Sim wi' wean,   (son)
    That lived in Achmacalla:
He gat hemp-seed, [13] I mind it weel,
    And he made unco light o't;
But mony a day was by himsel',
    He was sae sairly frighted
        That very night."

Then up gat fechtin' Jamie Fleck,   (fighting)
    And he swore by his conscience,
That he could saw hemp-seed a peck;
    For it was a' but nonsense.
The auld guidman raught down the pock,   (reached)
    And out a handfu' gied him;
Syne bad him slip frae 'mang the folk,
    Some time when nae ane see'd him,
        And try't that night.

He marches through amang the stacks,
    Though he was something sturtin;   (timorous)
The graip he for a harrow taks,   (dung-fork)
    And haurls at his curpin;   (drags, rear)
And every now and then he says:
    "Hemp-seed, I saw thee,

---

[12] The leader of the reapers.

[13] Steal out, unperceived, and sow a handful of hemp-seed, harrowing it with anything you can conveniently draw after you. Repeat now and then; "Hemp-seed I saw thee, hemp-seed I saw thee; and him (or her) that is to be my true love, come after me and pou thee." Look over your left shoulder, and you will see the appearance of the person invoked in the attitude of pulling hemp. Some traditions say: "Come after me, and shaw thee" — that is, shew thyself; in which case it simply appears. Others omit the harrowing, and say: "Come after me, and harrow thee." — B.

And her that is to be my lass,
    Come after me, and draw thee
        As fast this night."

He whistled up Lord Lennox' march,
    To keep his courage cheery;
Although his hair began to arch,
    He was sae fley'd and eerie: (frightened)
Till presently he hears a squeak,
    And then a grane and gruntle;
He by his shouther ga'e a keek,   (peep)
    And tumbled wi' a wintle   (stagger)
        Out-owre that night.

He roared a horrid murder-shout,
    In dreadfu' desperation!
And young and auld cam rinnin' out,
    And hear the sad narration:
He swore 'twas hilchin Jean M'Craw,   (halting)
    Or crouchie Merran Humphie   (crook-backed)
Till, stop — she trotted through them a' —
    And wha was it but Grumphie   (the pig)
        Asteer that night!

Meg fain wad to the barn hae gaen,
    To win three wechts o' naething; [14]   (corn-baskets)

---

[14] This charm must likewise be performed unperceived, and alone. You go to the barn, and open both doors, taking them off the hinges if possible; for there is danger that the being about to appear may shut the doors, and do you some mischief. Then take that instrument used in winnowing the corn, which, in our country dialect, we call a wecht, and go through all the attitudes of letting down corn against the wind. Repeat it three times; and the third time an apparition will pass through the barn, in at the windy door, and out at the other, having both the figure in question, and the appearance or retinue, marking the employment or station in life. — B.

But for to meet the deil her lane,   (alone)
   She pat but little faith in:
She gies the herd a pickle nits,   (few)
   And twa red-cheekit applies,
To watch, while for the barn she sets,
   In hopes to see Tam Kipples
      That very night.

She turns the key wi' canny thraw,   (gentle twist)
   And owre the threshold ventures;
But first on Sawny gies a ca',
   Syne bauldly in she enters:
A ratton rattled up the wa',
   And she cried, "L———, preserve her!"
And ran through midden-hole[15] and a',
   And prayed wi' zeal and fervour,
      Fu' fast that night.

They hoy't out Will, wi' sair advice;   (urged)
   They hecht him some fine braw ane;   (promised)
It chanced, the stack he faddom't thrice, [16]
   Was timmer-propt for thrawin';   (timber, twisting)
He taks a swirly auld moss oak   (knotty)
   For some black grousome carlin;   (loathsome)
And loot a winze, and drew a stroke,   (oath)
   Till skin in blypes cam haurlin' (shreds, peeling)
      Aff's nieves that night.   (hands)

A wanton widow Leezie was,
   As canty as a kittlin;   (merry — kitten)

---

[15] A gutter at the bottom of a dung-hill.

[16] Take an opportunity of going, unnoticed, to a bean-stack, and fathom it three times round. The last fathom of the last time you will catch in your arms the appearance of your future conjugal yoke-fellow. — B.

But, och! that night, amang the shaws,	(woods)
She got a fearfu' settlin'!	
She through the whins, and by the cairn,	(gorse)
And owre the hill gaed scrieven,	(scrambling)
Where three lairds' lands meet at a burn, [17]	
To dip her left sark-sleeve in,	
Was bent that night.	

Whyles owre a linn the burnie plays,	(fall)
As through the glen it wimpl't;	(wheeled)
Whyles round a rocky scaur it strays;	(cliff)
Whyles in a wiel it dimpl't;	(eddy)
Whyles glittered to the nightly rays,	
Wi' bickering, dancing dazzle;	(racing)
Whyles cookit underneath the braes,	(suddenly vanished)
Below the spreading hazel,	
Unseen that night.	

Amang the brackens, on the brae,	(fern)
Between her and the moon,	
The deil, or else an outler quey,	(unhoused cow)
Gat up and gae a croon:	(moan)
Poor Leezie's heart maist lap the hool;	(case)
Near lav'rock-height she jumpit,	(lark)
But mist a fit, and in the pool	(foot)
Out-owre the lugs she plumpit,	(ears)
Wi' a plunge that night.	

--- 🎃 ---

[17] You go out, one or more, for this is a social spell, to a south running spring or rivulet, where "three lairds' lands meet," and dip your left shirt-sleeve. Go to bed in sight of a fire, and hang your wet sleeve before it to dry. Lie awake, and sometime near midnight an apparition, having the exact figures of the grand object in question, will come and turn the sleeve, as if to dry the other side of it. — B.

In order, on the clean hearth-stane,
    The luggies[18] three are ranged   (dishes)
And every time great care is ta'en
    To see them duly changed:
Auld Uncle John, wha wedlock's joys
    Sin' Mar's year[19] did desire,
Because he gat the toom dish thrice   (empty)
    He heaved them on the fire
      In wrath that night.

Wi' merry sangs, and friendly cracks,
    I wat they did na weary;
And unco tales, and funny jokes,
    Their sports were cheap and cheery;
Till buttered so'ns,[20] wi' fragrant lunt,   (smoke)
    Set a' their gabs a-steerin';
Syne, wi' a social glass o' strunt,   (spirits)
    They parted aff careerin'
      Fu' blithe that night.[21]

[18] Take three dishes; put clean water in one, foul water in another, leave the third empty; blindfold a person, and lead him to the hearth where the dishes are ranged; he (or she) dips the left hand — if by chance in the clean water, the future husband or wife will come to the bar of matrimony a maid; if in the foul a widow; if in the empty dish, it foretells, with equal certainty, no marriage at all. It is repeated three times, and every time the arrangement of the dishes is altered. — B.

[19] The year 1715, when the Ear of Mar raised an insurrection in Scotland.

[20] Sowens, (a dish made of the seeds of oat-meal soured) with butter instead of milk to them, is always the Hallowe'en supper. — B.

[21] The most of the ceremonies appropriate to Hallowe'en, including all those of an adventurous character, are now disused. Meetings of young people still take place on that evening, both in country and town, but their frolics are usually limited to ducking for apples in tubs of water — a ceremony overlooked by Burns — the lottery of the dishes, and pulling cabbage-stalks. The other ceremonies are discountenanced as more superstitious than is desirable, and somewhat dangerous.

Tam O'Shanter: A Tale

By Robert Burns

[Within a mile of Burns's birthplace, near Ayr,
stands the ruin of old Alloway Kirk, surrounded by a
graveyard, two minutes' walk from the River Doon.
The legend of Tam's adventure was well known in
Burns's time.]

Of Brownyis and of Bogillis full is this buke.
— GAWIN DOUGLAS

When chapman billies leave the street,
And drouthy neibors meet,
As market-days are wearing late,
And folk begin to tak the gate;
While we sit bousin at the nappy,
And gettin fou and unco happy,
We think na on the lang Scots miles,

The mosses, waters, slaps, and stiles,
That lie between us and our hame,
Whare sits our sulky, sullen dame,
Gathering her brows like gathering storm,
Nursing her wrath to keep it warm.

This truth fand honest Tam o' Shanter,
As he frae Ayr ae night did canter:
(Auld Ayr, wham ne'er a town surpasses,
For honest men and bonie lasses.)

O Tam! had'st thou but been sae wise
As taen thy ain wife Kate's advice!
She tauld thee weel thou was a skellum,
A bletherin, blusterin, drunken blellum;
That frae November till October,
Ae market-day thou was na sober;
That ilka melder wi' the miller,
Thou sat as lang as thou had siller;
That ev'ry naig was ca'd a shoe on,
The smith and thee gat roarin fou on;
That at the Lord's house, ev'n on Sunday,
Thou drank wi' Kirkton Jean till Monday.
She prophesied, that, late or soon,
Thou would be found deep drown'd in Doon;
Or catch't wi' warlocks in the mirk,
By Alloway's auld haunted kirk.

Ah, gentle dames! it gars me greet,
To think how mony counsels sweet,
How mony lengthened sage advices,
The husband frae the wife despises!

But to our tale: — Ae market night,
Tam had got planted unco right,
Fast by an ingle, bleezin finely,

Wi' reamin swats that drank divinely;
And at his elbow, Souter Johnie,
His ancient, trusty, drouthy crony:
Tam lo'ed him like a vera brither;
They had been fou for weeks thegither.
The night drave on wi' sangs and clatter;
And ay the ale was growing better:
The landlady and Tam grew gracious
Wi' secret favors, sweet, and precious:
The souter tauld his queerest stories;
The landlord's laugh was ready chorus:
The storm without might rair and rustle,
Tam did na mind the storm a whistle.

Care, mad to see a man sae happy,
E'en drown'd himsel amang the nappy:
As bees flee hame wi' lades o' treasure,
The minutes wing'd their way wi' pleasure;
Kings may be blest, but Tam was glorious,
O'er a' the ills o' life victorious!

But pleasures are like poppies spread,
You seize the flow'r, its bloom is shed;
Or like the snow falls in the river,
A moment white — then melts forever;
Or like the borealis race,
That flit ere you can point their place;
Or like the rainbow's lovely form
Evanishing amid the storm.
Nae man can tether time or tide:
The hour approaches Tam maun ride, —
That hour, o' night's black arch the key-stane,
That dreary hour he mounts his beast in;
And sic a night he taks the road in,
As ne'er poor sinner was abroad in.

The wind blew as 'twad blawn its last;
The rattling show'rs rose on the blast;
The speedy gleams the darkness swallow'd;
Loud, deep, and lang the thunder bellow'd:
That night, a child might understand,
The Deil had business on his hand.

Weel mounted on his gray mear, Meg, —
A better never lifted leg, —
Tam skelpit on thro' dub and mire,
Despising wind and rain and fire;
Whiles holding fast his guid blue bonnet,
Whiles crooning o'er some auld Scots sonnet,
Whiles glowrin round wi' prudent cares,
Lest bogles catch him unawares.
Kirk-Alloway was drawing nigh,
Whare ghaists and houlets nightly cry.

By this time he was cross the ford,
Whare in the snaw the chapman smoor'd;
And past the birks and meikle stane,
Whare drucken Charlie brak's neck-bane;
And thro' the whins, and by the cairn,
Whare hunters fand the murder'd bairn;
And near the thorn, aboon the well,
Whare Mungo's mither hang'd hersel.
Before him Doon pours all his floods;
The doubling storm roars thro' the woods;
The lightnings flash from pole to pole,
Near and more near the thunders roll;
When, glimmering thro' the groaning trees,
Kirk-Alloway seemed in a bleeze:
Thro' ilka bore the beams were glancing,
And loud resounded mirth and dancing.

Inspiring bold John Barleycorn!
What dangers thou can'st make us scorn!
Wi' tippenny we fear nae evil;
Wi' usquebae we'll face the devil!
The swats sae ream'd in Tammie's noddle,
Fair play, he car'd na deils a boddle.
But Maggie stood right sair astonish'd,
Till, by the heel and hand admonish'd,
She ventur'd forward on the light;
And, wow! Tam saw an unco sight!

Warlocks and witches in a dance;
Nae cotillon brent-new frae France,
But hornpipes, jigs, strathspeys, and reels
Put life and mettle in their heels:
A winnock bunker in the east,
There sat Auld Nick in shape o' beast;
A towzie tyke, black, grim, and large,
To gie them music was his charge;
He screw'd the pipes and gart them skirl,
Till roof and rafters a' did dirl. —
Coffins stood round like open presses,
That shaw'd the dead in their last dresses;
And by some devilish cantraip sleight
Each in its cauld hand held a light,
By which heroic Tam was able
To note upon the haly table
A murderer's banes in gibbet airns;
Twa span-lang, wee, unchisten'd bairns;
A thief, new-cutted frae the rape —
Wi' his last gasp his gab did gape;
Five tomahawks, wi' blude red-rusted;
Five scymitars, wi' murder crusted;
A garter, which a babe had strangled;
A knife, a father's throat had mangled,
Whom his ain son o' life bereft —

The gray hairs yet stack to the heft;
Wi' mair o' horrible and awfu',
Which ev'n to name wad be unlawful'.

As Tammie glowr'd, amaz'd and curious,
The mirth and fun grew fast and furious:
The piper loud and louder blew,
The dancers quick and quicker flew;
They reel'd, they set, they cross'd, they cleekit,
Till ilka carlin swat and reekit
And coost her duddies to the wark
And linket at it in her sark!

Now Tam, O Tam! had thae been queans,
A' plump and strapping in their teens!
Their sarks, instead o' creeshie flannen,
Been snaw-white seventeen hunder linen! —
Thir breeks o' mine, my only pair,
That ance were plush, o' gude blue hair,
I wad hae gien them aff my hurdies,
For ae blink o' the bonie burdies!
But withered beldams, auld and droll,
Rigwoodie hogs wad spean a foal,
Lowping and flinging on a crummock,
I wonder didna turn thy stomach.

But Tam ken'd what was what fu' brawlie;
There was ae winsom wench and walie,
That night enlisted in the core
(Lang after ken'd on Carrick shore:
For mony a beast to dead she shot,
And perish'd mony a bonie boat,
And shook baith meikle corn and bear,
And kept the country-side in fear);
Her cutty sark o' Paisley harn,
That while a lassie she had worn,

In longitude tho' sorely scanty,
It was her best, and she was vauntie.
Ah! little kent thy reverend grannie,
That sark she coft for her wee Nannie,
Wi' twa pund Scots ('twas a' her riches),
Wad ever graced a dance o' witches!

But here my Muse her wing maun cow'r,
Sic flights are far beyond her pow'r;
To sing how Nannie lap and flang,
(A souple jad she was and strang,)
And how Tam stood like ane bewitch'd,
And thought his very een enrich'd;
Even Satan glowr'd and fidg'd fu' fain,
And hotch'd and blew wi' might and main:
Till first ae caper, syne anither,
Tam tint his reason a' thegither,
And roars out, 'Weel done, Cutty-sark!'
And in an instant all was dark:
And scarcely had he Maggie rallied,
When out the hellish legion sallied.

As bees bizz out wi' angry fyke,
When plundering herds assail their byke;
As open pussie's mortal foes,
When, pop! she starts before their nose;
As eager runs the market-crowd,
When 'Catch the thief!' resounds aloud,
So Maggie runs, the witches follow,
Wi' mony an eldritch skriech and hollo.

Ah, Tam! ah, Tam! thou'll get thy fairin!
In hell they'll roast thee like a herrin!
In vain thy Kate awaits thy comin!
Kate soon will be a woefu' woman!
Now, do thy speedy utmost, Meg,

And win the key-stane of the brig:
There at them thou thy tail may toss,
A running stream they dare na cross.
But ere the key-stane she could make,
The fient a tail she had to shake!
For Nannie, far before the rest,
Hard upon noble Maggie prest,
And flew at Tam wi' furious ettle;
But little wist she Maggie's mettle —
Ae spring brought aff her master hale,
But left behind her ain gray tail:
The carlin claught her by the rump,
And left poor Maggie scarce a stump.

Now, wha this tale o' truth shall read,
Ilk man and mother's son, take heed,
Whene're to drink you are inclin'd,
Or cutty-sarks run in your mind,
Think, ye may buy the joys owre dear,
Remember Tam o' Shanter's mear.

Broomstick Train;
Or Return of the Witches

By *Oliver Wendell Holmes*

I

Look out! Look out, boys! Clear the track!
The witches are here! They've all come back!
They hanged them high, but they wouldn't lie still,
For cats and witches are hard to kill;
They buried them deep but they wouldn't die, —
Books say they did, but they lie! they lie!

II

A couple of hundred years, or so,
They had knocked about in the world below,
When an Essex deacon dropped in to call,

And a homesick feeling seized them all;
For he came from a place they knew full well,
And many a tale he had to tell.
They longed to visit the haunts of men,
To see the old dwellings they knew again,
On their well-trained broomsticks mounted high,
Seen like shadows against the sky;
Crossing the tracks of owls and bats,
Hugging before them their coal-black cats.

III

Well did they know, those gray old wives,
The sights we see in our daily drives:
Shimmer of lake and shine of sea,
Brown's bare hill with its lonely tree,
(It wasn't then as we see it now,
With one scant scalp-lock to shade its brow;)
Dusky nooks in the Essex woods,
Dark, dim, Dante-like solitudes,
Where the tree-toad watches the sinuous snake
Glide through his forests of fern and brake;
Ipswich river; its old stone bridge;
Far off Andover's Indian Ridge,
And many a scene where history tells,
Some shadow of bygone terror dwells, —
Of "Norman's Woe" with its tale of dread,
Of the Screeching Woman of Marblehead,
(The fearful story that turns men pale:
Don't bid me tell it, — my speech would fail.)

IV

For that "couple of hundred years, or so,"
There had been no peace in the world below;
The witches still grumbling, "It isn't fair;
Come, give us a taste of the upper air!
We've had enough of your sulphur springs,

And the evil odor that round them clings;
We long for a drink that is cool and nice, —
Great buckets of water with Wenham ice;
We've served you well on earth, you know;
You're a good old — fellow — come, let us go!"

V

I don't feel sure of his being good,
But he happened to be in a pleasant mood, —
As fiends with their skins full sometimes are, —
(He'd been drinking with "roughs" at a Boston bar.)
So what does he do but up and shout
To a graybeard turnkey, "Let 'em out!"

VI

To mind his orders was all he knew;
The gates swung open, and out they flew.
"Where are our broomsticks?" the beldams cried.
"Here are your broomsticks," an imp replied.
"They've been in — the place you know — so long,
They smell of brimstone uncommon strong;
But they've gained by being left alone, —
Just look, and you'll see how tall they've grown."
— "And where is my cat?" a vixen squalled.

VII

"Yes, where are our cats?" the witches bawled,
And began to call them all by name:
As fast as they called the cats, they came:
There was bob-tailed Tommy and long-tailed Tim,
And wall-eyed Jacky and green-eyed Jim,
And splay-foot Benny and slimlegged Beau,
And Skinny and Squally, and Jerry and Joe,
And many another that came at call, —
It would take too long to count them all,
All black, — one could hardly tell which was which,

But every cat knew his own old witch;
And she knew hers as hers knew her,—
Ah, didn't they curl their tails and purr!

VIII

No sooner the withered hags were free
Than out they swarmed for a midnight spree;
I couldn't tell all they did in rhymes,
But the Essex people had dreadful times.
The Swampscott fishermen still relate
How a strange sea-monster stole their bait;
How their nets were tangled in loops and knots,
And they found dead crabs in their lobster-pots.
Poor Danvers grieved for her blasted crops,
And Wilmington mourned over mildewed hops.
A blight played havoc with Beverly beans,—
It was all the work of those hateful queans!

IX

Now when the boss of the beldams found
That without his leave they were ramping round,
He called,—they could hear him twenty miles,
From Chelsea beach to the Misery Isles;
The deafest old granny knew his tone
Without the trick of the telephone.
"Come here, you witches! Come here!" says he,—
"At your games of old, without asking me!
I'll give you a little job to do
That will keep you stirring, you godless crew!"

X

They came, of course, at their master's call,
The witches, the broomsticks, the cats, and all;
He led the hags to a railway train
The horses were trying to drag in vain.
"Now, then," says he, "you've had your fun,

And here are the cars you've got to run.
The driver may just unhitch his team,
We don't want horses, we don't want steam;
You may keep your old black cats to hug,
But the loaded train you have got to lug."

XI

Since then on many a car you'll see
A broomstick plain as plain can be;
On every stick there's a witch astride, —
The string you see to her leg is tied.
She will do a mischief if she can,
But the string is held by a careful man,
And whenever the evil-minded witch
Would cut some caper he gives a twitch.
As for the hag, you can't see her,
But hark! you can hear her black cat's purr,
And now and then, as a train goes by,
You may catch a gleam from her wicked eye.

XII

Often you've looked on a rushing train,
But just what moved it was not so plain.
It couldn't be those wires above,
For they could neither pull nor shove;
Where was the motor that made it go?
You couldn't guess, *but now you know.*
Remember my rhymes when you ride again
On the rattling rail by the broomstick train!

Shadow March

By Robert Louis Stevenson

All around the house is the jet black night,
It stares through the window-pane,
It creeps in the corners hiding from the light
And it moves with the moving flame.
Now my little heart goes a-beating like a drum,
With the breath of the bogie in my hair,
While all around the candle the crooked shadows come
And go marching along up the stair.
The shadow of the baluster, the shadow of the light,
The shadow of the child that goes to bed,
All the wicked shadows come a tramp, tramp, tramp,
With the black night overhead.

Little Orphant Annie

By James Whitcomb Riley

Little Orphant Annie's come to our house to stay,
An' wash the cups and saucers up, an' brush the crumbs away,
An' shoo the chickens off the porch, an' dust the hearth, an' sweep,
An' make the fire, an' bake the bread, an' earn her board-an'-keep;
An' all us other children, when the supper things is done,
We set around the kitchen fire an' has the mostest fun
A-lis'nin' to the witch-tales 'at Annie tells about,
An' the Gobble-uns 'at gits you
                Ef you
                Don't
                Watch
                Out!

Onc't they was a little boy wouldn't say his pray'rs —
An' when he went to bed at night, away up stairs,

His mammy heered him holler, an' his daddy heard him bawl,
An' when they turn't the kivvers down, he wasn't there at all!
An' they seeked him in the rafter-room, an' cubbyhole, an' press,
An' seeked him up the chimney-flue, an' ever'wheres, I guess;
But all they ever found was thist his pants an' round-about!
An' the Gobble-uns 'll git you
                    Ef you
                        Don't
                            Watch
                                Out!

An' one time a little girl 'ud allus laugh an' grin,
An' make fun of ever'one, an' all her blood-an'-kin;
An' onc't when they was "company," an' ole folks was there,
She mocked 'em an' shocked 'em, an' said she didn't care!
An' thist as she kicked her heels, an' turn't to run an' hide,
They was two great big Black Things a-standin' by her side,
An' they snatched her through the ceilin' 'fore she knowed what
                    she's about!
An' the Gobble-uns 'll git you
                    Ef you
                        Don't
                            Watch
                                Out!

An' little Orphant Annie says, when the blaze is blue,
An' the lampwick sputters, an' the wind goes woo-oo!
An' you hear the crickets quit, an' the moon is gray,
An' the lightnin'-bugs in dew is all squenched away, —
You better mind yer parents, and yer teachers fond and dear,
An' cherish them 'at loves you, an' dry the orphant's tear,
An' he'p the pore an' needy ones 'at clusters all about,
Er the Gobble-uns 'll git you
                    Ef you
                        Don't
                            Watch
                                Out!

The Ghost's Confession

By *Lewis Carroll*

[From "Phantasmagoria"]

"Oh, when I was a little Ghost,
　A merry time had we!
Each seated on his favourite post,
We chumped and chawed the buttered toast
　They gave us for our tea."

"That story is in print!" I cried.
　"Don't say its' not, because
It's known as well as Bradshaw's Guide!"
(The Ghost uneasily replied
　He hardly thought it was).

"It's not in Nursery Rhymes? And yet
  I almost think it is —
'Three little Ghosteses' were set
'On posteses,' you know, and ate
  Their 'buttered toasteses.'

"I have the book; so, if you doubt it — "
  I turned to search the shelf.
"Don't stir!" he cried. "We'll do without it:
I now remember all about it;
  I wrote the thing myself.

"It came out in a 'Monthly,' or
  At least my agent said it did:
Some literary swell, who saw
It, thought it seemed adapted for
  The Magazine he edited.

"My father was a Brownie, Sir;
  My mother was a Fairy.
The notion had occurred to her,
The children would be happier,
  If they were taught to vary.

"The notion soon became a craze;
  And, when it once began, she
Brought us all out in different ways —
One was a Pixy, two were Fays,
  Another was a Banshee;

"The Fetch and Kelpie went to school,
  And gave a lot of trouble;
Next came a Poltergeist and Ghoul,
And then two Trolls (which broke the rule),
  A Goblin, and a Double —

"(If that's a snuff-box on the shelf,"
    He added with a yawn,
"I'll take a pinch) — next came an Elf,
And then a Phantom (that's myself),
    And last, a Leprechaun.

"One day, some Spectres chanced to call,
    Dressed in the usual white:
I stood and watched them in the hall.
And couldn't make them out at all,
    They seemed so strange a sight.

"I wondered what on earth they were,
    That looked all head and sack;
But Mother told me not to stare,
And then she twitched me by the hair,
    And punched me in the back.

"Since then I've often wished that I
    Had been a Spectre born.
But what's the use?" (He heaved a sigh).
"*They* are the ghost-nobility,
    And look on *us* with scorn.

"My phantom-life was soon begun:
    When I was barely six,
I went out with an older one —
And just at first I thought it fun,
    And learned a lot of tricks.

"I've haunted dungeons, castles, towers —
    Wherever I was sent:
I've often sat and howled for hours,
Drenched to the skin with driving showers,
    Upon a battlement.

"It's quite old-fashioned now to groan
   When you begin to speak:
This is the newest thing in tone — "
And here (it chilled me to the bone)
   He gave an *awful* squeak.

"Perhaps," he added, "to *your* ear
   That sounds an easy thing?
Try it yourself, my little dear!
It took *me* something like a year,
   With constant practising.

"And when you've learned to squeak, my man
   And caught the double sob,
You're pretty much where you began:
Just try and gibber if you can!
   That's something *like* a job!

"*I've* tried it, and can only say
   I'm sure you couldn't do it, e-
ven if you practised night and day,
Unless you have a turn that way,
   And natural ingenuity.

"Shakespeare I think it is who treats
   Of Ghosts, in days of old,
Who 'gibbered in the Roman streets,'
Dressed, if you recollect, in sheets —
   They must have found it cold.

"I've often spent ten pounds on stuff,
   In dressing as a Double;
But, though it answers as a puff,
It never has effect enough
   To make it worth the trouble.

"Long bills soon quenched the little thirst
  I had for being funny.
The setting-up is always worst:
Such heaps of things you want at first,
  One must be made of money!

"For instance, take a Haunted Tower,
  With skull, cross-bones, and sheet;
Blue lights to burn (say) two an hour,
Condensing lens of extra power,
  And set of chains complete:

"What with the things you have to hire —
  The fitting on the robe —
And testing all the coloured fire —
The outfit of itself would tire
  The patience of a Job!

"And then they're so fastidious,
  The Haunted-House Committee:
I've often known them make a fuss
Because a Ghost was French, or Russ,
  Or even from the City!

"Some dialects are objected to —
  For one, the *Irish* brogue is:
And then, for all you have to do,
One pound a week they offer you,
  And find yourself in Bogies!"

I Saw Three Witches

By Walter de la Mare

I saw three witches
That bowed down like barley,
And straddled their brooms 'neath a louring sky,
And, mounting a storm-cloud,
Aloft on its margin,
Stood black in the silver as up they did fly.

I saw three witches
That mocked the poor sparrows
They carried in cages of wicker along,
Till a hawk from his eyrie
Swooped down like an arrow,
Smote on the cages, and ended their song.

I saw three witches
That sailed in a shallop,
All turning their heads with a smickering smile,
Till a bank of green osiers
Concealed their wild faces,
Though I heard them lamenting for many a mile.

I saw three witches
Asleep in a valley,
Their heads in a row, like stones in a flood,
Till the moon, creeping upward,
Looked white through the valley,
And turned them to bushes in bright scarlet bud.

The Cat!

By Joseph Payne Brennan

Who pads through the wood
  Where cypresses grow,
When the sun goes down
  And night-winds blow?
    The cat!

Who slinks through the cave
  In the side of the hill
Where black bats swoop
  From a cobwebbed sill?
    The cat!

Who purrs by the grave
  Of unshriven dead,
While witches dance
  And ghouls are fed?
    The cat! . . . SKAT!!!

The Hag

By Robert Herrick

The Hag is astride
  This night for to ride;
The Devil and shee together:
  Through thick, and through thin,
  Now out, and then in,
Though ne'r so foule be the weather.

A thorn or a Burr
  She takes for a Spurre:
With a lash of a Bramble she rides now,
  Through Brakes and through Bryars,
  O're Ditches, and Mires
She followes the Spirit that guides now.

No Beast, for his food,
  Dares now range the wood;
But hush't in his laire he lies lurking:
  While mischiefs, by these
  On Land and on Seas,
At noone of Night are a working.

The storme will arise,
  And trouble the skies;
This night, and more for the wonder,
  The ghost from the Tomb
  Affrighted shall come,
Cal'd out by the clap of the Thunder.

Halloween

By Molly Capes

Bolt and bar the front door,
    Draw the curtains tight,
Wise folk are in before
    Moonrise tonight.

Halloween, Halloween,
    Chestnuts to roast,
A gift for the fairy,
    A prayer for the ghost.

Who will have their fate told
This night is known,
Whose hand is full of gold,
Who goes alone.

Halloween, Halloween,
Snapdragon blue,
A lover for me
And a fortune for you.

Stars shiver blue and green,
Moon's wide and white;
There tattered clouds between
Witches take flight.

Halloween, Halloween,
Apples a-bob,
Elves at the keyhole
And imps on the hob.

"Twelve" calls the deep bell
To the hollow night;
"Twelve" whisper steeple tops
Far out of sight.

Halloween, Halloween,
Fires burn high,
Who shall say certainly,
Who can tell truthfully
What solemn company
Pass through the sky?

[Suggestion: This poem can be recited by two readers or two groups of readers, or a single reader with
a chorus reciting the italized lines.]

Witch Cat

By Rowena Bennett

I want a little witch cat
    With eyes all yellow-green.
Who rides upon a broomstick
    Every Halloween.
Who purrs when she is taking off,
    Just like a purring plane,
And doesn't mind a tailspin
    Even in the rain.

I want a cat who dares to light
    The candle of the moon
And set its jack-o'-lantern face
    A-laughing like a loon.

I want a cat who laps the milk
    Along the Milky Way,
A cat of spunk and character
    As daring as the day;
But gentle-looking kittens
    Are in the stores to sell
And which cat is a witch cat,
    I really cannot tell.

Theme in Yellow

By Carl Sandburg

I spot the hills
With yellow balls in autumn.
I light the prairie cornfields
Orange and tawny gold clusters
And I am called pumpkins.
On the last of October,

When dusk is fallen,
Children join hands
And circle round me
Singing ghost songs
And love to the harvest moon;
I am a jack-o'-lantern
With terrible teeth,
And the children know
I am fooling.

Hallowe'en

By Harry Behn

Tonight is the night
When dead leaves fly
Like witches on switches
Across the sky,
When elf and sprite
Flit through the night
On a moony sheen.

Tonight is the night
When leaves make a sound
Like a gnome in his home
Under the ground,
When spooks and trolls
Creep out of holes
Mossy and green.

Tonight is the night
When pumpkins stare
Through sheaves and leaves
Everywhere,
When ghoul and ghost
And goblin host
Dance round their queen.
It's Hallowe'en!

Ghosts

By Harry Behn

A cold and starry darkness moans
   And settles wide and still
Over a jumble of tumbled stones
   Dark on a darker hill.

An owl among those shadowy walls,
   Gray against the gray
Of ruins and brittle weeds, calls
   And soundless swoops away.

Rustling over scattered stones
   Dancers hover and sway,
Drifting among their own bones
   Like webs of the Milky Way.

Wicked Witch's Kitchen

By X. J. Kennedy

You're in the mood for some freaky food?
You feel your taste buds itchen'
for nice fresh poison ivy green?
Try Wicked Witch's kitchen!

She has corn on the cobweb, cauldron-hot,
She makes the meanest cider,
But her broomstick cakes and milkweed shakes
Aren't fit to feed a spider.

She likes to brew hot toadstool stew —
"Come eat, my sweet!" she'll cackle —
But if you do, you'll turn into
A Jack-o'-lantern's jackal.

From Ghoulies and Ghosties

From: *A Cornish Litany*

From Ghoulies and Ghosties,
And long-leggity Beasties,
And all Things that go bump
   in the Night,
Good Lord deliver us.

Wailed a Ghost in a Graveyard at Kew

By *Myra Cohn Livingston*

Wailed a ghost in a graveyard at Kew,
"Oh my friends are so fleeting and few,
   For it's gravely apparent
   That if you're transparent
There is no one who knows if it's *you!*"

Pumpkin People

By John Ridland

The Pumpkin People camp inside
Your Jack-o'-lantern's pumpkin hide,
Though you won't find them much about
Until you scoop the center out —
The seeds and all that stringy stuff.
Make sure you scrape it clean enough
And neatly carve eyes, ears, and nose,
And — carefully — the teeth in rows,
Since *that's* where Pumpkin People enter
To set up camp right in the center.
Around the brightly gleaming candle,
Which as you know's too hot to handle,
They toast marshmallows on long forks,
Pull sparkling-apple-cider corks,
And stuff themselves with tricks or treats —
The same that everybody eats —
Until their belts are stretched and groaning
(Just listen hard, you'll hear them moaning).
There while your Jack-o'-lantern glows
Through eyes and teeth and ears and nose,
The Pumpkin People loll inside.
You'll *almost* see 'em where they hide
Between the flame's flash and its flicker:
Look quickly! — Nope, they've scrambled quicker.
But when the candle stub is snuffed,

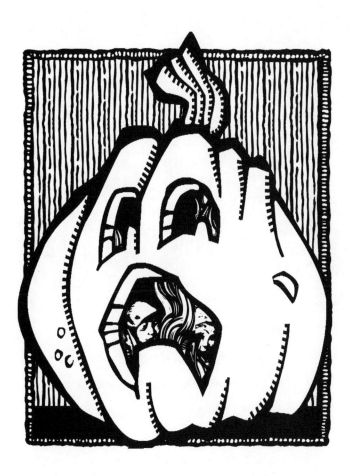

The Pumpkin People, crammed and stuffed
With sweets to hold them for a year,
And smiling still from ear to ear,
Roll round the floor and out the mouth
And far away — North, East, West, South —
Until next Halloween rolls round
When once again they — won't — be — found.

All Hallow's Eve

(My Mother Brings Me to Visit a Sicilian Cemetery)

By Emanuel di Pasquale

Below the hill, the cemetery sits,
a small city of the perfectly behaved.
Among the bushes and grass and pine trees
statues of angels rest their wings.
Like a goat, I hop on tombstones
and stone walls. My mother calls,
"Come down, you might get hurt."
I run to where two lions
guard the cemetery's gate.
One sleeps and one's wide-eyed.
I turn away from the sleeping lion.
Always, always I ride the wide-eyed beast.

Next Day

By Valerie Worth

Though fiends
Slink back
To their lairs,
And witches'
Grins go wan,
Some signs are
Yet to be found:

A splattered
Egg, a straggle
Of shaving cream,
And chalked
In the road
A gleefully
Wicked word.

To Pumpkins at Pumpkin Time

By Grace Tall

Back into your garden-beds!
    Here come the holidays!
And woe to the golden pumpkin-heads
    Attracting too much praise.
Hide behind the hoe, the plow,
    Cling fast to the vine!
Those who come to praise you now
    Will soon sit down to dine.
Keep your lovely heads, my dears,
    If you know what I mean . . .
Unless you sigh to be in pie,
    Stay hidden, or stay green.

The Haunted House

By Vic Crume

Not a window was broken
And the paint wasn't peeling,
  Not a porch step sagged—
  Yet, there was a feeling

That beyond the door
And into the hall
  This was the house of
  No one at all.

No one who breathed
Nor laughed, nor ate
  Nor said "I love,"
  Nor said "I hate."

Yet *something* walked
Along the stair
  Something that was
  And wasn't there.

And that is why weeds
On the path grow high,
  And even the moon
  Races fearfully by—

For something walks
Along the stair—
  Something that is
  And isn't there.

Pumpkin

By Valerie Worth

After its lid
Is cut, the slick
Seeds and stuck
Wet strings
Scooped out,
Walls scraped
Dry and white,
Face carved, candle
Fixed and lit,

Light creeps
Into the thick
Rind: giving
That dead orange
Vegetable skull
Warm skin, making
A live head
To hold its
Sharp gold grin.

Forbidden Sounds

By Eric James

When the banshees wail,
And the werewolves howl,
When the dead in the churchyard sigh.
When the witches scream,
And their demons hiss,
When you hear the song of the Lorelei.
When the bogies shout,
And when goblins yell.
When the shades call out
From the depths of Hell.
When the phantom drummer
Drums his drum,
When the midnight wraith
Whispers, "Come, oh come . . ."
Then who will go?

Not I.

All Hallowe'en

By Pauline Clark

Witch and warlock all abroad
Revels keep by field and yard.

In the firelight of the farm
Boy and maiden one by one
Place their chestnuts in the grate
And for omens quietly wait;
To a string their apples tie,
Twirl them till they fallen lie;
Those whose fruit fall in a hurry,
They shall be the first to marry.

Witch and warlock all abroad
Revels keep by field and yard.

Apples from the beam hang down
To be caught by mouth alone,
Mugs of ale on Nut-Crack Night
And many a tale of ghost and sprite,
Come to cheer and chill the heart,
While the candles faint and start,
While the flickering firelight paints
Pictures of the hallowed saints.

Witch and warlock all abroad
Revels keep by field and yard.

The Witch

By Jack Prelutsky

She comes by night, in fearsome flight,
In garments black as pitch,
the queen of doom upon her broom,
the wild and wicked witch,

a crackling crone with brittle bones
and desiccated limbs,
two evil eyes with warts and sties
and bags about the rims,

a dangling nose, ten twisted toes
and fold of shriveled skin,
cracked and chipped and crackled lips
that frame a toothless grin.

She hurtles by, she sweeps the sky
and hurls a piercing screech.
As she swoops past, a spell is cast
on all her curses reach.

Take care to hide when the wild witch rides
to shriek her evil spell.
What she may do with a word or two
is much too grim to tell.

The Bird of the Night

By Randall Jarrell

A shadow is floating through the moonlight.
Its wings don't make a sound.
Its claws are long, its beak is bright.
Its eyes try all the corners of the night.

It calls and calls: all the air swells and heaves
And washes up and down like water.
The ear that listens to the owl believes
In death. The bat beneath the eaves.

The mice beneath the stone are still as death.
The owl's air washes them like water.
The owl goes back and forth inside the night,
And the night holds its breath.

Plays

A Hallowe'en Husband

Anonymous

CHARACTERS

SISTER SNOOP
SISTER PINCH — *Witches of considerable renown*
SISTER SCREECH
JANE LEMON, *almost an old maid*
EBENEEZER SWEET, *a woman-hater*

SCENE: *The scene is the interior of the witches' home. It is just like any-one's home except that there is an old black pot standing on the floor in a far corner.*

COSTUMES: *The witches wear long black cloaks when they first appear. Underneath the cloaks are ordinary dresses. They have tall peaked hats with long wisps of gray hair fastened to the inside of the crown so that it hangs about their faces and conceals their features. Under the hats their hair is arranged in the fashion of today. They speak in ordinary voices in the first part of the play but when they resume their witches' costumes their voices are high, squeaky, shrill, and piercing. Very good effect can be obtained with a little practice.*

SISTER SNOOP *enters in full witches' regalia, carrying her broom. She pauses at the door to shoo a cat away.*

SNOOP. Shoo! Shoo! Scat! You nasty cat!

[*She limps wearily in, lays her broomstick aside and takes off her cloak and hat, revealing herself as a nice appearing young woman.* SISTERS PINCH *and* SCREECH *come with their broomsticks, also very tired.*]

PINCH [*putting cloak and hat aside*]. Thank goodness another Hallowe'en is over. Did you ever have such a tiresome evening?

SCREECH [*as she takes off her things*]. Never. I'm a wreck. I'm even forgetting how to ride my broomstick.

[*The witches seat themselves, putting their feet on foot stools, arranging pillows at their backs, etc.*]

SNOOP. A witch's life is certainly hard, even if we do only have to work one night a year now.

SCREECH. Thank goodness it's the only time folks believe in witches nowadays, anyway. Think how hard we had to work in the olden times — giving people rheumatism, fits, squint eye and goodness knows what all!

PINCH. Well, they make up for all that in one night. How many apple parings have I turned into initials tonight!

SNOOP. How many sweethearts have I revealed!

SCREECH. That's simply nothing. I'm hoarse from telling fortunes! But thank goodness we don't have to keep cats any more. Renting them for Hallowe'en was a great idea! Now if we could get rid of the brooms and those hats that make us look so awful!

SNOOP [*starting up in her chair in alarm*]. Did you hear something?

SCREECH. No. Why? Why, what's the matter, Snoop? You've fairly turned pale!

SNOOP [*weakly*]. And so would you if you'd had the awful night I had.

SCREECH. What was it? An old maid?

SNOOP. Not quite, but she will be next year and she knows it.

PINCH. You poor darling, they're the very worst kind.

SNOOP [*almost in tears*]. I couldn't find a husband for her high or low. She pestered me all evening. I declare she did everything from almost breaking her neck backing down the cellar stairs to eating an egg full of salt! I'm just a nervous wreck.

PINCH. Why, that sounds like a description of Jane Lemon!

SNOOP. It *was* Jane Lemon!

PINCH. Poor Snoop! I know just what you've been through. I had Jane Lemon last Hallowe'en and I've hoped and prayed ever since that she'd find a husband before another October.

SNOOP [*putting her hands over her ears*]. I can hear her muttering spells still. Hide me! Hide me! I just know she's following me! [JANE LEMON *appears in the door. She is a typical homely, old maid.*] Oh!

[SNOOP *collapses.*]

PINCH. Jane Lemon!

JANE [*of course she does not recognize the* WITCHES]. Is this where the witches live?

PINCH. Oh, no — that is, well, as a matter of fact, they do live here.

JANE. Humph! I thought so. I suppose they're still out galavanting around.

SCREECH. Yes. They won't be back for quite a long time.

JANE. Is that so? Well, then, I'll just wait around until they do come back. I mean to have them boycotted. They're nothing but a lot of fakes and I'm going to expose them. The sooner folks stop believing in them, the better. And if folks stop believing in them they'll be dead as a door nail!

WITCHES. [*starting, even* SNOOP]. Dead as a door nail!

JANE. Certainly. It's only believing in them that keeps them alive.

SCREECH. You wouldn't really boycott them, would you?

PINCH. You know, after all, there wouldn't be much fun on Hallowe'en without witches.

SNOOP. You aren't serious, are you?

JANE [*angrily*]. I should say I am! What did the witches ever do for me? I never went to a Hallowe'en party yet that I didn't bring home the *thimble*. I look in mirrors and jabber spells and what do I see? *Nothing*. Oh, you can't fool me. I'm going to wait on the door step for them and tell them what I think of them. And if they come down the chimney you can just tell them that Jane Lemon's here.

[JANE *marches out stiffly. The* WITCHES *look at each other in consternation.*]

SCREECH. If she does that we'll actually be *dead*. After all, it's superstition that keeps us alive. Take that away and where are we?

PINCH. There's only one way out. We've got to get a husband for her.

SNOOP [*wailing*]. But there isn't a man in the world that will have her! Don't I know? Haven't I been trying for hours to find one for her?

PINCH. But this is desperate. We've got to find one.

SCREECH. Let me think. [*Pause.*] Did you ever hear of Ebeneezer Sweet?

PINCH. Ebeneezer Sweet? Isn't he the young man who hates girls?

SNOOP. Yes. I know him by reputation. He never went to a Hallowe'en party in his life.

SCREECH. Ebeneezer Sweet is the answer to our problem.

SNOOP. I don't see what good he is to us.

SCREECH. Girls, I'm ashamed of you. Are we witches, or aren't we?

SNOOP. Of course we're witches.

SCREECH. Then let's get the kettle out and look up some incantations and get to work.

PINCH. Why, aren't you clever? I'd forgotten all about those old things. Where's the spell book.

SCREECH. Under those magazines. I always try to keep it hidden. If the neighbors ever picked it up it would look *queer*!

[PINCH *gets the spell book.*]

SCREECH. Now help me get the kettle out.

[*While* SCREECH *and* SNOOP *move the kettle out to the middle of the stage, front,* PINCH *looks through book.*]

SCREECH. My, this is heavy!

SNOOP. And to think that we used haul it around on heaths and moors every night!

SCREECH [*as they put it down*]. There. Now we must get into our costumes. This is going to be a real honest-to-goodness spell.

PINCH [*looking up from book*]. Here's a good one.

[*She shows them the book.*]

SNOOP. That's the very thing. Hurry into your clothes, Pinch.

[*They all put on witches' costumes.*]

SCREECH. I'll get the charm bag.

[*She gets a black bag full of old shoe strings, nails, old soles, etc. They gather around the kettle, their hair streaming over their faces as they bend over, completely transformed into witches. From now on their voices are high, shrill and piercing.* PINCH *reads the spell,* SNOOP *stirs and* SCREECH *casts the charms into the kettle. They may light incense in the pot to make smoke.*]

PINCH.   Bubble, bubble, cauldron, bubble,
Cast in owls' teeth, cast out trouble,
Cast in rats' tails, snakes and rubble,
Swiftly, cauldron, boil and bubble!

SNOOP. [*passing the stick to stir pot to* PINCH].
Brew! Brew! Witches' brew!
Ebeneezer, it's for you!
Drink it down without ado —
'Tis Jane Lemon you must woo!

[EBENEEZER *suddenly appears, but not from the entrance used by* JANE. *He is a cantankerous old bachelor and is far from handsome.*]

EBENEEZER. Witches! How did I get here? Speak, you wretched hags!

[*The witches cackle and stir their brew.*]

EBENEEZER. You're nothing but old frauds. You're trying to bewitch me but I don't believe in you for a minute.

[SNOOP *dips a cup in the kettle and holds it out to* EBENEEZER.]

SNOOP. Drink!

EBENEEZER. No, thank you, I don't care for any.

SNOOP *and* PINCH. *Drink!*

EBENEEZER. I won't. I don't want any of your nasty brew.

SNOOP, PINCH *and* SCREECH. DRINK!

[EBENEEZER *immediately drinks. The* WITCHES *watch him closely. He rubs his hand over his eyes and seems to be coming out of a dream.*]

EBENEEZER. Ah, who is that fair lady I am always thinking of? Jane! Jane! Beautiful Jane Lemon! Witches, I beseech you, tell me how I may find that fair damsel—Jane Lemon!

SNOOP [*crooking a finger at him*]. Follow me!

[*She leads* EBENEEZER *off in opposite direction from* JANE.]

PINCH. Quickly, Screech, fetch Jane in.

[SCREECH *hobbles to the door.*]

SCREECH. Jane Lemon, you may enter.

[JANE *comes in belligerently.*]

JANE [*speaking fast and angrily*]. I suppose you wonder what I'm here for. Well, I'll just tell you quick enough, you miserable old creatures! What do you mean by making an idiot out of me for ten years running? What do you mean—

PINCH. Peace, Jane Lemon! We will make amends. [*Handing her a mirror.*] Take this mirror, walk backwards from yonder door and you shall see your future husband.

JANE [*snatching mirror*]. Well, it's about time!

[*She goes to door which she has just entered and starts to walk backwards across the room.* PINCH *and* SCREECH *motion to* SNOOP *to bring* EBENEEZER *in and he is placed so that* JANE *catches sight of him in the mirror when she is about half way across the room.*]

JANE [*gasping*]. A man! A real man! And ain't he handsome!

EBENEEZER [*gasping*]. Jane! Ah, beautiful Jane Lemon! At last I have found you!

JANE [*embracing him*]. Ebeneezer Sweet! [*Leading him out.*] You come right along with me to the minister's.

[*Triumphantly the couple go out without another word to the witches. The three, laughing, gather around their kettle and begin stirring. They repeat the following in weird voices.*]

SNOOP. How happily extremes do meet in Jane and Ebeneezer!

PINCH. For she's no longer sour but Sweet!

SCREECH. And he's a Lemon squeezer!

[*As the curtain fall, or lights go off to mark end of play, the high shrill laughter of the witches is heard.*]

CURTAIN

The Haunted Cottage

(*Play for four boys and eight girls*)

CHARACTERS

MAY LOU
PATIENCE
JEAN
NESSIE   *who are having a party*
SUE
MADELEINE
ESTHER
ANN

LEN
PAUL   *who disturb the party*
JACK   *(no lines to speak)*
BING

COSTUMES

*Both boys and girls are dressed in ordinary school clothes,
but the boys have sheets wound about themselves
while they are impersonating ghosts.*

SCENE: *The interior of a haunted cottage on Halloween night. There is a door up center right, also a window up center left. Between the two, an ancient calendar is hanging askew on the wall. An inconspicuous cord is fastened to the calendar and strung along the wall so that a boy off stage can pull it and make the calendar move. On the back wall at right of door hangs a small, cracked mirror. It must be insecurely fastened, so that, when the cord tied to it is jerked from off stage, it will be sure to fall and break. At extreme left is an old, weatherbeaten rocking-chair, which also has a cord fastened to it, leading off stage.*

At center, two wooden boxes support a large board, which is used as a table. The box farthest up stage has a string, by which it can be pulled toward one side or the other by a boy off stage. On the table are several paper bags, a pail or similar container, paper cups, a dish of apples, and an unlighted candle. Three boxes of different sizes and a broken chair or two serve as seats. At right is a small oil heater which is supposed to furnish heat for the party. A small kerosene lamp, which should be wired for electricity, burns feebly on one of the broken chairs.

At rise of curtain, MAY LOU *is eating an apple at center front and picking out the seeds.* PATIENCE *is tuning her ukulele over by the window.* JEAN *is riding an old broom, witch-fashion, across back of stage.* NESSIE *is paring an apple, sitting on a box at left front.* SUE *is kneeling in front of a box at right, cracking nuts with a hammer.* MADELEINE *is trying on a tall witch hat before the mirror.* ESTHER *sits on the end of the table, near front, making a jack-o'-lantern out of a small pumpkin, and* ANN *is trying to make the oil heater burn.*

MAY LOU [*counting apple seeds*].

One I love, two I love, three I love, I say;
Four I love with all my heart, and five I cast away;
Six he loves, seven she loves, eight they both love;
Nine he comes, ten he tarries,
Eleven he courts, twelve he marries.

[*She hold up one extra seed. All the girls watch her.*] I say, girls, what does he do when there are thirteen?

MADELEINE [*flippantly, as she tilts hat to an absurd angle*]. He says, "My dear, go home to mother. Thirteen is an unlucky number."

NESSIE. Are there really thirteen, May Lou? [*She leans forward anxiously.*]

MAY LOU. Sure! There'd have to be thirteen in an apple that you ate in a haunted cottage; wouldn't there? [*She begins poking the seeds, one by one, down* ESTHER'S *back, but* ESTHER *threatens her with the knife, and* MAY LOU *desists.*]

NESSIE [*coming to front, shows her unbroken paring*]. Well, I'll try my luck. [*Throws paring over right shoulder and stoops to look at it, as others all crowd about her.*] Is it an L or an S, or what is it?

JEAN [*catching up paring on her broom handle*]. It's a question mark. Being a witch, I know.

NESSIE. Why a question mark?

JEAN. There's a question whether you'll ever change your initial. See? [NESSIE *starts for* JEAN, *who rides away to rear of stage on broomstick.*]

SUE [*nibbling a nut*]. We forgot a pan of water, girls, to sail our nutshell boats in.

ESTHER. Nutshell boats? [*She holds her pumpkin up for critical inspection.*]

SUE. Yes, of course. Haven't you ever done that? You put a tiny lighted candle in each shell, name it for some one, and set it afloat. If your boat stays close to the side of the pan, you will have a quiet life—nothing exciting. If it overturns and the candle goes out, you will die soon. [*Looks exaggeratedly mournful, hands clasped.*] If it floats near one that is named for a boy, he will be your husband. And the one whose candle burns longest will be the first bride.

PATIENCE [*crosses and sits cross-legged upon floor near* SUE, *taking a nut*]. How interesting! I wish we had thought of doing that, but when you are planning a Halloween party in a deserted cottage, which is haunted besides, you can't think of everything.

MAY LOU. Oh, we shall have excitement enough without the sailing party. [*She goes to window and looks out.*] Of course, we can expect a visit from the haunter or the hauntess of this place any minute now. I'll be downright disappointed if it fails us on Halloween, when that's its only chance.

NESSIE. Oh, don't May Lou! [*She glances about fearfully.*] We're all alone.

MADELEINE [*coming forward*]. Of course we're alone. Didn't we bet those boys that we could have our Halloween party all alone here? Don't begin to slip at this early hour, Nessie, my child.

ESTHER. No. It isn't the eerie hour of midnight yet. [*She rises, stooping, holding pumpkin out in front of her and creeps toward* NESSIE, *who laughs.*]

PATIENCE. No self-respecting ghost ever makes his debut until twelve o'clock.

ANN [*rising exasperatedly and glaring at heater*]. No self-respecting ghost will ever make his debut here. He'd freeze to death. I can't make this burn. [*Dusts off hands, goes over and takes an apple, then sits on table.*]

JEAN [*hopping to front of her broomstick, eyes glaring very witch-like*]. "Double, double, toil and trouble, fire burn and caldron bubble!"

SUE [*rising and catching* JEAN *by the hair*]. The First Witch of Macbeth, ladies and not a gentleman in sight. The Ghost of Banquo will follow soon.

NESSIE [*crouching down near* ANN]. Gracious! I wish you wouldn't keep talking about ghosts. There's no need of inviting them in; is there?

PATIENCE [*pointing finger at* NESSIE]. Ho, ho, ho! Nessie's 'fraid o' gobble-uns. [*Strums on her ukulele and chants.*] "And the gobble-uns 'll git you ef you don't watch out."*

MADELEINE [*beside* NESSIE]. I foresee that we'll have to be stern with you, Miss Clinging Vine. [*She drags* NESSIE *to her feet.*] Look here! Do you or do you not want to win that five-pound box of chocolates from those four boys? Are you going to let Len and the others laugh at us for the next ten years by breaking up our party? Speak, woman! [*Shakes* NESSIE.]

NESSIE. Oh, I shan't break up the party. I'll eat my share of those chocolates.

* See quoted poem on page 162, "Little Orphant Annie"

MADELEINE. Then just remember the bargain: We must have our party out and go home in good order and not let anything frighten us away — not even one of us! Remember, now!

NESSIE. Yes; all right. [*She glances to left, and, at that instant, the rocking-chair rocks several times in response to pull on the cord by some one off stage.* NESSIE *starts, frightened, looking at* ESTHER, *who happens to be nearest to chair but who does not see it rock.*] Did you rock that chair with your foot, Esther?

ESTHER. Me? [*She steps back and looks at rocking-chair, which is not rocking now.*] Me? What do you think I am? A sleight-o'-hand artist? My foot is a mile away from that chair.

NESSIE [*in a half whisper, backing to the table*]. It — it rocked. [*She tries a board in floor with the toe of her right foot.*] Maybe I stepped on a loose board. Never mind. [*She sits beside* ANN.] I'll not be the one to give up five pounds of candy without a struggle. Don't worry. [*Eats an apple.*]

ANN [*going to study idly the old calendar on back wall*]. Why should you give it up? There's nothing here to frighten you save a few ancient and venerable spiders, that I can see. So far, nothing unusual has hap — [*She stops to stare at the calendar which is swaying gently from side to side, as the invisible cord attached to it is pulled from off stage.*]

MAY LOU. What's the matter, Ann? Seeing things?

ANN [*looking out at window*]. N-no. The wind's blowing; isn't it?

PATIENCE. Not a whiff. Why? [*She goes to door, is about to open it, when it blows wide open, apparently by itself, but is really pulled open by a boy from without. She steps back in surprise.*] Well! [*She reaches out for knob to close door, which closes with a bang in dangerous proximity to her nose. She steps back again.*] The wind must be blowing. It must be! [*She comes thoughtfully down front and sits on floor.*]

JEAN [*sitting on table at center*]. What are you watching, Ann? Come here. I'm going to tell fortunes.

ANN. A — all right. [*Suddenly she slaps the calendar vigorously and then, with her shoulders squared, comes to center.*]

ESTHER [*laughing*]. Having a brainstorm, Ann? Why treat the work of art so rough?

ANN. It was acting too giddy for a calendar of its age. Well, go ahead with your fortunes, Jean. [*Holds out her hand to* JEAN.]

[*The rocking-chair rocks gently, and* NESSIE *jumps up.*]

NESSIE. Esther, stop rocking that chair, please! It makes me so nervous!

ESTHER. Say, Ness, lay off me; will you? I tell you I — [*Chair rocks harder.*] Why, who is rocking it? [*Rubs her eyes hard, then stares at chair again.*]

MADELEINE [*coming near chair*]. Now, don't you be silly, too, Esther! It will rock every time you just step on a loose board. Move the chair up a little off that board, Nessie. [*She steps to mirror again.*]

NESSIE [*shrinking*]. Oh, I c — can't. You do it, Madeleine.

MADELEINE [*turning sharply*]. Of all things! [*She marches up to chair, which is still, and pulls it a little down front.*] There! [*Shakes a finger at* NESSIE.] If you don't mend your ways, young lady, we'll make you go around the house outside in the dark, with water in your mouth.

NESSIE. Me? Alone! Never!

SUE [*laughing*]. What's that one, Madeleine?

MADELEINE. The first man you meet, as you go silently around the house, will be your husband.

SUE [*grasping* NESSIE *in mock alarm*]. Don't do it, Nessie. The nearest neighbor is squint-eyed and hasn't a hair on his head! [*Thrusts her hand out to* JEAN.] Tell my fortune first, Jean.

JEAN [*taking her hand and examining it*]. But you'll all have to keep quiet. There must be silence, and plenty of it, while I search the future. [*The other girls giggle.*] Sh! Not a noise!

[*From off stage, in the pause, comes the loud clank of a dragging chain.*]

ALL THE GIRLS [*starting and squealing*]. Ee-ee! Oh!

PATIENCE. What was that? [*Rises.*]

ANN. Sounded like a chain, but— [*Rises and looks behind her fearfully.*]

MAY LOU. Or a truck going past, maybe? [*She goes to window.*]

MADELEINE. My goodness! Don't hold your breaths, all of you! It's probably a brick off the chimney, rattling down the side of the house.

ESTHER [*in relief*]. That's just what it sounded like. My, but you're sensible, Madeleine! Nothing would ever frighten you. [*Sits, down left.*]

PATIENCE. Of course that's what it is: a brick that the wind dislodged. You know there must be quite a wind, because it blew the door open and shut a little while ago. Old doors don't fit tightly. [*She resumes her seat on floor.*]

ANN. And it blew the calendar back and forth, too. That's what I was watching back there. [*Points to back.*] But, of course, old walls have big cracks in them. [*She is satisfied and plumps down upon floor.*]

MAY LOU. Let the wind blow! Who cares? [*She dances a few grotesque steps at back and comes to right of table, looking into a bag.*] Did anybody say, "eat"?

NESSIE. I thought that chair rocked again.

[*The girls look, but the chair is still.*]

MAY LOU. Well, can't you let the poor old granny ghost have a wee bit rock, if she wants to, you hard-hearted creature? Come and get a sandwich. The table isn't rocking, anyway.

[*The box under the table begins to move slowly at a gentle tug on its cord, and then more quickly. The board which forms the table*] suddenly drops with a consequent scattering of the things upon it. The girls scream.]

PATIENCE. May Lou, you pushed the box away! [*She laughs, as she picks up the apples.*]

MAY LOU [*in a small voice*]. We—well, maybe I did, but I—I don't think so.

ANN [*picking up a bag*]. Why, you didn't, either; no one was near the box.

MADELEINE [*holding up the board and shoving box into place under it*]. It was the board that got pushed off, that's all. Come, Nessie. Don't stand there with your mouth wide open. Get the eats back on the table.

[NESSIE *helps pick up the fallen food with many a backward look and start.*]

JEAN. We're not getting anywhere. We've not done half the Halloween stunts. [*She leans on her broom at right.*]

SUE. No. Who is going down cellar backward with a candle in one hand and a mirror in the other?

MADELEINE. Oh, yes. She will surely see the face of her future husband looking into the mirror over her shoulder. Nessie'd love to do that. [*Takes* NESSIE'S *arm to lead her to mirror.*]

PATIENCE. Oh, yes! Go on, Nessie dear. [*Pushes* NESSIE *laughingly.*]

NESSIE [*struggling*]. Oh, no! I wouldn't go down into that cellar alone for all the chocolates in the world [*She backs down extreme left and, wild-eyed, points at the chair which rocks, first slowly, then faster and faster.*] Look at that chair! [*She continues to back across the stage, bumping into the table.*]

ANN. I declare, it does rock! That isn't the wind—that isn't! [*She goes to right and backs up center slowly, watching the chair.*]

SUE. No; you can't blame the wind for that; it just—rocks. [*She shrugs and nods calmly around upon all.*] Come, Madeleine. It's up to you to explain this chair's actions. You're good at explaining.

MADELEINE. I tell you it will rock every time any one takes a step; the floor is so uneven. Forget it now. [*The chair continues to rock moderately.*] Watch me! [*She goes to table and takes candle.*] Got a match, anybody? I'm going downstairs with the mirror myself! [*Starts toward back, and door flies open.*] Mercy! Some breeze! [*The door bangs shut.*] Humph!

PATIENCE. I'll fasten that door with something. [*As she approaches door it flies open.*] Gracious!

    [*Door bangs shut.* PATIENCE *looks at* MADELEINE. *The other girls turn toward back, and those who are sitting rise.*]

NESSIE [*growing more and more panicky*]. O-oh! and, Patience, look at the chair! [*Puts hands before her face and nestles against* ANN.]

ANN [*shaking* NESSIE *off and pointing at calendar, which is swaying rapidly from side to side*]. And see that calendar! [*All look.*]

MADELEINE. Oh, give me a match, somebody! Here I go down cellar. [*Reaches for the mirror, which falls with a crash to the floor. All scream and rush back.*]

MAY LOU. Glory! There goes seven years of bad luck!

SUE [*standing with hands on hips at center, surveying the debris*]. You don't need to worry about the seven years, May Lou. This is probably your last night on earth. [*Puts out both hands suddenly, as box moves from under the board table again.*] Whoa, there! Look out, Jean!

JEAN [*watching the box and running over to* SUE'S *side*]. I declare, the table's falling again! Something's funny!

MAY LOU [*her hand on the door knob, determined*]. Well, maybe it is funny, but it is not my idea of humor! I'm going home!

    [*The chair, calendar, and box move.*]

NESSIE [*running to clutch* MAY LOU'S *arm*]. Oh, take me with you, May Lou. [*Door flies open, revealing darkness.* NESSIE *shrinks back.*] Oh, dear, it's so dark out there! I'm scared to death!

ANN [taking NESSIE'S arm]. Well, I'll go with you, if you're afraid.

ESTHER [taking NESSIE'S other arm]. Let me. I live nearest. I'll go, Ness.

[ANN, NESSIE and ESTHER step into the open doorway, and a weird "O-oh! Oo-oo-oh!" rising and falling like a groan, is heard just before the door bangs shut once more.]

PATIENCE [clutching ESTHER'S arm]. I don't — don't [her teeth chatter] — l-ll-like that, exactly. Do you, Madeleine?

SUE. It may be the wind [table falls, and they all jump but make no move to retrieve articles rolling on floor], and I do hate to lose five pounds of candy. [Shakes her head regretfully, going slowly to door, then turns toward MADELEINE undecidedly.] And I don't really believe in ghosts —

JEAN [carefully giving rocking-chair a wide berth, as she comes up center]. Oh, of course we don't believe in ghosts —

MADELEINE [glaring at the group near door, as she stands up right]. You girls are quitters! Ghosts! [Very scornfully.] What rubbish! [She lights her candle at the lamp, and stands up right.] Ghosts! [Her candle goes out.] Oh! [She drops it.]

All the girls huddle near door. There appear two "ghosts" in white sheets from the right and two more from the left wing, creeping with hands outspread under the sepulchral robes. The nearest "ghost" blows or turns out the lamp, leaving the room dark. The wildest confusion reigns. All the girls push against door, which finally opens so suddenly as to precipitate the first girls out in a heap. The strident tone of MADELEINE's voice are heard above all the din.

MADELEINE. Let me out! This place is haunted!

[All the girls exeunt, and the door bangs shut behind them. One of the ghosts immediately turns on the lamp.]

[The four boys, impersonating the ghosts, silently move about the room, removing the cords which they had about box, chair, calendar, and mirror. Then, as they are winding the strings around their hands *and putting them into their pockets, all four come down front. They put the box back in place under board table. Each picks up an apple, and all sit in a row on the board, push sheets off their heads, and look at one another solemnly, then, raising their apples to bite, suddenly burst into silent laughter, rocking against each other and slapping one another's knees.]*

CURTAIN

Halloween Magic

TIME OF PLAYING: *About fifteen minutes*

CHARACTERS

SUE, *twelve years old*
JEAN, *twelve years old*
OLD WOMAN, *with the aspect and voice of a witch*
GHOST, *a tall child*

COSTUMES

SUE *and* JEAN: *Clothing suitable for school.*

OLD WOMAN: *A long black dress. A black shawl around her shoulders. Hair whitened with powder, hanging in straight wisps around her face. Her face should be lined with a black pencil to show age.*

GHOST: *Draped sheet. Face whitened with powder.*

TIME: *Late afternoon on Halloween.*

SCENE: *The front porch of* SUE'S *house. At left front, a bench large enough for two people to sit on. Near it, two wicker chairs. Potted plants on table, right rear. At right front of stage, a table with a lighted lamp. Center rear, an exit arranged to look like the porch steps. Stage dimly lighted, as action takes place at dusk. During last few minutes of the play the stage should be darkened still more by turning off a light or two.*

> *As the curtain rises,* SUE *is seated on the porch bench, cutting a black cat out of crepe paper. Near her on the seat are two or three medium-sized boxes.*

SUE. Oh, dear, will I ever get through? Seems as if I've cut out a million of these crazy cats. I always get the last minute jobs to do. I don't see any sense to Halloween anyway. [*Steps are heard off stage.* SUE *calls out without rising.*] I'm here on the porch, Jean. Come on up.

[JEAN *enters, carrying a large box.*]

JEAN. Aren't you finished yet, Sue?

SUE. Not quite. Here's an extra pair of scissors. Won't you help me?

[JEAN *takes scissors, sets box on floor, seats herself on chair near the bench, and begins to cut out the cats.*]

JEAN. Okay, but we should hurry. We'll have to put these things up after we get to school.

SUE [*irritated*]. I know, I know. I hate to rush. I'm disgusted with this Halloween entertainment. We're too big to believe superstitions.

JEAN. Well, why did you vote for a Halloween party if you didn't want it?

SUE. Oh, I don't know. Just to be doing something, I guess. You voted for it, too.

JEAN. Sure I did. I like Halloween. I kinda believe in it.

SUE [*sneering*]. Don't be so stupid.

[JEAN *lays her scissors down, gets to her feet, and puts her hands on her hips.*]

JEAN [*angrily*]. I'm not stupid, and if you think I am, you can just finish your old cats by yourself!

SUE. Oh, come on, Jean. I didn't mean you were *that* kind of stupid. Let's forget it.

JEAN [*sitting down*]. Well, I don't care what *you* think, but I don't want any black cats crossing my path, and I wouldn't think of looking at a new moon over my left shoulder.

SUE [*in amazement*]. For goodness' sakes, why not?

JEAN. Brings you bad luck, that's why.

SUE [*gathering up cutouts and putting them in box*]. Well, if that's the way you feel, we better get started for the school before it gets pitch dark, or you'll be too scared to go.

JEAN. I'm not afraid, really I'm not, only my brother declares he saw a ghost one time.

[GIRLS *finish packing the cutouts into boxes. They start toward exit at rear of stage.*]

SUE. Next thing you'll be telling me somebody you knew saw a witch. I wonder where we ever got the idea for Halloween, any way.

[GIRLS *are close to rear of stage when* OLD WOMAN *appears.*]

JEAN [*startled*]. Oh–h–h! [*She and* SUE *step to center of stage, as the* OLD WOMAN *comes forward.*]

OLD WOMAN. Maybe I can tell you about Halloween.

SUE. Who are you, and where did you come from?

OLD WOMAN [*at center of stage*]. Don't be frightened. I was just passing by and heard you talking. I am tired. May I sit down?

SUE [*more composed*]. Yes, certainly. Do sit down.

OLD WOMAN [*sitting down in chair at right and sighing loudly*]. Ah–h–h, thank you. [*Pauses as* SUE *takes previous place on bench.* JEAN *sits on chair nearer to back of stage.*] So you were wondering who ever thought up Halloween, eh?

JEAN. Well, — er — yes, we were.

OLD WOMAN [*smiling queerly*]. That isn't so strange. Lot's of people wonder that — and [*mysteriously*] a few — know.

JEAN. [*excitedly*] Do you know? Do you? [*Leans toward the* OLD WOMAN *expectantly.* SUE *shakes her head and fumbles with the boxes, in a disgusted way.*]

OLD WOMAN. No, I can't rightly say that I do. But I know why we have it.

SUE [*very bored*]. I suppose everyone knows why we have it. All Saints' Day or something like that. Some people even think that ghosts walk tonight. [*While she is talking,* GHOST *enters from right and stands behind the* OLD WOMAN. SUE *sees* GHOST, *just as she finishes her speech. She partially rises from her chair, claps her hand over her mouth as* GHOST *makes upward and outward motion with hands and backs off stage.* SUE *is the only one who sees* GHOST. *She seats herself, but every now and then she looks toward spot where* GHOST *appeared.*]

OLD WOMAN [*to* SUE]. Old superstitions, you don't believe in them, do you?

SUE [*trying to be calm*]. Certainly *not.*

OLD WOMAN. Perhaps you are right. But do you know that centuries ago people in the old world thought that their loved ones who were dead returned to them on the first day of November?

SUE. No, I didn't know it. I think it's silly.

[JEAN *has her elbows propped on her knees, and her chin is resting in her cupped hands. She is looking intently at the* OLD WOMAN.]

OLD WOMAN. Silly? They didn't think so. In fact, they believed it so strongly that they prepared a feast for them the night before. They called it the Feast of the Dead — or Holy Evening.

JEAN [*pulling her chair up closer to* SUE]. Holy Evening! Why that must be where we get the word Halloween — from Holy Evening. Oh, I like that.

OLD WOMAN. Yes, that is the reason we call it Halloween.

. SUE. It is just a myth, but it is interesting.

JEAN. What else do you know about Halloween?

OLD WOMAN. Haven't you ever heard that in Ireland they make a special dish for Holy Evening? [GIRLS *shake their heads as the* OLD WOMAN *continues, counting on her fingers.*] Yes, they put three things in it, potatoes, fish, and parsnips. Before it is cooked, a ring is hidden in the dish, and whoever finds the ring is sure to have very, very good luck.

SUE. That's a strange custom. What else do they do?

OLD WOMAN. Well, of course, you won't believe it, but they do tell that the old Dutch housewives were extremely afraid of witches.

[*Off stage is heard the hoot of an owl.* SUE *jumps up and speaks quickly.*]

SUE. What in earth is that? [*Looks up and around as if trying to discover where the sound came from.*]

OLD WOMAN [*speaking rather eerily*]. Sit down, my dear. It's just my friend, the owl. He can't hurt you.

SUE [*trying to cover up her nervousness*]. Of course, I knew all the time what it was.

JEAN [*to* OLD WOMAN]. Oh, yes, Sue, knew what it was — she says. Now go on about the old Dutch housewives. [*She moves her chair nearer to* SUE.]

OLD WOMAN. As I was saying, they were so afraid of the witches that they finally discovered how to find out who was and who wasn't a witch.

SUE [*showing interest*]. Did they really?

OLD WOMAN. Yes. They would put a live chicken in a pot and pour boiling water over it. Whoever passed their door while the chicken was squawking was sure to be a witch.

SUE. Oh, boy! I bet people stayed away from a person like that, didn't they?

JEAN [*smirking at* SUE]. I thought you weren't superstitious, Sue.

SUE. I'm not, but this is thrilling.

OLD WOMAN. Listen! [*She cocks her head, listening.*]

SUE. I don't hear a thing.

JEAN. Neither do I.

[OLD WOMAN *half risen from her chair, is listening intently. Off stage a faint rustling is heard, loud enough for the audience to hear.* GIRLS *look around, but seem not to hear the sound.*]

OLD WOMAN. I hear something. [*Sighs and sits down.*] I know just what it is. It's the people hiding in the corn fields, waiting to hear what the ghosts have to say.

[JEAN *moves to the seat beside* SUE.]

SUE. I still don't hear anything. Why would people want to hear a ghost [*shudders*] talk, even if they could?

OLD WOMAN. The ghost always tells you what will happen to you in the year to come.

[SUE *moves toward the end of the bench. In doing so she accidentally pushes the boxes off.* JEAN *jumps up at the noise and screams.* SUE *pulls her back to the bench.*]

SUE. Sit down, Jean. What are you yelling for? I just pushed a box over.

JEAN [*trying to laugh*]. Oh, but that scared me!

SUE. You're nothing but a fraidy cat.

OLD WOMAN [*chuckling*]. There's one more thing. The walnut tree is the meeting place for the witches, and any girl who is not afraid to walk around the walnut tree is sure to see the man she is going to marry.

[GIRLS *laugh easily.* OLD WOMAN *rises and starts toward exit.* GIRLS *spring to their feet.*]

JEAN. Oh, don't go. This is such fun.

SUE. Yes, please stay a while longer. I am just beginning to be interested.

OLD WOMAN [*near exit*]. I am late now, and I must go before the moon rises.

JEAN. Why must you go? You've never even told us who you are!

SUE. No, you haven't. Where are you going?

[OLD WOMAN *has reached exit, and, as she begins her last speech, she reaches off stage, presumably by porch steps, and picks up a witch's hat and broom.*]

OLD WOMAN. You want to know who I am? Well, I am the witch that you might meet down by the walnut tree. Do you want to know where I'm going? I'm going to climb upon my broomstick and ride to the Feast of the Dead!

[*She laughs shrilly, straddles broomstick, and makes a rapid exit.* GIRLS *look at each other wildly, scamper across stage, and stare in direction* WITCH *has gone.*]

CURTAIN

The Halloween Ghost

TIME OF PLAYING: *About twenty-five minutes*

CHARACTERS

WILLIAM GRAY, *the boy who is having the Halloween party*
AUSTIN GRAY, *William's younger brother, the ghost*
NORTON ROBERTS, *the boy who can always explain everything*
JAMES ROBERTS, *the boy who is very skeptical*
JOHN METCALF, *willing to try anything the first time*
DOROTHY KANE, *believes the barn is haunted*
NATALIE KANE, *also believes the barn is haunted*
ANNA METCALF, *not afraid of anything*
FRANCES FROMM, *always making suggestions*
PENELOPE DWIGHT, *always asking questions*

COSTUMES

All members of the cast wear children's ordinary apparel,
except the GHOST, *who wears a sheet.*

SCENE: *The barn of the Gray homestead. Stacks of cornstalks stand about the barn. Here and there are the yellow faces of pumpkins. Flickering lanterns hang along the wall, making the place look dim and dusky. In the middle of the floor is a tub half-filled with water in which float several apples. A mirror hangs on the back center wall.*

The curtain rises upon an empty stage. Presently the GHOST *slips in by left center entrance. Glances furtively about him and then hides behind one of the large stacks of cornstalks. Presently* WILLIAM *enters, followed by the other children.*

WILLIAM [*in a jovial tone*]. I hope everyone will have a good time at my party.

NATALIE. We ought to—with all the things you've planned.

PENELOPE. Do you like Halloween?

NORTON. Of course.

DOROTHY. William, did you ever hear your barn was haunted?

WILLIAM [*indignantly*]. Whoever said that?

DOROTHY. Our cook told us so this afternoon, when I told her you were going to have a party in your barn.

ANNA. Haunted by what?

DOROTHY. A horse-thief ghost. He comes every Halloween.

WILLIAM. That's nonsense! My father wouldn't *own* a haunted barn. [*Looks at the tub.*] Come on. I think we'd better get started. Let's duck for the apples first.

JOHN. You go first, William.

WILLIAM. All right [*Gets down on his hands and knees before the tub of water.*] I'll begin. [*Opens his mouth wide.*]

GHOST [*in a deep voice*]. Beware!

William [*leaping to his feet and glaring at the others*]. Who said that?

NATALIE. Don't look at me like that, William. I didn't say it.

DOROTHY. Nor I.

PENELOPE. I didn't.

NORTON. Nor I!

JAMES. Nor I!

WILLIAM. Did you, Anna?

ANNA [*indignantly*]. Of course not!

WILLIAM. That's very queer. I'll try it again. [*Gets down again on his hands and knees and opens his mouth.*]

GHOST [*in a deep voice*]. Stop!

WILLIAM [*leaping to his feet the second time*]. Who said that?

[ALL *silently shake their heads.*]

NORTON. It was probably the limb of a tree bumping against the barn.

DOROTHY [*shuddering*]. I tell you, our cook says this barn is haunted!

ANNA [*bravely*]. Well, who's afraid?

WILLIAM. I tell you, that's perfectly ridiculous! This barn is *not* haunted! I won't *have* it haunted! Someone else try this time.

NORTON. I will. [*Gets down on his hands and knees and opens his mouth.*]

GHOST. Halt!

NORTON [*jumping to his feet*]. You said that, William Gray! You've been saying these things all along and blaming them on us.

WILLIAM [*amazed*]. I? Why, I did not!

NATALIE [*glancing furtively about the room*]. All this is very odd!

NORTON. Maybe a board creaked.

JAMES. I never heard a board creak like that.

WILLIAM [*hastily*]. Let's do something else. Maybe we'll bob for apples later.

PENELOPE. What shall we do?

WILLIAM. We'll have our fortunes told by the mirror.

PENELOPE. What do you mean?

WILLIAM. It's this way. Each one of us will look into the mirror and see our future mate in it. Only *one* person is allowed in the room at a time. You have to say the rhyme—the one we learned last year. [*Hastily*] I shan't go first this time.

PENELOPE [*looking about the group*]. Who will?

JOHN. I don't want to.

NATALIE. Nor I.

DOROTHY. Nor I.

WILLIAM. Someone has to go first.

ANNA. I will.

WILLIAM. Very well. We'll go out and leave you alone.

[ALL *go out left center exit and leave* ANNA *alone.* ANNA *gazes a little wistfully after them. Then she slowly walks up to the mirror and, staring steadily into it, repeats the following lines:*]

> I approach the magic glass
> To consult my fate.
> I implore most earnestly
> To see my future mate.

[GHOST *glides out from behind the pile of cornstalks and gazes steadily over* ANNA'S *shoulder into the mirror.*]

ANNA [*shrieking at the top of her lungs*]. Oh – oh – oh!

[ALL *the children come running in pell-mell by left center entrance.*]

WILLIAM. What is the matter?

DOROTHY. Why, Anna — you're always so calm!

ANNA [*gasping*]. A ghost looked over my shoulder!

DOROTHY. I *told* you this barn was haunted!

NORTON. It must have been a shadow!

DOROTHY. You don't have to tell me —

WILLIAM [*very indignantly*]. I tell you, this barn is *not* haunted! It's the reflection of those cornstalks in the mirror! [*Pulls the cornstalks back away from the mirror.*] Now you can try again, and we'll all get out.

ANNA. I won't try again! Someone else can, but not I!

JOHN [*after a pause*]. I will.

WILLIAM. Now, John, remember, there's nothing to make you nervous. What Anna saw was only the reflection of the cornstalks in the mirror.

JOHN [*with great confidence*]. Oh, of course. [*The children go out, leaving* JOHN *alone.* JOHN *slowly approaches the mirror and repeats the rhyme*]. "I approach the magic glass —

GHOST [*in a loud voice*]. So do I! [*Slips out from behind the pile of cornstalks and stares into the mirror over* JOHN'S *shoulder.*]

JOHN [*calling lustily*]. Help! Help! Help!

[GHOST *disappears. The children come flocking in.*]

JAMES. John — did you *see* anything?

JOHN [*shaking*]. See? I should say I did! I saw and I heard!

DOROTHY. I told you this barn was haunted!

WILLIAM. It is not!

NORTON. I guess what you heard was the squeaking of a mouse!

JOHN [*indignantly*]. I never heard a mouse like that!

FRANCES [*hastily*]. Let's do something else.

PENELOPE [*at a loss*]. What shall it be?

FRANCES. Ten fingers. We can all be in the room together then.

PENELOPE. How do you play it?

FRANCES. We all sit down in a ring on the floor. [*They all do so.*] And put an apple in the middle —

WILLIAM. I'll get the apple. [*Walks over to the tub and picks out an apple.*] Here it is. [*Places the apple in the middle of the ring.*] There! [*Sits down again.*]

FRANCES. Now you all close your eyes. [ALL *do so.*] Now you grab for the apple — first count to ten. Ready?

ALL. Yes!

[ALL *close their eyes. Before they begin to count,* GHOST *slips out from behind the pile of cornstalks, creeps up to the circle, and snatches the apple. Then he goes back to his hiding place.*]

ALL [*counting*]. One, two, three, four, five, six, seven, eight, nine, ten! [ALL *grab for the apple. Then they open their eyes. Of course, the apple is not there.*]

WILLIAM [*looking about him*]. Who has the apple?

ANNA. I haven't!

PENELOPE. Nor I!

JAMES. Nor I!

    [ALL *show their empty hands.*]

WILLIAM [*much excited*]. Someone's hiding that apple!

FRANCES. I'm not!

NORTON. Neither am I!

DOROTHY. Nor I!

NATALIE. I'm not the guilty one.

WILLIAM. Then it must have rolled away somewhere. We'll look for it.

    [*As they are looking about the barn for the apple,* GHOST *comes out and quickly puts the apple down on the floor, then goes back.*]

WILLIAM. I don't see where that apple can be! [*Turns and catches sight of the apple on the floor.*] There it is! [*They gather about him as he picks the apple up from the floor.*] Someone *was* hiding it!

DOROTHY. I tell you, no one hid it. This old barn is haunted!

WILLIAM. And I tell you, I *won't* have it haunted!

NORTON. Maybe the apple just naturally rolled away!

JAMES. Humph! That's *very* queer!

WILLIAM. Well, we'll try the game again. Everyone sit down on the floor. [ALL *sit.*] Now — [*Puts the apple in the middle of the ring.*] We'll close our eyes and count.

    [*They close their eyes and begin to count again.* GHOST *glides out from behind the pile of cornstalks and hits* WILLIAM *a sounding whack over the head with one of the stalks.*]

WILLIAM [*leaping to his feet*]. Who did that?

ALL [*opening their eyes*]. What?

WILLIAM [*ruefully rubbing his head*]. Hit me on the head.

NORTON. You imagined that! As if anybody here would hit you on the head!

WILLIAM [*indignantly*]. I imagined it? Who did it? [*Glares at the others.*] Who hit me on the head?

ANNA. I didn't.

FRANCES. Neither did I!

PENELOPE. Nor I!

JAMES. No one did!

WILLIAM. I never had a Halloween party like this one!

NATALIE [*shuddering*]. Queer things happen on Halloween!

DOROTHY. This barn—

WILLIAM [*almost shouting*]. I tell you, this barn is *not* haunted!

PENELOPE. Can't we do something else?

FRANCES. Yes. Why not have something to eat? We haven't eaten anything yet.

WILLIAM. Oh, of course. The candy. [*Walks over to the basket of candy that stands in one corner of the barn. The candy is in boxes.*] Here it is. A box for everyone.

> [*Picks up the basket and carries it around with him, giving a box to each guest. They stand facing the audience, eating the candy. When no one is looking, GHOST glides up behind WILLIAM and sprinkles some pepper and salt over his candy. Then GHOST scurries back behind the cornstalks.*]

FRANCES [*obviously enjoying her candy*]. This is good candy, William.

JAMES [*agreeing*]. Yes, it is.

PENELOPE. Did you get it at Doe's?

WILLIAM [*in a pleased tone*]. Yes. Their candy's always good. [*Puts a piece of candy in his mouth. His expression changes to dismay.*]

NATALIE. Why, what is the matter, William?

NORTON. Perhaps he's going to be sick! [*Stares steadily at WILLIAM.*]

WILLIAM [*looking at the others*]. Does your candy taste queer?

ANNA. No. Mine's fine!

NORTON. I guess you imagine it.

WILLIAM [*indignantly*]. I don't imagine it!

JOHN. Try another! Maybe the one you took just happened to be that way!

WILLIAM [*doubtfully*]. Well— [*ALL gather about him while he carefully chooses another piece. Naturally, since the barn is dusky, he cannot see the salt and pepper on the candy.*] I'll take this one. [*Puts it in his mouth.*]

PENELOPE. How's that?

WILLIAM [*sputtering*]. Oh – er – This is worse than the other!

FRANCES. Come — get a lantern and look at the candy! [*Runs over to the wall and takes down one of the lanterns. Then runs back to WILLIAM with it.*] Here — we'll look at it! [*Holds the lantern directly over the box of candy.*]

NORTON. It looks like pepper and salt.

WILLIAM [*putting his finger in the box and tasting it*]. It is pepper and salt!

JAMES. You'd better buy your candy some other place, next time.

DOROTHY [*shuddering*]. I knew this barn was haunted!

WILLIAM. I tell you it isn't. There's somebody here, and I know it! John, you and James and Norton stand over by the door so what's here can't get out. [*The boys obey.*] Now, the rest of us'll chase him. [WILLIAM *and the girls run behind one pile of cornstalks.* GHOST *runs from behind one pile of cornstalks to the other.*]

DOROTHY [*shrieking*]. It's a ghost! It's a ghost. [*A lively chase follows. Finally they* ALL *corner* GHOST *and tear the sheet from him. There stands* AUSTIN.]

WILLIAM. Austin!

ANNA. So it's you who's been doing all this, Austin Gray! [*All gather about him.*]

FRANCES [*severely*]. You should be ashamed to spoil your brother's party like this!

WILLIAM. Why did you do it?

AUSTIN. I'll tell you why. You never invited me! Just because I'm younger you never invited me!

PENELOPE. Didn't you invite him, William?

WILLIAM [*in a hesitating tone*]. Well, no, I didn't. I had just an even number of boys and girls.

FRANCES. William, you should have asked him.

NORTON. I think so, too.

JOHN. It wasn't right to leave him out.

AUSTIN [*gazing intently at* WILLIAM]. Am I invited now?

WILLIAM [*hastily*]. Oh, of course — of course. [AUSTIN *quickly tosses the discarded sheet into the corner.*]

WILLIAM [*in a brisk business-like tone*]. We'll start all over again, now that we're rid of the Halloween ghost.

CURTAIN

Activities

Classic Pumpkin-Carving

How well a jack-o'-lantern lights up and how long it lasts depends a great deal on how it is carved. To carve a jack-o'-lantern lasting about ten days in chilly weather or five days in warm weather or at room temperature, the following procedure is recommended.

You'll need:

- paper and pencil
- pumpkin (preferably at least nine inches tall) with a firmly attached stem
- several layers of newspaper, piled up in open, two-page spreads
- big, long-handled spoon
- large bowl
- black water-based felt pen (preferably with a big, blunt tip)
- sharp, thin knife
- small dish of water
- paper towels

- short votive candle in a clear glass container (available at most supermarkets, drug stores, and hardware stores; provides about 2½ to 3 hours of light)
- a saucer or plate as big as the bottom of the pumpkin
- long fireplace matches (or a short wooden match held in pliers)

Directions:

On a sheet of paper, draw several sample faces until you have the combination of eyes, nose, and mouth you want. If desired, include eyebrows in your design. Try drawing different types of faces: scary, scraggly toothed, laughing, winking, frightened, dopey, cross-eyed, sleepy, scowling, angry, and plain old ugly.

1. Spread out the newspapers for your work area, and place the pumpkin on top. With the felt pen, draw a circular lid for the jack-o'-lantern. The stem should be in the center of the lid, and the opening should be big enough so that you can easily get your hand inside to work (to pull out the pulp, press out the features, and put in the candle).

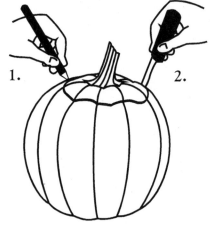

2. Cut the lid with the knife. Be careful to cut as clean a line as possible, so that there won't be any jagged spaces where light can escape. Also, cut at a slight angle toward the center of the pumpkin. As necessary, clean the dirty knife blade for easier cutting.

After cutting all the way around, *gently* test the lid to see if it will lift off easily (the stem should always be handled with care so that it doesn't break off). If the lid won't lift off easily, try recutting the same line. Test again.

3. Once you can easily lift the lid, clean away the stringy pulp from the bottom of the lid. Scrape the bottom flesh off the lid so that it, too, is relatively smooth and flat.

4. Use the big spoon (and, if necessary, your hands) to scoop out the stringy pulp and seeds from the inside of the pumpkin. Place the pulp and seeds in the large bowl for disposal (unless you want to pick out the seeds for toasting: see *Recipes*). Gently scrape the inside pumpkin shell so that it is clean and smooth, with all the wet stuff removed. Pat the inside dry with a paper towel.

5. Carefully draw the features you've chosen on the smoothest, roundest side of the pumpkin with the felt pen. If you make mistakes in drawing, wash them off with a paper towel and water. Here are some pointers to keep in mind:

- The features of your pumpkin face should be centered on the pumpkin — not too close to the bottom or top and not too far around the sides. This way your pumpkin face will be lit up more effectively with the candle inside, and will have a solid frame.

- Each cutout feature should be large enough so that a good amount of air and light can get through. Avoid very narrow slits.

- Don't make cutout features too close to each other (they may decay into each other very quickly).

- Avoid mouths that have very big
  open spaces or that are very long horizontal-
  ly, or the pumpkin may quickly collapse at the mouth.
- If you are carving teeth into the mouth or pupils into the eye,
  make sure that the teeth/pupils are relatively big; if they're
  too small, they'll quickly shrivel up.

6. Neatly cut each feature out at an angle toward the center of the
   pumpkin. Clean the knife as necessary.

7. Reach inside the pumpkin and gently press out the features. If a
   piece won't come out easily, recut the lines. Pull any remaining
   stringy pulp or seeds away from the cutout areas. Using the big
   spoon and/or the knife (as necessary), make a smooth, flat spot
   for the votive candle in the center of the bottom of the
   pumpkin.

8. Set the pumpkin on the saucer or plate, for security and safety
   (you can't tell if or when the bottom will rot).

9. Place the votive candle inside the pumpkin. Light it with the
   fireplace match or a wooden match held in pliers. Place the lid
   on top.

Turn out all the lights and stand back and look at your jack-o'-lantern. See if the candlelight illuminates the features.

If the features don't appear big enough, or if the angle of the cut obscures them, blow out the candle and do some fine-cutting with the knife to correct the problem. Just be sure to proceed *slowly* with any recutting, so that you don't go too far.

If the candle won't stay lit, it's a sign that more air needs to get inside the jack-o'-lantern, so one or more of the features should be made a bit bigger. Also make sure the lid of the pumpkin is not too close to the flame. Check to see if the inside of the lid is blackened. If so, scrape or cut away the singed flesh, plus a little bit more.

Once the features are the way you like them, make sure they're clean of stringy pulp or seeds. Pat the edges dry.

Professional carvers (and they do exist) keep their jack-o'-lanterns fresher for a greater length of time by misting their shells, including all cut-flesh areas, with lemon juice. Another way to prolong the life of your jack-o'-lantern is to keep it outside in a sheltered (but frost-free) place, or in a cool rather than a warm place inside, as much as possible.

ALTERNATIVES TO THE CLASSIC METHOD

- Instead of cutting out a lid in the top of the pumpkin, cut out a similar-sized hole in the bottom of the pumpkin. Scrape out the seeds and stringy pulp from the bottom, with the pumpkin resting on its side.

  After you've cut the features, illuminate the jack-o'-lantern by sitting it over the candle or over a low-wattage electric bulb

(15-40 watts, depending on the size of the jack-o'-lantern). For a ghoulish variation, try a green- or red-colored bulb.

- If you can't find a votive candle, use any short candle (so-called "plumber's candles" are appropriately stubby and relatively long-lasting). Before placing it inside the jack-o'-lantern, light it and drip some wax on the inside bottom where you're going to set the candle. Then blow the candle out and quickly press the bottom end into the molten wax. Hold it for a few seconds until the wax hardens.

- Carve different faces on opposite sides of the pumpkin. Make sure that there's lots of space between each face, and that the features in both faces are not too big. Otherwise, the light shining through one face will interfere too much with the light shining through the other face, and/or the pumpkin may cave in prematurely.

- Try enhancing the borders of the jack-o'-lantern features, and/or adding new features, by applying paint directly on the shell. Slightly thick tempera paint in bold colors (red, yellow, black, dark green) works best.

How to Make a Halloween Lantern

To make a turnip lantern you need a large root such as a swede, a beet, or a mangel. These are the kind of roots which have a reddish skin and yellow flesh. The skin of these turnips can be carved (or scribed) to make a pattern that will glow when a small candle or flashlight is placed inside the lantern.

You will need:

- turnip, beet or mangel
- hard pencil
- small kitchen knife
- metal spoon
- modelling knife
- length of soft wire
- small candle or flashlight

Directions:

1. Carefully cut into the flesh with the kitchen knife to the depth of about ¾", keeping the walls of the lantern about ¼" thick. Be careful not to go too deep when cutting your edge.

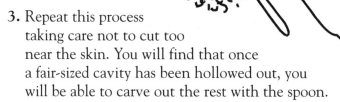

2. Draw the knife all over the flesh many times, keeping it at a constant depth so that the flesh becomes loosened. You will now be able to scoop cut the first ¾" with the spoon.

3. Repeat this process taking care not to cut too near the skin. You will find that once a fair-sized cavity has been hollowed out, you will be able to carve out the rest with the spoon.

4. Draw a pattern on the skin with a hard pencil, then carve the skin with the modelling knife, taking care not to cut too deeply.

5. Make a handle with the wire and place a nightlight or small flashlight inside the lantern ready for lighting on Hallowe'en.

Don't try to make the turnip lantern if you are not used to handling a knife. Ask a grown-up to do it for you.

A Halloween Mobile

To turn a bare branch into a Halloween Mobile with a witch, a ghost, a jack-o'-lantern, a skull, an owl, moon, and stars, you will need the following materials:

- white tissue paper
- construction paper and/or light cardboard
- poster paints and brushes
- needle and thread
- tape
- scissors
- pencil
- a branch from a tree

Directions:

1. ***To make a witch:*** Draw the witch on a piece of construction paper or lightweight cardboard and then paint in the details with poster paint. Give her a pointed hat and a long dress. You might want to give her a broomstick to ride, a large pot to stir, or a cat to keep her company. When the paint is dry, turn the witch over and paint the same thing on the back. Make a small hole at the top of the figure and run a long piece of thread through it. Use tape or a knot to secure the end of the thread.

2. To make a ghost: Crumple up a piece of tissue paper into a ball to make the head. Then tie a larger piece of tissue around the ball with a piece of thread and let the corners hang down. Draw a ghostly face on this outer layer of tissue with paint or a felt-tip pen. Insert a threaded needle, with a good-sized knot at the end of the thread, up through the inside of the head. Then cut off the thread near the needle. Your ghost is ready to hang.

3. To make a jack-o'-lantern: Cut the shape of a pumpkin with a stem out of a piece of construction paper or lightweight cardboard. Paint the body of the pumpkin orange and the stem brown with poster paints. When the paint is dry, turn the pumpkin over and paint the same thing on the back. Then, with a pencil, mark holes for eyes, nose, and mouth and then cut out. For added effect, you can border them with black paint. Make a small hole in the middle of the stem and run a long piece of thread through the stem and secure the end of thread with a knot or tape.

4. To make a skull and an owl: Draw the skull on black construction paper and paint in white eyes, a white nose, and teeth. If you don't know how to draw an owl, look in an encyclopedia or a book about birds. The owl can be drawn sitting on a branch or with his wings extended. Tie a long piece of thread to both the skull and the owl, and don't forget to paint both the front and the back.

5. To make a moon and stars: Cut the moon and several stars out of light cardboard and cover them with foil or paint them silver. Glitter adds a nice touch. Tie a piece of thread through each.

Putting the Mobile Together:
Tie each shape to a different point on the branch. If you vary the length of the thread, some will hang down further than others. When all of the pieces have been attached, tie a double length of thread to each end of the branch and tape or hang it from the ceiling. If you hang the mobile near a fan or open window, it will sway in the breeze.

Ten Quick and Easy Halloween Costumes

1. **Robber.** Wear a black turtleneck sweater, black pants, and a black mask. For added effect, stick a flashlight into your belt, and/or a small, stuffed, white cloth bag with a large dollar sign painted on it.

2. **Bum.** Wear old, ragged clothes, with a rope for a belt. Smear makeup on your face so that it looks like dirt (or a three-day growth of beard).

3. **Mummy.** Wrap your arms, legs, body, and head in gauze bandages or long strips of white cloth.

4. **Gypsy.** Wear your most peasantlike clothes. Accessorize heavily with scarves and jewelry. Wear a headkerchief, beret, or bowler hat. *Men:* Makeup could include moustache, sideburns, heavy eyebrows. *Women:* Makeup should be very florid and exotic.

5. **T-shirt Minimalism.** Have a T-shirt printed with a provocative statement. For example:
   - "How dare you assume I'm not wearing a costume!"
   - "I wore a costume at the office!"
   - "The dog ate my costume!"
   - "I'm disguised to look like [your name]."
   - "Generic Costume"

And, in conclusion, five costumes you can make with the classic Halloween costume material—a plain white sheet:

6. **Ghost.** Put a sheet over your head and mark holes for your eyes, nose, and mouth. Cut out the holes and border them in black. For added effect, drape chains and locks across your body, over the sheet.

7. **Baby.** Diaper yourself with the sheet (or part of the sheet) and wear a rattle around your neck. *Men:* Go barechested. *Women:* Wear a plain T-shirt or a top that looks like an infant's shirt. For added effect, wear a baby-like cap, or a banner that says "Baby New Year" or "Baby [your city or town]."

8. **Yogi.** Swaddle your loins in the style of an (Eastern) Indian yogi. It may take several practice attempts and, ultimately, some cutting of the sheet:
   - First, wrap a folded sheet around your hips.
   - Then, cross the ends of the sheet in front of you.
   - Holding the "underneath" end up against your chest, work the other end through your legs and tuck it into the waist at the back. Adjust so that the loincloth fits snugly.
   - Release the end you're holding against your chest and let it hang down the front slightly below the crotch.

- Discreetly safety-pin the two ends in place.
  Wear another length of sheet as a turban. *Men:* Go barech-ested. *Women:* Wear a plain T-shirt or a simple top that looks (Eastern) Indian.

9. *Toga.* Wear the sheet draped around your body and over one shoulder. Discreetly safety-pin the sheet so it stays in place. Wear with a head-wreath of green leaves. For added effect, cinch the toga with a Roman- or Greek-looking belt and/or wear it with Roman- or Greek-looking jewelry.

10. *Bedouin.* Cut a hole in the middle of a sheet for your head. Slip the sheet over your head and cinch it at the waist with yarn or an appropriate cord belt. Wear part of another sheet (or a pillowcase) as a hood, held in place by a "halo" of braided cord or cloth.

More Halloween Costume Ideas

Scarecrow

A scarecrow costume offers a tribute to the season, suggesting the autumn harvest. To make a scarecrow costume, you need the following materials:

- a long-sleeved shirt—preferably white or solid-colored—that is too big (to give you room for stuffing)
- an old or beat-up hat with a brim (preferably a straw hat or a "hobo" hat)
- a burlap, cloth, or paper bag that is just large enough to fit comfortably over the wearer's head, neck, and upper chest.
- a bandanna or other scarf
- patch-shaped scraps of cloth in different colors and patterns
- straw and/or dried grass and weeds
- a belt-length piece of rope
- old pants or blue jeans

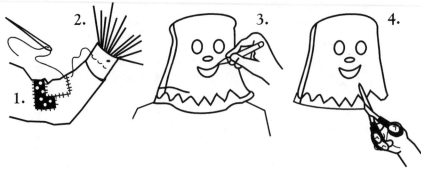

Directions for Making the Scarecrow Costume:

1. Sew the scraps of cloth randomly all over the shirt.

2. Sew or tape the straw all around the inside of each shirt sleeve cuff, so that the straw juts several inches out of the sleeve.

3. Slip the bag over the wearer's head and mark holes to be cut for the eyes, nose, and mouth. Also, mark a jagged neckline that will be low enough to cover the wearer's neck area completely *after* the bag is loosely tied at the neck with the bandanna.

4. Take off the bag and cut the holes and neckline. Outline the eye and mouth holes with thick black lines.

5. Wear the costume with old pants (preferably blue jeans) and old shoes. Tie the bag loosely at the neck with the bandanna. Stuff the shirt with paper, a small pillow, or more straw. Cinch the shirt at the waist with the piece of rope. Color the wearer's nose red or black with makeup.

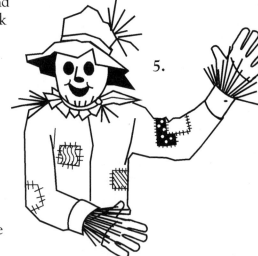

Witch

Few costumes are as evocative of Halloween and as easy to adapt to the wearer's individual preferences as a witch costume. Just keep in mind that males as well as females can be witches, and that witches (like any extraordinary beings) can be magically attractive as well as fearsomely ugly. For a basic-black witch costume, you need the following materials:

- a rectangular piece of black material for the robe: approximately twice the distance from the wearer's shoulder to the wearer's ankles and a few inches wider than the wearer's shoulders (an alternative to black cloth is a thin, black plastic tarp; for a small child, an alternative is a black plastic trash bag)
- a rectangular piece of black material for the cape: as long as the distance from the wearer's shoulder to the back of the wearer's calves; and approximately twice as wide as the wearer's shoulders (see above for alternative materials to cloth)
- a piece of heavy cardboard several inches bigger than the circumference of the wearer's head
- a rectangular piece of poster board or construction paper — black, if possible — approximately two feet by one foot
- black paint and brush
- aluminum foil for cutout decorations
- dark yarn for robe belt and cape drawstring
- glue, scissors, and clear tape

Directions for Making the Witch Costume:

1. Fold the robe material in half, across the width. In the center of the fold, cut out a neck hole.

2. An inch and a half below the neck of the cape material, draw a faint line. Every two or three inches along this line, make a small hole. Thread dark-colored yarn through these holes to make a drawstring for the cape.

1.

2.

3.

4.

5.

6.

7.

8.

3. Draw a circle on the heavy piece of cardboard as big as the wearer's hat size. Draw another, concentric, circle three or four inches outside the first circle, for the edge of the hat's brim. Cut out both circles.

4. Draw the largest half-circle you can on the poster board. Cut it out.

5. Bend the half-circle in half along the straight edge, and overlap the edges to form a cone that is about an inch wider all around than the inside circle of the hat brim. Tape or glue the seam of the cone on the inside, leaving a couple of inches from the base of the cone unfastened.

6. Insert the cone into the hat brim. When the cone is as far into the brim as it can easily go, cut small slits around the edge of the cone, bend edge sections up to the underside of the brim, and fasten them securely with glue or tape.

7. Paint the entire hat so that it is black. Cut out several small stars and crescent moons from aluminum foil and glue them to the hat.

8. Wear dark pants, shoes, and socks with the costume, and cinch the robe at the waist with dark-colored yarn.

Devil

Halloween is the one day of the year when being a devil is good fun, so why not take advantage of it? For a red-hot devil costume, you need the following materials:

- red leotards (alternatives include red pants, or red pantyhose under a red or black swimsuit or shorts)
- a rectangular piece of red material for the tunic that is as lor as the distance from the wearer's shoulders to the wear mid-thigh and a few inches wider than the wearer's shou'
- a rectangular piece of material for the hood (same shad as the tunic) that is twice the length from the top of '

wearer's head to the wearer's upper chest and wider than slightly over half the circumference of the wearer's head

- a rectangular piece of material for the tail (same shade red as the tunic and hood): length — from wearer's waist to back of wearer's knees; width — about one-and-a-half inches
- thin, red cardboard: enough for four, 4" x 2" pieces (an alternative to cardboard is poster board, and black may be substituted for red)

Directions for Making the Devil Costume:

1. Fold the tunic material in half across the width. Cut a hole for the head in the center of the fold. Sew together the sides of the material, leaving space at the top for the arms to poke through, and at the bottom to give the legs room to walk, The tunic will be turned *inside out* for wearing, so the seams won't show.

2. Fold the hood material in half across the width. Trace a rough outline of the wearer's head, neck, and top of the shoulders onto one half of the material, making sure that the outline is centered on the material with the top of the head close to the fold of the material. Mark holes for the eyes, nose, and mouth.

3. Cut the outline you have drawn through *both* layers of the hood material. Cut the eye, nose, and mouth holes through the front layer only. Sew the two layers of material together close to the edges of your outline. Leave the bottom open, leave a few inches unsewn on either side to fit across the shoulders, and leave two 1½-inch slits open at the top of the head for inserting the horns. Turn the hood *inside out* to wear.

1.

2. and 3.

4. Sew the tailpiece to the back of the tunic, so that it is attached to the *inside* of the tunic and the tip of the tailpiece hangs to the back of the wearer's knees. For the tip of the tail, cut two equal-size triangles with four-inch bases from the red cardboard. Fasten them to opposite sides of the end of the tailpiece, directly across from each other, with the point of each triangle aiming downward. Glue the two triangles together along their edges.

5. For the horns, cut two semicircles with 4-inch diameters from the red cardboard.

6. With each semicircle, bend the straight edge to form a cone whose base is slightly larger than one of the horn slits in the hood, with the two edges of the cone overlapping a bit. Insert the cone into the horn slit, bending the bottom edges back against the inside of the hood (i.e., the inside of the hood when it is worn). Glue the seam of the cone and fasten the bent-back edge of the cone to the inside of the hood as securely as possible.

7. The tunic is worn over the leotard, and the hood is worn over the tunic. If desired, use black or red yarn (or a near equivalent) to cinch the tunic, and/or wear a long-sleeved, solid red shirt or sweater underneath the tunic. Wear solid black or solid red slippers, shoes, or boots.

Angel

An angel costume is very striking on a dark Halloween night, and it reflects well on the wearer. For a heavenly angel costume, you need the following materials:

- a rectangular piece of white material for the robe: length should be about twice the length from the wearer's shoulders to the wearer's ankles, and width a few inches wider than the wearer's shoulders.
- a sheet of poster board (white is best) at least 18" x 24" for the wings, and newspaper for a pattern.
- glue
- scissors
- gold or silver garland tinsel
- gold or silver glitter
- optional items to decorate wings such as feathers or aluminum foil

Directions for Making the Angel Costume:

1. Fold the white robe material in half across the width. Midway across the fold, cut a circular hole large enough for the wearer's head to fit through, but not so big that the material slips off the shoulders. When the material is fitted over the head of the wearer it should not be too long in front or back to make walking difficult. This is the basic robe for the costume.

2. On a piece of scrap paper, practice drawing a set of wings for the angel. Make sure that your wing design includes at least 6 inches of connection between the wing for attaching to the costume. Also keep in mind the size of the wearer—wings too big will slip off, and too small will be hard to see from the front.

When you have drawn a wing size and design you like, cut it out of the newspaper to use as a pattern on the poster board. Then trace and cut out the design on the paperboard. Complete the next step *before* you go on to decorate the wings.

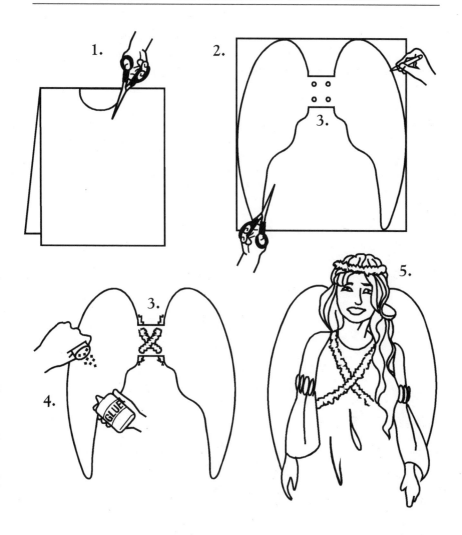

3. Poke four holes in the center of the poster-board wings. Use a length of garland to lace through these holes and go over the wearer's shoulders to crisscross in front, wrap around back again, and tie.

4. Now you can use glue, glitter, aluminum foil, feathers, or other bright, shiny material to decorate the wings. (Make sure you are decorating the parts of the wings that will be visible when worn.) For the simplest and easiest decoration, use a small scrap piece of poster board to spread a thin layer of glue just inside the outline of the wings. Sprinkle glitter over the glue, and let dry thoroughly (about four hours or overnight). You can also first paint the wings with silver or gold paint, allow to dry, then decorate with glitter.

5. Tie a length of the garland around your head for a halo.

"Bag" Costumes

You can make many different kinds of costumes using a large, sturdy garbage bag or its near equivalent. Among the possibilities are:

- **Sea Sprite.** Cut a hole for your head midway across the bottom of a green garbage bag, and holes for your arms on opposite sides of the bag at appropriate spots. Shred another green garbage bag into long, thin strips. Wear one strip as a headband (or wear a green cap), and attach other strips to it so that they dangle, like seaweed, around the sides and back of your head. Cinch your waist with another strip. For extra effect, wear appropriately marine-colored or marine-designed makeup and a seashell necklace (real or paper).

- **Peter Pan.** Cut a hole for your head midway across the bottom of a green garbage bag, and holes for your arms on opposite sides of the bag at appropriate spots. Cut a zigzag edge around the opening of the bag (which will be the bottom of your Peter Pan "tunic"). Cinch at the waist with a green ribbon or its near equivalent. Wear it with green leotards or pantyhose, and a green cap with a feather. For added drama, sprinkle the cap, your face, and the shoulders of the bag with gold glitter (pixie dust).

- **Grape Cluster.** Cut a hole midway across the bottom of a green garbage bag, and holes for your arms on opposite sides of the bag at appropriate spots. Cover the bag with light green or purple balloons, or plate-sized circles of light green or purple, to represent grapes. Tie a thick green cord or its near equivalent around your neck, so that one end of the cord dangles for about a foot as the "stem." All around the cord at the neck, attach "leaves" cut out of dark green construction paper or another green garbage bag.

- **Olive.** Cut holes for your legs in the bottom of a green trash bag, and holes for your arms on opposite sides of the bag at appropriate spots. After stepping into the bag, pack it with wadded newspapers so that it assumes a round, olive shape. Tie the opening of the bag at the neck with an unobtrusive cord. Wear a red hat—or red head covering—for the pimento.

- **Leaf Pile.** Cut a hole for your head midway across the bottom of a garbage bag (any color); and holes for your arms on opposite sides of the bag at appropriate spots. All over the surface of the bag, attach paper leaf cutouts in various fall colors.

- **Trash Pile.** Cut a hole for your head midway across the bottom of a garbage bag (any color), and holes for your arms on opposite sides of the bag at appropriate spots. All over the surface of bag, attach small cardboard boxes and cans of familiar consumer products, as well as small wadded clumps of different types of materials (e.g., cloth, paper, netting, ribbon).

"Box" Costumes

For a standout costume, be inventive with large cardboard boxes, or panels cut from large cardboard boxes. Here are some suggestions:

- **A Die (one of a pair of dice).** Find or make a cardboard cube, with each square side being a few inches wider than your shoulders. On one side, cut a circular hole big enough for your head to slip through comfortably. On appropriate opposing sides, cut holes big enough for your arms to fit through comfortably (mindful that you should be able to remove the box yourself). On the "bottom" side, cut an oval hole big enough to fit over your body. You might even want to cut out the whole bottom side, leaving just a small "support triangle" at each corner.

  Paint the entire box white. Then paint each side with a different number of black dots, arranged as they are on a die. Wear with black shirt or sweater, black pants or leotard, and, if available, an eye visor such as professional gamblers use. Your partner may also want to wear a die costume, so that you can be a pair!

- **A Robot.** Find or make two rectangular or square boxes with no "bottoms:" one into which your body can comfortably fit (shoulders to waist), and one into which your head can comfortably fit. The "head box" should be tall enough so that it rises a few inches *above* the top of the head when it is worn on top of the "body" box, and the "face" side should be fairly close to the face.

  Cut rectangular holes for the arms and head on the "body" box. Cut rectangular holes on three sides of the "head" box: on the "face" side, a hole just big enough to go from the tops of your eyes to the top of your lips, and just as wide as your two eyes; on each adjacent side, a bar-shaped hole going almost from side to side at ear level, and just as high as the ear is long. Cover all the "head" box holes with wire or cloth mesh fastened on the inside, so that you can see out fairly clearly, but others can't easily see in.

  Spray-paint the outside of both boxes silver. Then paint or attach robotlike eyes and nose above the mesh face hole, so that the face hold resembles a large robotlike mouth. Paint or attach robotlike ears at appropriate spots on the side of the "head" box. Paint or attach various robotlike knobs, dials, and gizmos to both boxes. Wear with silver or black sleeves, silver or black pants or leotards, and robotlike gloves and shoes.

- **A Card.** Cut out or create two flat cardboard "cards," a few inches wider than each shoulder and one-and-a-half times as long. Paint one side of each card to resemble your favorite playing card or tarot card. Paint the other side of each card black.

  Next, create shoulder straps so that you can wear the two cards as "sandwich boards." First, securely attach two lengths of black yarn, cord, or cloth strip to the back of one of the cards: one length near each "top" corner of the card. Then, hang this card over your shoulder, "face"-side out, so that it falls against your back at the desired height. Finally, figure out how much yarn, cord, or cloth strip you need to cut so that the front card will hang well when it's attached. Wear the cards with a long-sleeved black shirt or sweater and black pants or leotard.

- **A Television Set.** Find or make a "bottomless" rectangular box that is a few inches wider than your shoulders, and long enough to extend from a few inches above the top of your head to your waist. Viewing the box as a TV set, cut out a TV-screen-shaped hold big enough to frame the entire head, with an inch or so to spare above the head.

  Slip the box over your head, figure out where the tops of your shoulders should be, and draw a horizontal line all around the inside of the box at this point. Securely fasten two shoulder straps of yarn, cord, or cloth from the front of the box to the back of the box on this line.

  Cut out appropriate holes in the sides of the box for each arm, big enough for your arm to bend back inside the box for easy removal. Paint the outside of the box to look like a TV set. If desired, make up face and/or adorn head to look like a TV personality. Wear the box with black sleeves and black pants or leotard.

- **A Cereal Box.** Find or make a "bottomless" rectangular box that is a few inches wider than your shoulders and that extends from the top of your shoulders to approximately your knees. On the "top" side, cut out a circular hole big enough for your head to fit through comfortably. Cut out oval arm holes on opposing vertical sides of the box, so that the box can "hang" from your shoulders, and so that your arm has room to bend back inside the box for easy removal. Paint the box to resemble your favorite cereal box.

Regular Clothes as Costumes

The following costumes can be made with clothing articles that are probably around the house. Second-hand and used clothing stores are also a good source for authentic costumes and accessories at reasonable prices.

- *Gangster.* A dark, preferably double breasted suit, with a dark shirt and a white tie create the basics for a gangster costume. A carnation or fake flower in the lapel, a big cigar and a violin case should be added. A wide brim hat provides the final touch.

- *Harpo Marx.* Harpo can be created with a plaid shirt, a plain pair of baggy trousers supported by a pair of suspenders and an oversized rain or trench coat.

  A cheap red or yellow curly wig can be used or bits of yellow yarn can be attached to the inside of a novelty crushed top hat. All that's needed to complete the costume is Harpo's taxi horn.

- **Pirate.** This costume requires either a full-sleeved white shirt or a tattered sleeved shirt open at the neck and tied at the waist. Wear dark pants, preferably black, which are tattered at the bottom. A head scarf can be made by using a triangular piece of cloth. A sash for the waist can be made from a piece of material 8" wide x 72" long. Another option is to mark an undershirt with a black magic marker to make a striped shirt worn underneath the outer shirt. A big gold earring, an eye patch and sword can be added as accessories.

- **Lady Pirate.** Use a white sleeved blouse open at the neck and tied in a knot under the bust. Wear either black shorts or a short black skirt tattered at the bottom. Use a piece of cloth 8" wide x 72" long to make a sash for the waist. A red kerchief should be worn around the head. An earring and sword make the costume complete.

- **Gypsy.** Use almost any type of white or colorful blouse and wear as many strings of beads or necklaces as possible to form the basic top of the costume.

  Use a colorful full skirt, and add trim if desired. Tie a long strip of colorful material around the waist for a sash and let the ends hang down at one side. Boots, a head scarf, an earring, and a piece of lace or shawl thrown over the shoulders adds the final touch.

How to Make a Mask

If you dress up for your party you may decide that the easiest thing will be to buy a mask from a novelty store in order to give your face the appearance you require.

You may, however, want to make your appearance completely unique by devising your own mask. You will get a great deal of enjoyment and satisfaction from creating something all of your own, but if you decide to do this, prepare it in plenty of time; otherwise, you may be disappointed. You'll probably have to experiment, as you may not get the results you hoped for the first time.

You will need:

- a large round balloon
- newspaper
- wallpaper paste
- scissors
- 1" paintbrush
- paints and felt-tip markers
- eggbox

Directions:

1. Begin by tearing the newspaper into small pieces about 2" square. Blow up your balloon and make up a thick wallpaper paste in a jar (use about a tablespoon of flour).

2. Paste the pieces of paper to the balloon so that the edges just overlap. Be systematic about this or you'll get a difference in thickness. You'll need about three or four layers of newspaper. If you get folds or crease-crinkles, snip them carefully with fine scissors and paste them flat.

3. Allow the covered balloon to dry slowly. Don't put it near any source of heat to dry.

4. Deflate and remove the balloon, then cut the shape you require. You can "tailor" the mask by cutting, overlapping the cut edges, and then resticking.

5. To fit a nose, use a single section from an eggbox cut lengthways. Paste this over a hole cut in the mask using newspaper layers.

6. When the mask is dry, paint it. To achieve a flesh color, add white powder or poster paint to burnt sienna until you get the tone you need. (Don't use red or pink paint for flesh colouring.)

7. Ask a grown-up to let you finish off with a coat of clear varnish.

Fortune-Telling Activities

The ancient Celts, to whom we are indebted for the Halloween holiday, considered Halloween the best time of the year for divination, because of the exceptional proximity of the supernatural world to the real wold. Besides using tarot cards, throwing runes, casting the I-Ching, consulting a Ouija board, or reading a crystal ball, you might try the following fortune-telling activities that have a much more direct association with Halloween:

- *"Ring in a Cake."* Bake a ring in a cake or cookie. The person who finds the ring will find true love. This is an old Irish custom. For safety's sake, make sure that the ring is fairly big, and that everyone knows about it!

- *Play "Snap Apple."* An apple is hung on a string from a doorway or the ceiling. The string is set in motion before each play. Players, holding their hands tied behind their backs, take turns trying to bite the swinging apple. Whoever succeeds will have good fortune.

  This custom has prevailed in scattered parts of Great Britain for centuries. Until recent times, it was so popular in these parts, as well as in parts of America, that October 31 was known as "Snap Apple Night." A more traditional and complicated form of "Snap Apple" involves fixing a lit candle and an apple to opposite ends of a horizontal pole that is suspended at midpoint from the ceiling. The horizontal pole is twirled. The player then has to brave the candle in trying to bite the apple. (It might be safer *not* to try this one at home.)

- **"Chestnut or Walnut Crack."** For each person who counts as a possible beau, place a chestnut or walnut on a grate in the fire. Then watch what happens. If a nut burns "true" (i.e., without popping), that person is worth trusting. If a nut pops, that person is *not* worth trusting.

  This custom has long been popular in northern England and Scotland, where nuts are abundant at harvesttime. As was the case with "Snap Apple Night" (see above), many people in England, Scotland, and colonial America honored this custom by referring to October 31 as "Nut Crack Night."

- **Play "Three Luggies."** Before each play, the player is blindfolded and three bowls are lined up in random order on a table. One bowl is filled with clear water (signifying good luck), one is filled with dirty water (signifying "mixed" luck or no change in luck), and one is empty (signifying bad luck). The first bowl in which the player dips his or her fingers reveals his or her fortune.

  This game is a traditional favorite in Ireland, Great Britain, and parts of the United States (such as Appalachia). In its most ancient form, the divination applied strictly to marriage: If a player picked the clear bowl, he or she would marry a virgin; a dirty bowl, he or she would be widowed; an empty bowl, he or she would remain single. In the American version, "Three Luggies" is often played with a bowl of apples (good luck), nuts ("mixed" luck or no change), and soot (bad luck).

- **"Apple Swing."** Peel an apple in one long winding piece. Then swing it over your head three times clockwise with your right hand and cast it over your left shoulder. If you can read an initial into that fallen paring, then it is the initial of your true love.

  As far as experts can determine, this game came to England and Ireland via ancient Rome. On October 31, the Romans

– 265 –

celebrated the Feast of Pomona, goddess of fruit, whose main symbol was an apple.

- **"Count the Seeds."** Cut an apple in half from top to bottom. Choose one half (if you're by yourself, the left half) and count the number of seeds. Here's a key to what your fortune will be:
  one seed = same luck as the year before
  two seeds = lucky in love
  three seeds = a financial windfall
  four seeds = a long trip
  five seeds = happiness in work
  six seeds = good health
  seven seeds or more = many blessings in life

  Variations of this game have been played throughout history wherever apples are grown, being especially popular at Halloween, wherever Halloween is celebrated. The numerical interpretations have remained surprisingly consistent.

- **"Candlelit Mirror."** Look into a candlelit mirror at midnight on Halloween. The image of your true love is supposed to appear over your left shoulder. This is an English custom of long standing transferred to the American colonies. The last mention of its practice to any widespread degree was in the final decade of the nineteenth century.

- **"Walnut Fortunes."** For a group of people, carefully crack more than enough walnuts ahead of time so that the two shell halves are intact. Clean out these halves, and insert either (a) a slip of paper with a fortune written on it, or (b) a slip of paper saying "yes" or "no" (alternate the two responses evenly among the walnuts). Choose either (a) or (b); don't do a combination of both. Reattach the halves together with rubber cement.

  When the group has assembled, ask each person to choose a walnut. Then, depending on how you've stuffed the walnuts, have the person (a) crack the walnut for his or her fortune, or (b) silently or audibly pose a question he or she wants answered, then crack the walnut for the "yes" or "no" answer.

This divination technique is a modern adaptation of ancient European nut divinations at harvesttime, when the fortune or answer was derived from the nutmeat itself: its look, taste, or "split" (the walnut didn't have to be cracked evenly). Nutmeat-interpreting skills are sure to be much rarer today than they were in ancient times!

- **Try "Hot Wax Fortunes."** First, melt old candle stubs into liquid wax. One easy and relatively mess-free way to do this is to put the old candle stubs into a clean tin can, and then put the can in a saucepan partway filled with water. Using low heat, warm the water in the pan until the candle stubs have melted completely. If you want to use paraffin instead of candle stubs, it's best to use a double boiler: **Paraffin is flammable if exposed to too much heat.**

  Next, set the can or pan of melted wax on a pot holder or heat-resistant dish. Have each person spoon out a small amount and drip it into a wide dish, bowl, or bucket of cold water. Then, read the person's fortune (using your imagination) from the shape of the hardened wax. For example, a heartlike shape might indicate "love," a shape like a letter might indicate a "significant initial," a stairstep shape might indicate "progress," and so on.

  This is an updated version of a custom popular in Ireland at Samhain-Halloween time during the Middle Ages. Sometimes lead was used instead of wax, and often the wax or lead was poured through an important object, such as a wedding ring (for divinations relating to marriage or family), a broken pot (for divinations relating to crops), or a circle of rope, leather, or steel (for divinations relating to trades).

Ghostly Antidotes

- As you are getting ready for bed, place one shoe with the toe pointing under the bed. Place the other shoe pointing in the opposite direction. Now you will be safe from ghosts and goblins throughout the night.

- Keep ghosts away. Turn your pockets inside out.

- Carry a piece of bread crust in your pocket. It will protect you from creatures that roam in the night,

- You can get rid of a ghost by throwing a key at it.

- If you should meet a witch, cross your fingers and you'll stay safe.

- Hang a mirror on the front porch. It will keep ghosts from coming into your house.

- At the first light of day ghosts, goblins, witches, and zombies disappear.

Halloween Superstitions

Here are some Halloween superstitions for your own entertainment or to share — however you wish — with your family, friends, and guests during Halloween festivities:

- If a candle flame suddenly turns blue, a ghost is near at hand.

- Knocking on wood (preferably oak — sacred to the Celts) keeps evil away.

- To prevent ghosts from coming into the house, especially at Halloween, bury animal bones near the doorway, or bury the image of an animal in a sealed box or jar.

- If you see a spider on Halloween, it's a departed spirit from your past that is watching you.

- A child that has teeth when it is born will grow up to be a vampire.

- If Halloween night occurs on the night of a full moon, the spirit world is all the closer, so intuition and divination are stronger (and caution and care are more advisable!).

- A fire lit or burning after sunset on Halloween should be kept burning until after midnight, or spirits may come around and do harm.

- In the United States, if an all-black cat crosses your path, it's bad luck. If an all-white cat crosses your path, it's good luck. In Great Britain and Ireland, it's just the opposite.

- Wear a ring on Halloween, especially if you are sick, and you are safe from harm.

- Ring a bell to scare evil spirits away.

- Before sunset on Halloween, walk around your home backwards three times, counterclockwise, to ward off evil that night.

- Make friends on Halloween, and you'll be one in spirit for (at least) the coming year — i.e., until next Halloween. If you quarrel with someone on Halloween, make up before midnight or your estrangement will last for (at least) a year — i.e., until next Halloween.

- A dream on Halloween night is especially potent. Here are some traditions regarding specific dreams:

  — If you dream of someone you know, even from the distant past, contact that person and share your dream. It could involve an important spirit message.

  — If someone speaks to you in a dream, mark those words.

  — If you have a nightmare, write it down, then write down a happier version, and sleep with the happier version tucked under your mattress.

  — If you dream of trouble or danger threatening something in your real life, take pains to guarantee the safety of that thing.

  — If you dream of someone dying (even yourself), be especially kind and solicitous to that person (even yourself).

- A couple married on Halloween is well bonded in spirit.

- A child born on Halloween can see spirits and even converse with them.

- A person who dies on Halloween becomes the most active ghost there can be, forever travelling back and forth between the real world and the spirit world.

How to Make a Spider's Web

You will need:

- needle with a very large eye
- heavy jute string
- scissors
- black thread
- poster paint
- tape

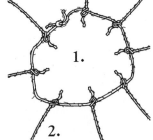

Directions:

1. Using a fairly heavy jute string made out of separate strands twisted together, make a loop about 20 inches in diameter.

2. Place the loop in the center of the room. Tie eight to ten pieces of string to the loop that are long enough to reach the walls. Make the knots loose at first so you can adjust and tighten them when the center ring is a good shape. If you have a picture-rail, you can attach the strings to it at several points around the room. Otherwise, try taping them to the ceiling molding so that the center ring hangs just above your head.

3. Take another piece of string and thread it through a needle with a very large eye. Then make a concentric ring around the center loop by passing the needle through the twisted strands that make up the web's "arms." Don't make the rings look too symmetrical or evenly spaced. Repeat this process until you have several concentric rings in your "web." Dab the points where the strings cross with thick poster paint to hold them in place.

4. Fasten spiders and bats to the cobweb and let pieces of black thread dangle from it. Make sure they're long enough to brush against the face of anyone who walks into the room.

Halloween Games and Stunts

Bobbing for Apples

This is a traditional Halloween game that is a lot of fun, even for adults. Fill a large (and leakproof!) tub with water—adding ice cubes will increase the challenge. Take the stems off several apples, and float them in the tub. Have barrettes, hairbands, or scarves that girls can tie around their heads to keep their hair out of the way.

Players should kneel in front of the tub with their hands tied behind their backs and try to pick up an apple with their teeth. An interesting variation on this game is to have one person tuck an apple under his or her chin and try to transfer it to somebody else's chin while both keep their hands behind their backs. The gyrations they will have to go through to complete the transfer successfully are guaranteed to keep everyone else entertained!

Supernatural Levitation

This trick requires the participation of five people. Have one of them — preferably someone of average height and weight — sit upright in an armless, straight-backed chair with arms crossed. Ask the other four people to try and lift the seated person by placing their hands under his/her upper arms and thighs. The lifters will probably be able to raise the person a few inches or not at all.

Now tell two of the lifters to place their first and second fingers under the seated person's knees, while the other two lifters each place two fingers under the person's arms at the shoulder. Tell all five to take three deep breaths in unison. On the third inhalation, give the command to "Lift." Much to their surprise, the lifters will be able to raise the seated person much further — using only eight fingers!

Another approach to levitating someone is to have each lifter place a hand, palm down, on the seated person's head so that all eight hands are eventually stacked on top of each other. They should all press gently downward while taking a deep breath and holding it to a count of 20. As soon as they exhale, they should immediately try to lift the person.

The Ghostly Touch

Invite a friend or party guest into a dimly lit room and explain that it is haunted by a very shy, gentle ghost. Allow the guest to look around and make sure there is no one else hiding in the room. Then set up two chairs opposite each other and ask your guest to sit in one while you sit opposite him or her.

Summon the ghost by asking, "Are you there? Will you give us a sign?" When nothing happens, explain that the guest has to be completely relaxed before the ghost will appear. To help the person relax, move both hands toward his or her eyes, index fingers extended, and say that you're going to place your fingers on his or her closed eyelids. Explain that the ghost often makes its presence known by a current of air, a rapping noise, or sometimes by touching. But nothing is guaranteed.

Take your hands away from your guest's eyes as you call the ghost again. Chances are, your guest will open his/her eyes to see what is going on. When nothing happens, move your hands toward the guest's face again and place your two fingers on his/her eyelids. The point here is to establish in your guest's mind the idea that you're using *both* hands to close his/her eyes. Withdraw your hands a second time and try to summon the ghost. But this time, as you move your hands back toward his/her face and your guest begins to close his/her eyes, place two fingers from the *same* hand on his or her eyelids. This leaves the other hand free — but your guest won't know it.

Don't be in too much of a hurry to use your free hand. Allow 20 or 30 seconds to pass in complete silence. Then quietly put your free hand on the back of your guest's head and touch his or her hair lightly. The gentler your touch, the more convincing it will be. You can also tap the person on the shoulder, lift a piece of his or her clothing slightly, or give other indications of the ghost's presence. Watch your guest shiver as he or she experiences the "ghostly touch."

Ghostly Noises

You can make any Halloween stunt more effective by making ghostly noises in the background. Here are some suggestions:

- Have several people blow gently across the tops of different-sized bottles to make a chorus of moaning sounds.

- Ask someone who can make a spine-chilling scream or ghostly laugh to do it into a large jug or through a paper tube. Whispering, humming, or breathing heavily into a bucket will produce a hollow, echoing noise.

- Wet your finger and run it around the rim of a wine glass to make a high-pitched sound that will set your friends' teeth on edge. Filling the glass partially with water will change the pitch of the sound.

- Make a bull-roarer. All you need is a ruler or thin piece of wood about the size of a ruler (1½ x 12 inches). Make a small hole in one end and attach a piece of string. Then, holding it by the end of the string, swing the piece of wood around your head repeatedly to produce a ghastly roaring noise.

The Exhumed Corpse

Have everyone sit in a circle in the middle of the room and either blindfold them or turn the lights out and tell them to keep their eyes closed. Tell them that they will be examining body parts from a dead man's corpse (make up a good story about why the body had to be exhumed). Then, one by one, pass the following items around the circle:

- the dead man's hand (a rubber glove filled with wet sand)
- an ear (dried apricot)
- eyes (olives or hard-boiled eggs)
- intestines (cold, cooked spaghetti)
- liver (raw liver)
- pancreas (a cold oyster)
- teeth (hard kernels of corn)
- hair (cornsilk)
- brains (a whole cooked, greased cauliflower)

With a little imagination, you can probably come up with other "body parts" that are very convincing.

How to Conduct a Spirit Seance

One of the highlights of a Halloween party is a seance in which you make contact with the spirit world.

To present the seance you will need:

- 2 school slates
- a sheet of black construction paper
- a bell
- a horn
- 4 aluminum pie plates
- a squirt gun
- 6 to 12 ping pong balls that have been painted with luminous paint
- a card table and 4 chairs

You will also need the help of a secret assistant who will be willing to practice the seance stunts so they go off smoothly.

Begin the seance by announcing it in a ghostly tone of voice and asking for three volunteers. One of these must be your secret assistant. The four of you should then take your places at a card table, which must be placed near a light switch at one end of the room. Your back must be to the wall, and your assistant must be facing you with his or her back to the guests.

Before a single candle is lit and the room lights are turned off, gothic organ music or eerie sound effects should be playing in the background to set the proper mood. You are now ready to perform "spirit table lifting."

Spirit Table Lifting

Instruct each person at the table to grab his left wrist with his right hand, and place the left hand flat upon the table. Then, tell the group that they will attempt to lift the table through "psychic energy."

While everyone places their left hands on the table, you and your secret helper extend your right forefingers beneath your left hand and under the edge of the table. The table can then be slowly lifted with your forefingers.

Spirit Slate Writing

Next, conduct an experiment in "spirit slate writing." Two slates, blank on both sides, are placed together and a piece of chalk is placed on top of them. The slates are separated and a message has mysteriously appeared.

This stunt requires two black school sates, a piece of chalk, and a piece of black construction paper. The black paper should be cut to fit inside the border of one of the slates. It should be loose enough to fall out when the slate is turned over.

Before the seance, write a message on one slate, cover it with the black paper, and leave both slates on the table. Show your trick slate first, front and back. As you are showing the second slate, tilt the first slate back and let the "insert" fall into your lap.

With a candle on the table and the other lights out, this move will go unnoticed. All that remains is to place the slates together, wait for several seconds, and "discover" the communication from the spirit world.

A Host of Ghosts

The last seance stunt will make your guests believe that a host of ghosts actually did manifest at the party. Have everyone at the table change seats, and make sure that your secret helper is now sitting next to you.

Place the bell, horn, and aluminum pie plates on the card table, and instruct everyone at the table to hold each other by the wrist. Mention that this is necessary to prove that no one at the table is aiding the ghosts. Tell your guests that you are going to extinguish the candle and try to contact the spirit world.

When the candle is out, you and your secret helper release your grip on each other. This will give both of you a free hand with which to carry out the spirit manifestations.

Either you or your secret helper can now reach on the table and sound the horn in the darkness. Next, one of you ring the bell while the other tosses the aluminum pie plates across the room.

For a real fright, remove the ping pong balls from your pocket. The balls must have been previously painted with luminous paint, and exposed to a bright light for several hours before the seance. Toss these "comets" around the party room. As your guests pick up these glowing objects and also toss them around the room, it will produce an eerie visual effect.

While this continues, your secret helper can remove the toy water pistol which has been filled with ice cold water from his or her pocket. He or she should squirt the water around the room at your guests, giving them cold, damp, spirit kisses.

At a given signal, your helper should place the water pistol back in his or her pocket. You should both join hands, announce that the seance has ended, and turn on the house lights.

How to Stage a "Chamber of Morbius"

The "victims" are sent to wait outside the room. They are told that they will shortly be able to enter the Chamber of Morbius, where they will undergo a trial of their courage and fortitude. If they survive the horrors which guard the Chamber, they will be allowed to enter the inner sanctum and discover for themselves the secret of Morbius.

Meanwhile, the room is being made ready with whatever props and effects are needed for the stunt.

Then, one by one, the victims knock on the door, which is opened by the doorkeeper. The following dialogue takes place (the victim's answers can be written on a card):

"What seek you?"
"The secret of Morbius."
"Do you promise to do as you are commanded?"
"I do."
"Do you promise to ask no questions and to tell no one what
    you discover?"
"I do."
"Enter."

The victim is led into a room which is divided off by screens. (Old sheets could be used for this.) The room is lit by a dim colored light. Some weird music is playing.

The victim is asked to stand on a short plank which rests on bricks or small boxes. A blindfold is placed over his eyes. His hands are placed on the shoulders of two attendants who stand on either side of him.

He is told that if he is a worthy candidate, the power of Morbius will raise him up into the air. In fact, he is such a suitable candidate that his head bumps gently against the ceiling. (The victim thinks he is rising when the attendants sink slowly down towards the floor while others gently rock the plank. The "ceiling" is a book which is gently bumped on the victim's head.)

Safely back on the ground, the victim is asked if he is willing to undergo a test of courage. He is told that he must walk barefoot through the snake pit which guards the entrance to the inner sanctum. No harm will come to him if he has led an honest and completely blameless life.

In the pit is a mass of snakes' eggs. Unfortunately the victim walks over several which crush beneath his tread. In fact the eggs are simply polystyrene egg-boxes or apple dividers.

The victim is now able to enter the inner sanctum where he is to be asked to hold the brain of Morbius which will allow him to look into the past and future at the same time.

A gong is struck (an old tin tray will do) and the brain is placed in the victim's hands. At the same time the blindfold is removed.

The brain is made from cold, congealed spaghetti.

The impact is considerable, but it soon dissolves into the general laughter which follows. The victim can then join the "silent" onlookers and enjoy the next candidate for the Chamber of Morbius.

How to Haunt a House

Decorations

The first step in "haunting" your house is to create a spooky atmosphere outside, especially if you have a good-size lawn, yard or porch. The yard can be turned into a cemetery by placing several cardboard tombstones painted with day-glow paint on the ground. An ultraviolet light hiding behind a tree can cast a chilling glow on the "stones" when the sun goes down. The names of friends and neighbors could be written on the tombstones.

Dig a hole the size of a grave and have the tombstone's inscription reading: "It's empty . . . but not for long." Have a pile of dirt and a shovel next to the grave marker. Make sure that the fresh grave is not too deep, and be sure to keep it off to the side so that no one accidentally falls in.

Dig a shallow ditch in the walkway, place several old pillows or cushions in it, and cover them with dirt. When your guests arrive and step on the path, it will feel as if they are walking into quicksand.

Hang a cloth dummy from an upstairs window and have several dummies on the porch sitting in rocking chairs. If you have an intercom system, place one of the speakers on the porch, and have a recorded voice welcome your guests as they arrive.

A headless man or ghost could greet your guests at the front door, saying in a weird voice "Greetings, I am your M.C., otherwise known as the Master of Cemeteries."

Inside, cover the furniture with white sheets to give the house that "unlived-in" look. This effect can be enhanced by soaping windows to create a spooky film. Silhouette figures cut from black construction paper can be taped in the windows. Large foot prints cut from white paper can be placed on the floor, up the walls and across ceilings.

Carve several pumpkins and have these jack-o'-lanterns grinning from dark corners. Corn stalks can also be placed in several corners.

The traditional black and orange crepe paper streamers can be hung around doorways or across the corners of a room to the chandelier. Buy some large plastic skulls and cut the bottoms out. Set the skulls over the lights for a spooky chandelier, and for a really ghostly effect, substitute red light bulbs.

The walls of the house can appear "haunted" by hanging pictures or paintings upside down or on angles. You can also create an unusual effect with a wall clock. Wind the clock and remove the pendulum. This will cause the clock to "tick" faster and the hands to move more rapidly than normal. You and your guests will actually see time "fly."

Hang strips of aluminum foil from the ceiling. They will reflect any light source, and add to the other effects. The streamers can be kept moving by placing a small electric fan behind them.

Write ghoulish messages on the mirrors with red lip-stick. Try "Let me out!" or, "I'm trapped on the other side!" backwards to add to the confusion.

One of the best "spook" effects is to hang several rows of black thread in the doorways. The thread dangles down and brushes across your guests' faces, to create a feeling of spider webs. Make sure that the lights are dim so that the thread can't be easily seen.

Spider webs can also be made out of string (see "*How to Make a Spider's Web*") and hung in the corners of a room. They should be painted with bright day-glow paint. An ultraviolet light will make the spider webs glow. Tie a few hangsmen's nooses and scatter them throughout the house.

Place several buckets of dry ice in different rooms to give the appearance of fog pouring in from the streets. Hot water must be poured on the dry ice and changed frequently to sustain the effect of a ground-covering mist.

You can buy weird-looking rubber masks and grotesque hands from the local costume shop. Have the fake hands sticking out of a vase or a piano, or attach a fake hand onto a light switch or door-knob. Imagine the reaction when someone reaches for one of these and finds another hand already there. A fake head or mask could also be sticking out of an attic door.

Buy a pair of inflatable fake legs and have these protruding from under a sofa. Rubber bats, fake spiders, plastic skulls, realistic snakes, chattering teeth, and pooh cushions can be placed around the house and under sofa pillows. Your budget and imagination are the only limits to the unearthly atmosphere that can be created.

Now that you've decorated your haunted house, let's look at some of the tricks that you can play on those who have enough nerve to come inside.

Spooky Stunts

If you really want to scare the wits out of your guests, arrange one corner of a room as a funeral parlor, complete with flowers and an open casket. A fake coffin can be easily made out of large sheets of cardboard. Place an accomplice in the casket wearing a scary false face. When one of your guests pays his "last respects," have the accomplice jump up from the coffin and let out a blood-curdling scream.

Hang a cloth-made dummy or luminous skeleton on the back door of the bathroom. When someone enters and shuts the door, behind him, imagine his surprise when he finds he is not "alone." Better yet, hide one of your intercom speakers in the bathroom. When someone goes inside, count to ten and then say "I see you."

For a real thriller, send in a plague of worms to crawl through a room. Get several rubber worms from a fishing tackle shop, and tie them in 3 foot intervals to a thin line from a fishing rod. Before your guests arrive, feed the line out into the room, keeping the line close to a wall or furniture to prevent people from tripping over it. The worms should be hidden either under a curtain or a table. Your fishing rod is in the next room with the fishing line hooked onto it.

At the proper moment, reel in the worms. This effect will play havoc on your guests as they watch the squirming worms slither by them, especially if the worms have been coated with luminous paint and the room is dark.

Dress an accomplice as a scarecrow, and stand him in a corner before the guests arrive. Place several chairs in front of him, and instruct him to stand perfectly still. At the right moment, have your scarecrow put his straw arms around the group of people sitting in front of him.

Though tricky, it's possible to rig a tape recorder to one of the doors upstairs. Have the sound effects of a party on this tape. This tape will play for sometime until someone's curiosity causes him to open the door. As soon as the door is opened, the music and talking should stop. When he shuts the door, the party sound will continue.

Another tape recorder stunt is to record the sound of a thunderstorm. Have a flashing light in the hallway leading upstairs. The sound of a thunderstorm and the flashes of light will chill those who dare to ascend the steps.

Imagine blood dripping from the ceiling in your haunted house! All that is required is one bottle of theatrical stage blood, a piece of thin plastic tubing, a basin, and a cooking syringe (bulb). Fill the bulb and tube with as much stage blood as they will hold. Hook the tube to a pipe in the house or through a ceiling panel. A helper pumps on this bulb, forcing the "fake" blood out a drop at a time. The basin underneath catches the blood. You may find it more practical for the blood to drip into a bathtub or sink.

Buy several vibrating hand buzzers from your local novelty store. After winding the buzzers properly, scatter them on chairs throughout the house. Make sure the flat part of the buzzer is placed down. To hide them, cover the seats of the chairs with lightweight seat mats. Imagine the "shock" when someone sits on the chair and gets a surprising jolt.

By now your guests should really be in the mood for ghostly illusions. The next section outlines 13 different "special effects" that you can create.

13 G*h*osts

No haunted house would be complete without real "live" (or dead) ghosts, and this section provides 13 ways to create these unearthly visitors in your home. While some of these methods are simple, others are quite elaborate and require preparations. You should use these stunts sporadically throughout your house to create the atmosphere you desire.

Most of the items needed to produce spirits can be bought at hardware or department stores. Some of the ghost illusions, however, require luminous paint. If your local hardware store or hobby shop does not carry this item, it can be mail ordered.

There are several important details to remember about producing manifestations. Effective background music will enhance the appearance of any horrible haunt you produce. If a "ghost" is coated with luminous paint, expose it to a strong light for several hours prior to its appearance. Also, remember that a luminous ghost will require either total darkness, or a semi-lit room. Finally, test your ghost ahead of time to ensure that it works smoothly.

Disembodied Spirits

Just about any "ghostly" activity can be duplicated with the use of strong black thread. Doors can be made to open, pictures to fall from walls, chandeliers to sway, chairs to "walk" across the room, and books to drop from shelves. A button can be hooked to the end of each thread to make it easier to find.

Frightening Apparitions

Here is an easy method for producing a specter in your haunted house. As a guest walks down the hallway, he will see a phantom-like face appear, and then vanish right before his eyes.

The secret involves a mirror. Place a mirror on a 45-degree angle in a corner of a hallway or corridor, so that you see both your face and the face of anyone approaching. For this effect to work properly, the area should be as dark as possible.

As a person approaches the mirror, shine a flashlight on *your* face. When your guest looks at the mirror, your ghostly reflection will appear. To vanish, simply turn off the flashlight and exit through another room.

Foreboding Skeleton

To create this apparition, you will need a cardboard skeleton that has been treated on one side with luminous paint. Luminous skeletons are easily available at department stores, card shops, or novelty stores. Cover the side of the skeleton that is *not* luminous with wall paper or paint that is identical to that of the room to be used.

Next, insert small screw eyes into opposite walls near the ceiling. Run a piece of strong black thread up the side of one wall through the first screw eye, across the room through the second screw eye, and back down the other wall. The thread should be tied to either a tack or a small nail on both sides of the wall.

Place the skeleton with the luminous side facing one of the walls so that the skeleton is flush against it. This should go unnoticed in a semi-lit room, since the side of the skeleton that is covered with wall paper or paint should blend into the wall.

Finally, hook the skeleton to the thread so that it can be pulled away from the wall and travel across the room. It is now up to you and your secret helper to control the movements of the haunted skeleton while the lights are off.

Green Grinning Ghosts

More macabre effects can be achieved through the use of luminous make-up, which is available at most costume shops. Apply the make-up to several of your ghostly helpers and at the right moment, turn out the lights. The painted faces will shine in the dark like grinning ghosts. This make-up can also be applied to hands and fingers, so that when the lights are out, these ghastly hands will appear in the dark, float around, and tap your guests on their shoulders. The illusion of the glowing faces and waving hands will vanish when the lights are turned on.

Floating Heads in the Basement

This hideous apparition requires several yards of black cloth (either corduroy, velvet, or velveteen) and three 25-watt red light bulbs with reflectors facing the audience.

Cover one end of the wall in a large room with sheets of black cloth. Also cover the windows so there is no trace of light. Next, take the black material and make two ponchos. These will be placed over two friends, covering their entire bodies except their heads.

Place the three red lights about six feet in front of the curtain; these will be the only lights in the room. Your two helpers will be performing between the three red lights and the black curtain. Since this effect demands that it be viewed from a distance, a section of the room should be appropriately roped off so the illusion is not ruined.

This effect creates an astonishing feeling of the unreal. Your guests will witness two human heads without bodies hovering in mid air.

Ghost-Infested Room

Here is another method for conjuring elusive spirits and unseen ghosts.

You will need several dozen balloons and a balloon bag, which are used by large dance groups. Suspended from the ceiling, the bag will cascade balloons upon your guests when a rip cord is pulled.

If you can not find a balloon bag through a supplier of party goods or through a dance group, one can be made out of two large sheets of plastic. Take the sheets and secure one side of each to the ceiling so that they are parallel. The free ends of the hanging sheets should overlap when they are raised to the ceiling. Punch holes in both plastic sheets. To keep them together, run a piece of cord through the holes, weaving the cord through the holes in the sheets. The cord should be tied to wall and hidden so that no one releases it too soon. Next, fill the plastic sheets with balloons.

When the room is dark and the time is right, release the balloons. At first your guests will be surprised. After they realize what has happened, however, they will have fun laughing in the dark knocking the balloons about the room.

Vampire Bats

Luminous paint always produces eerie effects, and the next is no exception. A glowing bat will instantly appear in a pitch dark room, then flutter about before vanishing.

This trick is as simple as it is effective. All one needs is a cheap paper fan. Department stores will carry them, if there isn't one lying about the house. Paint an image of a bat on the fan with luminous paint, and expose it for several hours to a strong light before the effect is to be created. Immediately prior to the manifestation, fold the fan up and place it in your coat pocket. In a dark room the fan can be taken from your pocket, opened, and waved in an up and down motion to create the bizarre image of a glowing bat fluttering about the room.

Portable Ghost

At your command, a ghost will appear in the center of a room, float about, then suddenly vanish.

This effect requires two 12-inch rulers and two pieces of black material, 2 by 4 feet. Paint the image of a ghost on one side of the black material with luminous paint. After the paint has dried, sew the second piece of black material onto the back of the ghost. (This is to prevent the painted image from seeping through to the other side.) Along the two foot edge, at the top, attach the two rulers end to end.

Expose the ghost to a brilliant light for several hours. When you are ready to put the spirit in operation, fold it in half lengthwise, roll it up, and place it in your pocket. All that remains is to unroll the material and wave the ghost about in the dark room.

Galloping Ghost

You may want to have a ghost haunting the outside of your house, as well as the inside.

To create this illusion, tie a long piece of black elastic string onto the end of a long pole. Next, roll a towel into a bundle and place it in the middle of a large square of cheese cloth, or some other light material. Picking up the four corners of the square material and tying the elastic string immediately above the towel will form the image of a ghost.

At the proper moment, stick the pole out of an upstairs window and wave it about. The cloth, animated by the weight of the towel and the elastic, will appear to be a galloping ghost.

The Uninvited Guests

During the evening, when the lights are out, a ghost materializes in a most uncanny manner. It wavers, floats about, then suddenly vanishes towards the ceiling.

This creepy spook is nothing more than a rolled-up window blind. First cover the windows to block out any trace of light. Then hang a window blind with a painted luminous figure of a ghost on the side of the shade that will be facing the room. Expose the ghost to a bright light, and roll it up just prior to the arrival of your guests. Simply pulling the blind down in a dark room creates a wonderfully hair-raising effect.

Spectral Phenomena

This next stunt is supernatural enough to fool and horrify anyone who sees it. In the dark, a glob of light appears to hover in mid air. This vaporous light pulsates like an amoeba, and then expands as it floats through the air.

You will need an old umbrella. It is best to use a standard umbrella rather than one that opens automatically. After removing the covering from the hinged ribs, attach small round cardboard circles to the center and the ends of the rods. Next, coat the circles with luminous paint.

After the circles have been exposed properly to a light source, the umbrella can be hidden anywhere in the house. When the lights are out, grab the umbrella by the handle and wave it slowly around the room. Opening and closing the umbrella will make the circles of light seem to multiply, for a truly startling effect.

Ethereal Forms

This effect is rather complicated, but it is well worth the effort. When the lights are turned out, a horde of unearthly phantoms, shrouds, and peering ghosts rise in the air and then suddenly vanish.

This illusion requires a roll of black material at least 36 inches wide. The longer the material, the more spooks you can produce. Use luminous paint to draw ghosts and ectoplasmic forms on the long ribbon of black material. Fold the cloth in an accordion fashion, and place the material in a deep box.

Just before the lights are turned out, place the box near a pipe or rod that has been securely attached to the ceiling. There should also be a dark curtain hanging from the pipe. When the lights are turned off, remove the black material with the ghosts from the box and feed it over the pipe behind the curtain. Stepping behind the curtain, slowly pull the material towards you. It will look as if an endless procession of disjointed zombies, hobgoblins, and spirit enigmas are rising from the damp earth and vanishing into the mist of the heavens.

Wandering Skeleton

While all the lights are out, a headless skeleton suddenly appears in the middle of the room. After it has walked about and performed a few crazy antics, the lights are turned back on, and— to the amazement of all—the supernatural visitor is nowhere to be found.

You will need a helper to accomplish this effect. Get an old suit from a second-hand clothing store. On the back of the suit, using luminous paint, paint a skeleton: the skeleton's legs and pelvis on the pants, rib cage, arms, and neck on the coat.

Expose the "skeleton suit" to a strong light for several hours. After your friend has put on the suit, he should nonchalantly walk into the room, keeping his back towards the wall, away from the other guests. At a precise moment, turn out all the lights. Your secret helper should now turn his back *towards* the people and stroll through the room. It will appear as if a gruesome skeleton is searching for its head. The skeleton can vanish by simply mingling with the other guests as the lights are turned back on.

Recipes

10 Fun Food Ideas for Halloween

If you're looking for easy dishes to serve at a Halloween party, consider the ideas listed below. Most can be made with ingredients you can find around the house or buy at your local grocery store.

1. *Halloween party mix:* In a large bowl, combine equal amounts of roasted pumpkin seeds (see recipe on page 299), peanuts, raisins, candy corn, and Chex cereal. Mix well (without crushing the ingredients!) and serve as a snack.

2. *Green veggie dip:* Buy a sour-cream-based dip mix and add a few drops of green food coloring to the dip itself. Garnish with small pieces of red and yellow bell pepper scattered across the top.

3. *Edible spiders:* Use a dried prune for the body, pieces of licorice or stick pretzels for the legs, and two "red hot" candies for the eyes.

4. *Apple jack-o'-lanterns:* Don't try to hollow out an apple the way you would a pumpkin! With a sharp knife, cut away portions of the skin to form eyes, a nose, and a mouth.

5. *Edible witch's hat:* Use a large, flat, chocolate cookie about five inches in diameter for the brim and a sugar cone for the crown. Fill the cone with ice cream just to the rim and center it, upside down, on top of the cookie. You might want to cover the "hat" with a thin layer of chocolate frosting.

6. **Halloween punch:** Combine a 12-ounce can of orange juice concentrate, a 12-ounce bottle of white grape juice, a 2-liter bottle of 7-Up, a pint of lemon or lime sherbet, and several drops of green food coloring. Serve with plastic spiders floating on top.

7. **Jack-o'-lantern pizza:** Use pepperoni slices, green pepper strips, black olives, pimento-stuffed green olives, pineapple chunks, and whatever else you can think of to make a jack-o'-lantern face on a regular cheese pizza. Another idea is to make mini-pizzas using English muffins.

8. **Gingerbread ghosts:** Make regular gingerbread men and turn them into ghosts by covering them in white icing and giving them two raisins or chocolate chips for eyes (see recipe later in this section). You can also turn regular round cookies into pumpkins by icing them in orange, or you can partially ice one side of the cookie in yellow to make a Halloween crescent moon.

9. **Jack-o'-lantern sandwiches:** With a small, sharp knife cut eyes, a nose, and a mouth into the top layer of bread, letting whatever is inside the sandwich (preferably something much darker — or lighter — than the bread) show through.

10. **Pumpkin fruit salad:** Make a fresh fruit salad and serve it in a large, hollowed-out pumpkin. Make sure the inside of the pumpkin is clean before you add the fruit. You can also serve fruit individually in small pumpkins with a jack-o'-lantern face painted on the outside.

Homemade Pumpkin Filling

For fresh and delicious pumpkin filling, try making your own instead of relying on canned filling. You'll need:

1 **four-pound pumpkin ("cheese" variety)**
1 **teaspoon ground cinnamon (optional)**

Directions:

1. Preheat oven to 350 degrees F.

2. Cut off the top of the pumpkin, making a big enough "lid" so that you have easy access to the interior.

3. Using a large metal spoon, scrape away stringy pumpkin pulp and seeds from the interior and from the bottom of the "lid."

4. Cut the entire pumpkin shell, including the lid, into small squares, roughly 4 inches on a side.

5. Rinse the squares in cold water, pat them dry, and arrange them on a greased baking sheet.

6. Bake for one hour (until soft), flipping the pieces from time to time. Then remove and allow to cool.

7. Using a paring knife, cut each piece into four sections and peel the skin away from the pulp itself.

8. Strain the pulp through a sieve, or process it in a blender or food processor to remove any lumps. If desired, knead cinnamon into the pulp puree. A four-pound pumpkin should yield slightly over 4 cups of smooth pumpkin filling.

Pumpkin Pie

Here's a recipe for a good, classic pumpkin pie. Vary it as you please, and at your peril! You'll need:

2 cups pumpkin filling (preferably homemade filling [see recipe in this section] or canned pumpkin, *not* pie filling)
2 tablespoons butter or margarine
2 large eggs (beaten)
1 cup milk
1 cup light brown sugar
1½ teaspoons ground cinnamon
½ teaspoon salt
½ teaspoon ground nutmeg
½ teaspoon ground ginger (or fine-chopped crystallized ginger)
9" pie shell (unbaked)

Directions:

1. Preheat oven to 350 degrees F .

2. Combine filling, butter, eggs, and milk into a large bowl and mix until blended.

3. Slowly stir remainder of ingredients into filling mixture and beat thoroughly.

4. Pour filling mixture into pie shell and bake for 50 minutes (or until filling is firm, indicated by a knife blade remaining clean after insertion into the middle).

5. Allow to cool for at least five minutes, and serve with whipped cream, ice cream, yogurt, or lightly sweetened sour cream. The pie will yield six generous or eight slim servings.

Roasted Pumpkin Seeds

Don't throw out the seeds after you've cleaned out your prospective jack-o'-lantern! They make tasty and nutritious snacks (high in phosphorus). You'll need:

1¹/₂ tablespoons vegetable oil
¹/₂ teaspoon Worcestershire sauce
³/₄ teaspoon salt (optional)
2 cups pumpkin seeds
(a four-pound pumpkin yields about 1 cup of seeds)

Directions:

1. Preheat oven to 225 degrees F .

2. Using a mesh colander, rinse seeds well in cold water and pat dry.

3. Combine seeds, vegetable oil, and Worcestershire sauce in a large bowl and mix thoroughly.

4. Spread seeds across baking sheet and bake for 30 minutes (until golden brown), stirring seeds every six or seven minutes.

5. Remove seeds from oven, drain on a paper towel.

6. After seeds are drained, sprinkle with salt if desired. For maximum freshness, store uneaten seeds in a jar with a tight lid.

Pumpkin Bread

Neither man nor woman nor Halloween ghoulie can live by plain bread alone. Try this palate-charming variation at mealtimes as well as snack times. You'll need:

1½ cups all-purpose flour
1 teaspoon baking powder
½ teaspoon salt
½ teaspoon baking soda
1 teaspoon ground cinnamon
1 teaspoon ground nutmeg
1 teaspoon ground ginger
⅛ teaspoon ground cloves
1 cup sugar
2 large eggs (beaten)

½ cup vegetable oil
½ cup water
¾ cup chopped pecans or walnuts (optional)
½ cup raisins, preferably golden (optional)
1 cup pumpkin filling (preferably homemade filling or canned pumpkin, *not* pie filling)

Directions:

1. Preheat oven to 350 degrees F.

2. Combine flour, baking powder, salt, baking soda, all seasonings, and sugar into a large bowl. Mix thoroughly.

3. In another large bowl, combine eggs, oil, water, and pumpkin filling. Mix thoroughly.

4. Slowly stir flour mixture and (if desired) nuts and/or raisins into filling mixture.

5. Pour filling into a greased, 9" x 3" x 5" loaf pan.

6. Bake for one hour (or until bread is firm, indicated by a knife blade coming out clean after insertion in the middle).

7. Allow bread to cool *in the pan* at least 10 minutes before removing. Bread tastes and slices better if it is wrapped in a cloth and left to set for a day.

Pumpkin Soup

This wholesome and hearty soup will put you, your family, and your guests in good shape for the rigors of a scary Halloween night. You'll need:

1 clove garlic, minced
1 tablespoon butter or margarine
4 cups homemade pumpkin filling
(see recipe in this section)
5 cups chicken stock or canned broth
3 cups milk
1 cup heavy cream
1 teaspoon onion powder
1 teaspoon curry powder
1/2 teaspoon salt (optional)
2 tablespoons chopped parsley
2 cups croutons, preferably fried in butter or margarine
(optional)

Directions:

1. In bottom of large saucepan, sauté garlic in butter until tender.

2. Lower the heat and add pumpkin filling, gradually stirring in chicken broth.

3. Slowly add milk and cream to pumpkin mixture, stirring constantly.

4. Cook over low heat, stirring from time to time. Do not allow to boil.

5. Before the soup is fully cooked, stir in onion powder, curry powder, and (if desired) salt.

6. Serve with parsley and (if desired) croutons sprinkled on top. For a festive touch, you may want to serve the soup in a hollowed-out, well-scraped pumpkin (about 30 pounds). This recipe yields about 12 servings.

Flap Jack-o'-Lanterns

For the morning before or the morning after, nothing is more appropriate or more delectable than pancakes made with pumpkin. You'll need:

2 cups all-purpose flour	¹/₄ cup water
1 teaspoon baking soda	1¹/₂ cups milk
2 teaspoons baking powder	3 tablespoons butter or margarine (melted)
¹/₄ teaspoon salt	1 cup pumpkin filling
1 teaspoon ground cinnamon	(preferably homemade filling [see recipe in this section] or canned
¹/₂ teaspoon ground ginger	pumpkin, *not* pie
2 large eggs (beaten)	filling)
¹/₄ cup vegetable oil	

Directions:

1. In a large bowl, mix together flour, baking soda, baking powder, salt (if desired), cinnamon, and ginger.

2. In another large bowl, mix eggs, oil, water, milk, and butter.

3. Blend flour mixture into egg mixture until completely smooth.

4. Put lightly greased frying pan over medium-high heat. When hot enough, drop large spoonfuls of batter into the pan. Fry on either side until bubbles appear.

5. Serve immediately with maple syrup. This recipe makes about 8-10 flapjacks.

Harvest Squares

A heavenly dessert, harvest squares also make devilishly good bribes for trick-or-treaters. You'll need:

2¼ cups flour
2¼ teaspoons baking powder
½ teaspoon baking soda
1½ teaspoon ground cinnamon
½ teaspoon ground nutmeg
1¼ cup white sugar
¾ cup light brown sugar
4 large eggs, beaten

½ cup butter or margarine (melted)
2 tablespoons heavy cream
2 cups pumpkin filling (preferably homemade filling [see recipe in this section] or canned pumpkin, *not* pie filling)
1 cup chocolate chips
¾ cup chopped walnuts

Directions:

1. Preheat oven to 325 degrees F.

2. In large bowl, combine flour, baking powder, baking soda, cinnamon, nutmeg, white sugar, and brown sugar. Mix thoroughly.

3. In another large bowl, combine eggs, butter, cream, and pumpkin filling. Mix thoroughly.

4. Slowly blend flour mixture into filling mixture. Then add chips and nuts, stirring throughout mixture.

5. Pour mixture into greased 9" x 13" x 2" baking pan and bake for 45 minutes (or until mixture is firm, indicated by a knife remaining clean after being inserted into the center).

6. Allow to cool *in pan* for at least 10 minutes. Cut into squares before removing.

Pumpkin-Walnut Muffins

If you are a regular and enthusiastic muffin eater, pumpkin-walnut muffins will provide a welcome change of pace. You'll need:

2 large eggs (beaten)
1 cup pumpkin filling (preferably homemade filling [see recipe in this section] or canned pumpkin, *not* pie filling)
4 tablespoons butter or margarine (melted)
1/2 cup milk
1 1/2 cup all-purpose flour

1/2 cup light brown sugar (packed)
3/4 teaspoon ground cinnamon
1/4 teaspoon ground nutmeg
1/4 teaspoon ground ginger
2 teaspoons baking powder
1/2 teaspoon salt (optional)
3/4 cup chopped walnuts

Directions:

1. Preheat oven to 400 degrees F.

2. In large bowl, combine eggs, pumpkin filling, butter, and milk. Mix thoroughly.

3. In another large bowl, combine flour, sugar, cinnamon, nutmeg, ginger, baking powder, and (if desired) salt. Mix thoroughly.

4. Slowly stir flour mixture into filling mixture. Blend until smooth.

5. Sprinkle nuts into mixture and stir until distributed throughout.

6. Pour into two greased muffin pans (six 1/3-cup muffin molds each) and bake 25 minutes (or until muffin is firm, indicated by toothpick remaining clean after inserted in center).

7. Allow to cool *in pan* for at least 10 minutes. For a festive touch, coat top with orange or white icing and make a jack-o'-lantern face in the icing with candy corn, M & M's, and/or contrasting icing.

Pumpkin-Eater Cookies

Peter, Peter, pumpkin-eater might have kept his wandering wife at home by baking her these irresistible cookies. You'll need:

1 cup pumpkin filling (preferably homemade filling [see recipe in this section] or canned pumpkin, *not* pie filling)

2 large eggs (beaten)

3 tablespoons vegetable oil

1 teaspoon vanilla

1/2 cup milk

2 1/2 cups all-purpose flour

1 1/2 teaspoons baking soda

1 teaspoon ground cinnamon

1/2 teaspoon ground nutmeg

1/2 teaspoon ground ginger

1 cup dark brown sugar

1/2 cup white sugar

1 cup chopped walnuts

1 cup butterscotch chips

Directions:

1. Preheat oven to 325 degrees F.

2. In a large bowl, combine pumpkin filling, eggs, oil, vanilla, and milk. Mix thoroughly.

3. In another large bowl, combine flour, baking soda, nutmeg, cinnamon, ginger, and sugar. Mix thoroughly.

4. Slowly stir flour mixture into filling mixture. Blend until smooth.

5. Add nuts and chips, and stir until distributed throughout filling.

6. Drop by teaspoonfuls, two inches apart all around, onto greased baking sheet.

7. Bake 15 minutes (or until cookie is firm, indicated by a toothpick remaining clean after insertion into the center). Ice if desired. This recipe yields about 60 cookies.

Jack-o'-Lantern
Beef Stew

Adapted from *Carbonada Criolla*, a regional specialty of Argentina, this South American dish involves several steps and is a good project for several cooks to work on together. The stew and pumpkin are prepared separately, then baked and served together.

Utensils:

Vegetable brush
Paring knife,
   kitchen knife
Large spoon
Shallow oven-proof
   baking dish large
   enough to hold
   your pumpkin
Timer
Potholders
Table fork
Cutting board
Dutch oven with lid
Garlic press
Aluminum foil *or*
   soup bowl
Wooden spoon
Vegetable peeler
Measuring cups
   and spoons
Long-handled fork
Heat-proof pad
   or trivet
Black oil-base felt-
   tipped pen
   (optional)

Ingredients for pumpkin:

1 whole pumpkin — 6 pounds or
   larger
2 tablespoons butter *or* margarine
1/4 teaspoon cinnamon
1/4 teaspoon ground nutmeg

Ingredients for stew:

2 medium-sized yellow *or*
   white onions
3 tablespoons margarine or butter
2 cloves of garlic
2 pounds stewing beef — chuck
   cut into bite-sized pieces
1 large carrot
2 medium-sized sweet *or*
   white potatoes
2 medium-sized whole tomatoes
8 dried apricot *or* peach halves
1 1/2 cups frozen or fresh peas *or*
   corn kernels
1/4 cup seedless raisins
1/2 teaspoon salt
1/4 teaspoon pepper
1/4 teaspoon dried thyme
1/4 teaspoon cinnamon
2 cups beef bouillon *or* water

To Cook Pumpkin

Directions:

NOTE: Follow steps 1 to 4 to cook any fresh pumpkin. Instead of using it for this stew, you can also peel and cube or mash it and serve it as you would squash or sweet potatoes.

1. Turn oven on to 350 degrees F. Wash outside of pumpkin with vegetable brush and water to remove dirt. Cut out the lid of the pumpkin as you would for a jack-o'-lantern, *but* cut the lid about 2½" to 3" out from the stem. This opening must be large enough for you to reach inside holding the serving spoon.

2. With the lid off, scrape out seeds and membranes. Save seeds to toast (see recipe in this section).

3. Place butter *or* margarine and the spices inside pumpkin. Cover with lid, and place pumpkin on oven-proof dish. Set it in 350-degree F. oven and set timer to bake for 60 minutes. During this time, prepare the stew as described in stew directions following.

4. After 60 minutes, use pot holders to remove pumpkin (on its dish) *carefully* from oven. Set on heat-proof surface. To test doneness, lift lid, wait a few seconds for steam to subside, then stick a table fork into the pumpkin flesh near the opening. It should feel quite soft, like a baked potato. If done, set pumpkin aside on heat-proof surface and turn off oven. If still too hard, return it to oven and bake until soft. Pumpkin may be baked ahead of time and kept unrefrigerated up to 3 hours before filling and baking with stew.

To Make Stew:

Directions:

NOTE: Stew can be made the day before and refrigerated until needed.

1. Chop onions on cutting board.

2. Add butter or margarine to Dutch oven and set it on stove over medium heat. Add chopped onions. Press both cloves of garlic into pan with onions. Sauté (fry gently) onions and garlic until golden, stirring every now and then with wooden spoon. When done, spoon onion-garlic mixture out of pan and set it aside on foil or in soup bowl.

3. Cut beef into serving pieces, then add it to the same pan that onion was cooked in. Turn on heat to medium and brown beef on one side, then turn it with wooden spoon or long handled fork. After meat is browned on both sides, turn off heat. Sprinkle cooked onion garlic mixture over meat in pan.

4. Peel carrot, then cut it up into roughly 2" lengths and add them to beef.

5. Wash and peel potatoes. Cut them into approximately 1" cubes. Add to beef. Wash and remove stems from tomatoes. Cut them into small pieces and add to beef.

6. Add fruit, peas, raisins, and bouillon *or* water to meat mixture. Stir with wooden spoon. Cover pan with lid and set on stove over medium-low heat. When mixture boils, turn down heat and simmer (cook slowly over low heat) about 60 minutes, or until meat feels tender when stuck with a fork. When done, turn off heat, remove pan from stove and set it aside on heat-proof-surface until about 45 minutes before serving. (Refrigerate stew if waiting longer than a couple of hours.)

To Assemble

Directions:

1. 45 minutes before serving, preheat oven to 350 degrees F. Spoon stew into baked pumpkin, which should be sitting on its baking dish. Any stew that does not fit can be left in the pan to be reheated later. Put the lid on the pumpkin and return it to the hot oven. Set timer to bake 30 minutes.

2. To test doneness, lift pumpkin's lid. Stew inside should be steaming hot.

3. *Very carefully* use pot holders to remove pan with pumpkin from the oven. Remember, the pumpkin is full and extra heavy. You may need to ask an adult to help with this step. Set pan on heat-proof pad on table.

4. If you wish, you can use a felt tipped pen to draw a jack-o'-lantern face on the side of the baked pumpkin. *Be careful not to pierce the pumpkin's skin with the pen.* Do not eat the skin with the drawing on it! To serve, scoop or ladle out some pumpkin along with the stew.

All Souls' Bread

8 cups flour	1 teaspoon grated orange rind
2 cups milk	1 teaspoon grated lemon rind
4 yeast cakes	1/2 cup butter
8 egg yolks	1 teaspoon salt
2 cups sugar	poppy seeds

Directions:

1. Dissolve yeast in 1/2 cup milk. Mix yeast with milk and one cup flour. Sprinkle top with flour and let rise.

2. Add salt, egg yolks, beat until thick.

3. Add sugar and rinds and mix with other ingredients.

4. Add 2 cups flour, alternating with milk and knead for 1/2 hour.

5. Add remaining flour and butter and knead until dough comes away from hands.

6. Set dough in a warm place until it rises to double in bulk.

7. Separate into 4 parts, braid. Brush top with beaten egg yolks and sprinkle with poppy seed. Let rise.

8. Bake at 350 degrees F. for one hour.

Green Pepper Monsters

At a luncheon party, your guests might enjoy making their own monsters if you set out all the pieces. You'll need:

Utensils:	Ingredients for 1 monster:
Paring knife	1 whole raw green (or sweet red) bell pepper
Teaspoon	
Vegetable peeler	$1/2$ cup of your favorite egg or tuna-fish salad
Toothpicks	
	1 small raw carrot
	2 whole cloves
	3 or 4 flower clusters of raw broccoli *or* cauliflower *or* celery leaves
	1 lettuce leaf

Directions:

1. Wash pepper. Cut around stem end and lift it out. Use teaspoon or fingers to pull seeds and white membrane out of pepper. Rinse inside with water to remove loose seeds.

2. At end opposite stem, cut out a mouth with jagged teeth. Use pepper's lumpy shape for nose, chin, and so on. Fill pepper (from stem end) with any salad you like.

3. To make eyes, peel carrot. Then cut 2 slices, each about $1/4$" thick. Poke a hole in the center of each slice with toothpick, then stick a clove in each hole to make pupil of eye.

4. Break a toothpick in half. Stick broken end of each half into the edge of a carrot slice (like a lollipop). Then attach eyes by sticking sharp toothpick ends into top of monster's head.

5. To make end of nose, cut pointy tip off carrot (*or* carve cone shape from a small carrot section). Stick one end of a toothpick into flat end of shape, then poke other end of toothpick onto tip of monster's pepper nose.

6. To make arms, cut 2 carrot sticks, about ¹/₄" on each side and 3" long. Use point of paring knife to make 1 small arm hole on each side of monster. Poke a carrot stick into each hole.

7. For hair, break off 3 or 4 small flowers of broccoli *or* cauliflower, *or* use celery leaves. Use toothpicks to connect pieces. To do this, poke a toothpick into stem of each flowerlet *or* leaf, then poke other end of toothpick into top of monster's head. Set each monster on a lettuce leaf and serve. *Or* make monsters ahead of time and refrigerate until needed.

ᎶᏣᏝ

Baked Acorn Squash

If you have ever tried to cut a raw acorn squash in half, you know how hard that job can be. Try our simplified method in which the squash is baked whole, then sliced and seasoned. Serve baked squash in place of potatoes with any roast meat, a green vegetable, and a salad. You can use squash baked this way in any recipe calling for pumpkin or sweet potatoes.

Utensils:	*Ingredients for 4 servings:*
Vegetable brush	2 whole acorn squash
Shallow oven-proof	(¹/₂ squash for each serving);
baking dish	each about 2¹/₂ pounds
Timer	4 tablespoons butter *or* margarine
Potholders	4 tablespoons honey *or* brown
Knife	sugar *or* maple syrup
Large spoon	Dash of cinnamon and
Measuring spoons	ground nutmeg

Directions:

1. Turn oven on to 350 degrees F. Wash squash with vegetable brush and water. Place whole squash on baking dish and set in oven. Set timer to bake for 60 minutes.

2. Remove baked squash from oven with pot holders. Leave heat on. Cool squash until comfortable to touch—about 10 minutes—then cut each squash in half crosswise.

3. Use spoon to scoop out seeds and membranes and discard them.

4. Set halves, cut sides up, in baking dish. If they lean over too much, prop them upright against each other, *or* lean them against an overturned oven-proof custard cup. In each squash half add:

   1 tablespoon butter *or* margarine
   1 tablespoon honey *or* brown sugar *or* maple syrup
   Dash of cinnamon and ground nutmeg

5. Return pan to oven. Set timer to bake for 30 minutes, so seasoning cooks into squash. Remove pan from oven with pot holders. Serve each half squash upright in a small bowl.

Halloween Applesauce

Kids and adults alike will enjoy this hearty and flavorful apple-sauce: warm or cool, at breakfast, lunch, dinner, or snacktime. You'll need:

2 pounds apples (preferably tart — or "cooking" — apples)	1/2 teaspoon ground cinnamon
2/3 cup sugar	1/4 teaspoon ground nutmeg
1 cup water	1/4 teaspoon allspice
1 teaspoon lemon juice	1/2 cup golden raisins

Directions:

1. Quarter, core, and pare apples. Set raisins in 1/2 cup of the water to plump.

2. In medium-sized saucepan, bring 1/2 cup of the water to boil. Add apples and bring to second boil.

3. Leave on low simmer, covered, for 10 minutes, stirring occasionally.

4. Add raisins and, if apple mixture seems too thick, some or all of the water in which the raisins have been plumping. Leave on low simmer, covered, for another 10 minutes.

5. Add sugar, lemon juice, cinnamon, nutmeg, and allspice and mix thoroughly. Serve warm or cool (allow to cool at room temperature before refrigerating). This recipe yields about 3 1/2 cups.

Bobbing Apple Punch

1½ cups orange juice
4 cups apple cider
1 cup pineapple juice
2 tablespoons sugar

4 cups ginger ale, chilled
6 to 8 small red apples
1 orange, sliced

Directions:

1. In a punchbowl, mix the orange juice, apple cider, pineapple juice, and sugar.

2. Chill for a couple of hours.

3. Just before serving, add the ginger ale, apples, orange slices, and ice cubes. Makes 10½ Cups.

Mulled Cider

6 1-inch cinnamon sticks
1 tablespoon whole cloves
1 tablespoon whole allspice
2 pieces whole nutmeg

2 cups brown sugar
1 gallon apple cider
16 whole cinnamon sticks

Directions:

1. Tie the first four ingredients in a cloth bag.

2. In a large pot, stir together the sugar and the cider.

3. Add the spice bag.

4. Bring to a boil and simmer for about 20 minutes.

5. Remove the spice bag and serve hot with a whole cinnamon stick in each mug. Serves 16.

Candied Apples

12	red delicious apples	1	teaspoon red food
12	wooden ice-cream sticks		coloring
4¹/₂	cups sugar	1¹/₂	cups water
³/₄	cup light corn syrup	1	cup chopped peanuts

Directions:

1. Grease a large cookie sheet and set aside.

2. Wash and dry the apples. Insert a stick through the stem of each, leaving about 2 inches of the stick for gripping.

3. In a saucepan over medium heat, combine the sugar, corn syrup, food coloring, and water. Cook, stirring constantly, until the ingredients are dissolved and the liquid boils.

4. Set a candy thermometer in the mixture and continue cooking, without stirring, until the temperature reaches 290 degrees, in about 20 minutes. Meanwhile, place the chopped peanuts in a bowl.

5. Remove the syrup from the heat and dip the apples, one by one, to coat evenly. Work quickly so the sauce doesn't harden. As you finish dipping an apple, roll it around in the peanuts to coat evenly. Then set each down on the prepared cookie sheet. Let the apples cool for at least an hour before placing on a platter to serve. Makes 12.

German Apple Cake

This German recipe will give a delicious cake which can be served warm or cold. You'll need:

Utensils:	*Ingredients:*
Wooden spoon	1 lb apples
Mixing bowl	2-3 eggs
8" cake tin	4 oz sugar
	4 oz butter
Icing:	1-4 tablespoons of milk
confectioners' sugar	7 oz self-raising flour
	4 drops lemon flavouring

Directions:

1. Mix the butter, sugar and eggs. Add lemon flavouring.

2. Mix in the flour with the milk until the mixture is of a soft dropping consistency.

3. Put the mixture into the greased tin.

4. Peel and cut apples into quarters. Scored with a knife to decorate, and place the scored surface uppermost on top of the mixture.

5. Bake for 45 minutes at 375 degrees F.

6. Dust before serving with icing sugar (confectioners' sugar).

Skull Cake

This skull cake could form the centrepiece for your party food. The cake itself is easy to make and delicious to eat. You will need:

1 lb digestive biscuits (or graham crackers)
8 oz butter
2 dessert spoons (approx 1 oz) cocoa
2 tablespoons golden syrup
2 tablespoons sugar

This makes a flat shape approx 12" x 9"

Icing:
8 oz confectioners' sugar

Directions:

1. Dissolve the butter, sugar, golden syrup, and cocoa in a saucepan until just warm.

2. Crush the digestive biscuits well in a mixing bowl using the end of a wooden rolling pin. Add the liquid to this and mix well.

3. Now shape the mixture into the skull. Do this on to waxed paper on which you have drawn the outline of the skull. Make indentations for the eyes, nose, and mouth.

4. Allow the cake to firm up in the fridge for a few hours.

To ice the cake:

1. Mix a little water with about 4 oz confectioners' sugar, keeping the mixture as stiff as possible.

2. Ice the skull, avoiding the eyes, nose, and mouth. When the icing has hardened, apply a second coat, using the remaining sugar mixture.

3. Allow the cake to set completely in the fridge. Then remove it from the waxed paper and transfer it to a square cutting board which has been covered with black plastic (from a garbage bag).

Spooky Eyeballs

Utensils:

Egg-cup
Saucer
Wooden spoon
Mixing bowl
Greaseproof paper
Metal spoon
Sieve

Ingredients to make 40 to 45 cookies:

1 lb. icing sugar
   (confectioner's sugar)
1 egg-white
   peppermint essence
1 stick of black liquorice
   blue or green colouring

Directions:

1. Beat the egg-white lightly, and blend with sifted icing sugar and a few drops of peppermint essence. Mix in icing sugar until you get a fine dry paste.

2. Using finger-tips, knead the paste, adding small amounts of icing sugar for as long as the paste will absorb it.

3. Separate a small quantity to make the irises of your spooky eyeballs. Add a few drops of blue or green colouring and mix in with a metal spoon.

4. Roll the white mixture into small round balls. (You can do this easily if you sprinkle a little icing sugar on to the palms of your hands.) Press a hole in the top of the ball with your little finger or the end of the wooden spoon.

5. Make a flat button-shape with the coloured mixture big enough to fit in to the hole.

6. Cut out a small round section of the liquorice to make the pupil.

Gingerbread Ghosts

¹/₂ cup sugar	2 teaspoons ground ginger
¹/₂ cup butter or margarine, softened	³/₄ teaspoon baking soda
¹/₃ cup molasses	¹/₂ teaspoon ground cinnamon
2¹/₂ cups sifted all-purpose flour	Pinch of salt

Directions:

1. In a large bowl, blend together the sugar and butter. Add the molasses. Fold in the sifted flour, ginger, baking soda, cinnamon, and salt. Refrigerate for at least 2 hours.

2. Preheat the oven to 350 degrees F. Lightly grease a large baking sheet.

3. On a lightly floured board, roll out the dough until it is ¹/₈ inch thick. Cut out the cookies with a gingerbread-shaped cookie cutter and place on the baking sheet. Bake for 6 to 8 minutes, until lightly browned. Remove from the oven and let cool thoroughly on a wire rack before decorating with Frosting. Makes 2 Dozen.

Frosting

1 16-ounce box powdered sugar	3 to 4 tablespoons milk
1 teaspoon vanilla	1 8-ounce package minia-chocolate chips
Pinch of salt	

Directions:

1. Take half of the sugar and add the vanilla, salt, and 2 tablespoons of the milk. Mix well.

2. Now add the remaining sugar and mix again. Add as much of the remaining milk as you need to reach the desired consistency for spreading.

3. Spread the Frosting on each cookie until it is totally white and looks like a ghost. For eyes, use two miniature chocolate chips on each cookie.

Gingerbread Jack-o'-Lanterns

These delicious cookies can be made into any shape you want. Decorate them with raisins, nuts and candies. What you'll need:

$1/2$ cup butter	**Utensils:**
$1/2$ cup honey	small pan
1 cup molasses	mixing bowl
raisins, nuts, candies	mixing spoon
$3^1/2$ cups whole wheat flour	measuring cups and
1 teaspoon baking soda	spoons
2 teaspoons cinnamon	cookie sheet
2 teaspoons ginger	
1 teaspoon ground cloves	
$1/4$ teaspoon salt	
1 egg	

Directions:

1. Measure the correct amounts of butter, honey and molasses. Heat the mixture carefully in a pan, until the butter melts. Then let cool.

2. While the mixture is cooling, measure the flour, soda, spices and salt. Mix in a bowl until the spices are evenly distributed throughout the flour.

3. When the molasses mixture has cooled off a bit, add an egg to it and mix well.

4. Pour the molasses-egg mixture into the flour mixture. Mix well.

5. Turn the oven to 350 degrees F. Then put the batter in the freezer for about ten minutes.

6. After ten minutes, the batter will be easy to shape. Form balls of dough the size of a quarter. Put them on a lightly-buttered cookie sheet. Flatten them until they are about ¼-inch thick. Attach a small piece of dough to the circle so that it will look like the stem of the jack-o'-lantern. Decorate.

   You may want to try other shapes besides the jack-o'-lantern. It is easy to do this with cold dough. Sprinkle a little flour on a cutting board. Roll the batter and cut into any shape you like.

7. Bake for ten minutes at 350 degrees F.

Popcorn **Balls**

2½ quarts popped popcorn
 1   14-ounce package light
     caramels

¼ cup light corn syrup
2 tablespoons water

Directions:

1. Keep the popped corn warm in a 200-degree F. oven.

2. Melt the caramels in the top of a double boiler over simmering water. Add the corn syrup and water and mix until smooth. Slowly pour over the popcorn in a large bowl or pan. Stir to mix well. With greased hands, shape the mixture into balls about the size of softballs.

3. Let the balls cool and dry completely before wrapping (you can make them the day before). Wrap in plastic wrap or in corsage bags, available at any florist, and tie with orange and black ribbons. Makes about 15 balls.

Halloween Nut Balls

In England and Scotland, so many Halloween (All Hallow's Eve) games and foods have to do with nuts that the holiday is often called "Nut Crack Night." These cookies, made with chopped nuts and rolled in powdered sugar, are popular holiday treats in the British Isles as well as around the world. In each country they have a different name, but they are always called *delicious*. They taste best made with sweet butter, but lightly salted butter or margarine will work, too.

Utensils:

Cookie sheet
Large and small
  mixing bowls
Measuring cups
  and spoons
Wax paper
Sifter
Large spoon
Electric mixer *or*
  slotted spoon
Timer
Large platter *or* tray
  (optional)
Pot holders
Spatula *or* pancake
  turner
Airtight tin *or* cookie jar

Ingredients to make 40 to 45 cookies:

1 cup (2 sticks) *plus*
  2 tablespoons sweet butter
  at room temperature
2½ cups confectioners' sugar, sifted
1 teaspoon vanilla extract
¼ teaspoon almond extract
2½ cups all-purpose flour, sifted
½ teaspoon salt
1 cup finely chopped pecans

Directions:

1. Turn oven on to 350 degrees F. Wash your hands. Grease cookie sheets with 2 tablespoons of butter *or* margarine and set them aside.

2. Measure 1 cup (2 sticks) butter *or* margarine into large bowl and press it into small pieces with spoon.

3. Sift confectioners' sugar onto wax paper, then measure $1/2$ cup and add it to butter. Use electric mixer or spoon to beat them together until smooth.

4. Add vanilla and almond extracts to butter-sugar mixture and beat well.

5. Sift flour onto wax paper, then measure and add it to other ingredients in bowl. Add salt and mix well. Stir in pecans.

6. Sift about 2 cups confectioners' sugar into small bowl and set it aside.

7. Flour your hands, then pick up small lumps of dough and roll them between your palms, making balls about 1" in diameter. Set balls about 1" apart on greased cookie sheets.

8. Set timer to bake cookies 10 to 12 minutes in 350-degree F. oven or until just golden around the edges. Use pot holders to remove cookie sheet from oven. Place it on heat-proof surface.

9. Cut a sheet of wax paper approximately 14" long and set it on a large platter or tray. Beside it place the bowl of sifted sugar.

10. Let cookies cool a couple of minutes, until you can comfortably touch them, though still warm. Use spatula or pancake turner to loosen cookies from the sheet.

11. Pick each warm cookie up in turn and roll it in the sifted confectioners' sugar in the bowl. Then set cookies on wax paper to cool completely. When they are cold, roll cookies in sugar a second time. Store them in an airtight tin, sprinkling them with more confectioners' sugar.

Indexes

Author and Title Index

Index to
First Lines of Poetry